THE WAKEFIELD COURT ROLLS SERIES OF THE YORKSHIRE ARCHAEOLOGICAL SOCIETY

Volume XIV

THE COURT ROLLS OF THE MANOR OF WAKEFIELD

from October 1688 to September 1689

General Editor

C. M. Fraser

ISBN 1-9035-6435-2

THE COURT ROLLS OF THE MANOR OF WAKEFIELD

from October 1688 to September 1689

Edited and Calendared by

C. M. Fraser

Yorkshire Archaeological Society
Claremont, Clarendon Road
Leeds, LS2 9NZ

2004

CONTENTS

Introduction		vii
Map of Manor		between vii and viii
Great Court held at Wakefield	Friday 12 October 1688	1
Court Baron at Wakefield	Friday 2 November 1688	8
Court Baron at Wakefield	Friday 23 November 1688	14
Court Baron at Wakefield	Friday 14 December 1688	17
Court Baron at Wakefield	Friday 4 January 1689	22
Court Baron at Wakefield	Friday 25 January 1689	24
Court Baron at Wakefield	Friday 15 February 1689	29
Court Baron at Wakefield	Friday 8 March 1689	33
Great Court held at Wakefield	Friday 5 April 1689	39
Court Baron at Wakefield	Friday 26 April 1689	43
Court Baron at Wakefield	Friday 17 May 1689	56
Court Baron at Wakefield	Friday 7 June 1689	59
Court Baron at Wakefield	Friday 28 June 1689	67
Court Baron at Wakefield	Friday 19 July 1689	71
Court Baron at Wakefield	Friday 9 August 1689	72
Court Baron at Wakefield	Friday 30 August 1689	75
Court Baron at Wakefield	Friday 20 September 1689	78
Court Leet held at Wakefield	Saturday 13 October 1688	83
Court Leet held at Halifax	Monday 15 October 1688	90
Court Leet held at Brighouse	Tuesday 16 October 1688	104
Court Leet held at [Kirk]burton	Wednesday 17 October 1688	111
Court Leet held at Wakefield	Saturday 6 April 1689	127
Court Leet held at Halifax	Monday 8 April 1689	134
Court Leet held at Brighouse	Tuesday 9 April 1689	147
Court Leet held at [Kirk]burton	Wednesday 10 May 1689	156
Index of Names		173
Index of Places		195
Index of Subjects		206

It was originally proposed to publish the Wakefield court rolls for 1687/8 and 1688/9 as one volume. In the event the size of the index was decisive, and the rolls have been published separately. The decision to choose the years was influenced by a curiosity to see how the Manor dealt with the crisis of the deposition of James II and inauguration of William and Mary as the new monarchs. A notable feature of the manor rolls is their insulation from national events. The rolls, however, were dated by regnal years, and hence must necessarily show the point at which it was recognised that James had gone and William and Mary arrived. The answer was that the court held on 25 January 1689 was dated in the fourth year of the reign of James II, the court held on 15 February 1689 was dated AD1688 [Old Style], and that held on 8 March was dated in the first year of William and Mary.[1] Everything else carried on as usual.

It could be argued that the most important feature of the series as published is their comprehensive indexes, which list all persons occurring in the particular rolls, and all the places, including the names of closes, plots of land, and even strips in the town fields. The Subject Index highlights points of interest. The cumulative information is impressive, demonstrating the significant role of certain families in the administration of the manor both as a land registry and as a centre for local policing.

There is virtually no information about trade in the Manor in the present volume. While there is an incidental reference to a fulling

---

1 These dates are more revealing than might appear at first sight. According to the *Handbook of Dates* (new edition, 2000), published by the Royal Historical Society the Interregnum between the reigns of James and William and Mary lasted between 12 December 1688 and 12 February 1689. Hence the three courts held on 14 December, 4 and 25 January should not have ascribed to James II, and that on 15 February could have been safely ascribed to William and Mary, and not given a date in AD.

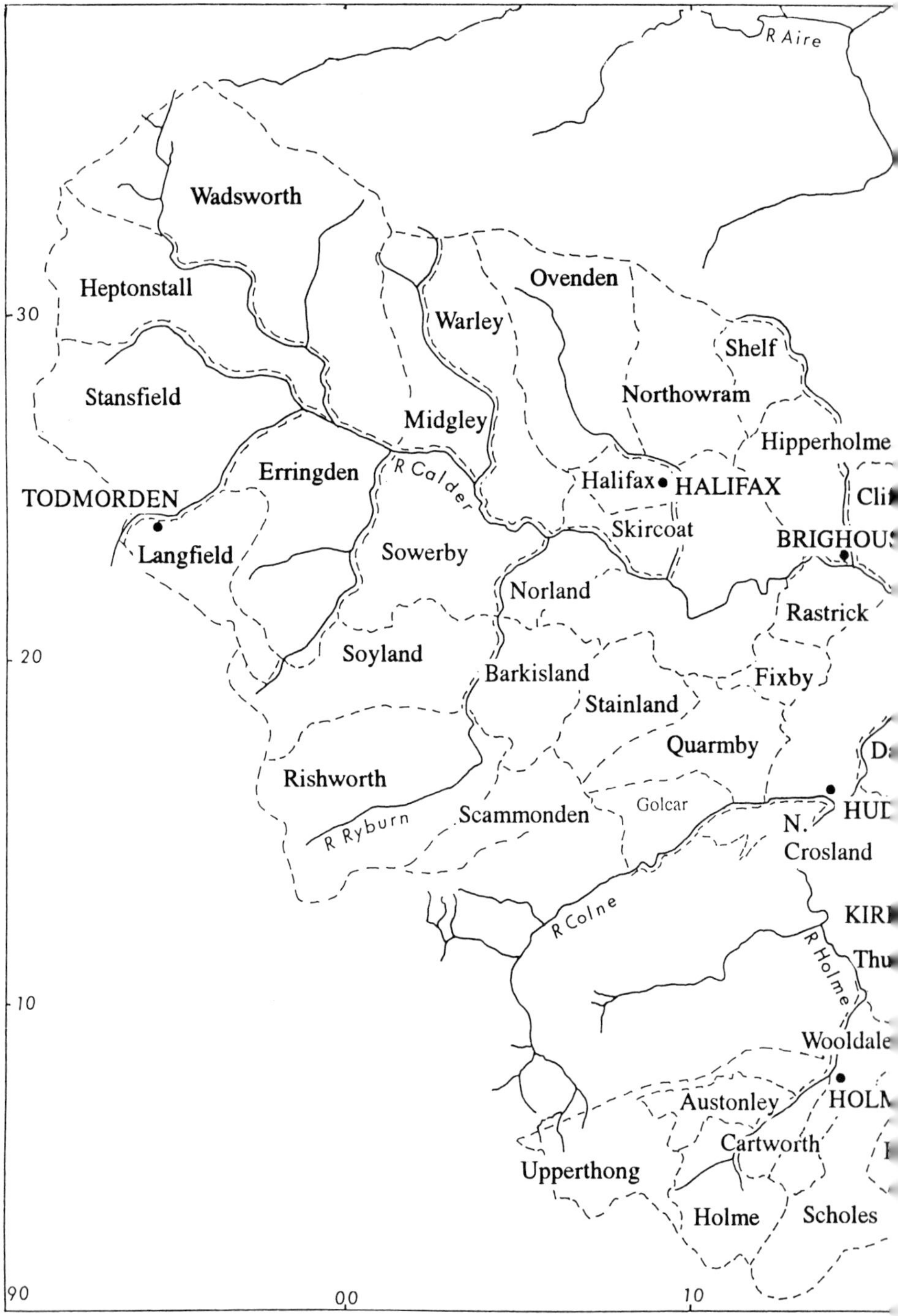

R Aire
Wadsworth
Heptonstall
Ovenden
Warley
Shelf
Stansfield
Northowram
Midgley
Hipperholme
Erringden
R Calder
Halifax
HALIFAX
TODMORDEN
Skircoat
Langfield
Sowerby
BRIGHOUS
Norland
Rastrick
Soyland
Barkisland
Fixby
Stainland
Quarmby
Rishworth
Golcar
Scammonden
R Ryburn
N.
Crosland
R Colne
KIRK
R Holme
Thu
Wooldale
HOLM
Austonley
Cartworth
Upperthong
Holme
Scholes
30
20
10
90
00
10

MAP OF THE MANOR OF WAKEFIELD and its townships

mill at Warley, and two smithies change hands, no close is called Tentercroft. There are three references to coal-working, once where the right to operate is reserved from a conveyance of land near Northowram (p 138). There is one reference to peat-digging, at Soyland (pp 138-9). There does seem to be concern about the state of the roads, particularly in the areas supervised in the Halifax and Brighouse courts leet. At Longfield it was presented on 15 October 1688 that there was 'a steap place joyning to the high way and very dangerous for travlers, lying in Eringden', and a fine of 10s was to be imposed on Abraham Sunderland if it were not repaired before the following Candlemas [2 February 1689] (p 101). The constable and sworn men of Heptonstall laid fines of 20s and 30s for repair of highways in Stansfield, although it is not clear on whom rested this responsibility (pp 101-2). Shelf came down heavily on a variety of persons to make good two foot-bridges and also paths, with fines totalling over £5 liable if the repairs were not completed by 1 December. However, the township was still agitating about non-compliance at the following April court leet (pp 106, 153). Quarmby on 9 April 1689 required Anne Clay and James Ryley of Lindley to 'repaire and make passable for horses with packs and loads the way betweene the Salter lane bottome and the Birchincliffe' under pain of 6s 8d. The constable and four sworn men also presented the inhabitants of Lindley for failure to shut the gates on Lidyate lane 'immediately after they have occasion to passe that way' on pain of 12d (pp 154-5). This may shed light on the charge brought by the constable and sworn men of Rastrick on Isaac Bates for failure to 'hang of his owne proper charge one yate at Bradley lane end, commonly called High Lane Yate, and hang the same yate there in the accustomed place' before 1 May 1689 on pain of 10s (p 151). Concern was also expressed about maintenance of hedges bordering the road, as well as the ditches, to prevent flooding.

One advantage of publishing consecutive rolls is that it provides an opportunity to compare business and the persons involved. Several wills figure in the 1688/9 roll, and just as Jonas Burnett had tried the previous year to influence from the grave the wish of his son Joseph to marry Mary Brookesbanck, to prevent which Jonas threatened to bequeath his land to a grandchild Jonas, so Mary Mawde of Halifax left her property in trust for the benefit of her grandsons John and Jonathan Mawde on the understanding that at the end of twelve years, when they would come into possession of the estate, they should make no provision for their mother Sarah out of its revenue 'or suffer her to dwell with them or have any releife livelyhood or succour from them or either of them during her naturall life'. Should this wish be disregarded, the property would remain with the trustees for their own benefit (pp 49-53). Mrs Mawde seems to have had a sour view of human nature, for in a codicil to prevent future dispute she amended her instruction to the trustees to split her estate equally between the grandsons, and explicitly named the pieces of land to go to each. She also left a legacy of £100 to 'their sister Mary Mawde', to be paid, £50 from each, by the brothers, 'this legacy [to be] kept private by my trustees till the summe become payable'. (She also bequeathed an eleven-year lease of six closes to her servants Martha Riddlesden and James Hoyle at a rent of £4 a year.)

Turning to personnel, one is struck by the regular appearance of certain jurymen at the Courts Baron. In 1687/8 Robert Cusworth served no less than 8 times, and appeared as many times in 1688/9. Thomas Totty served 7 times and 8 times respectively. Usually the attendance was less balanced. John Leake occurs 6 times in 1687/8 and 3 times in 1688/9. Gideon Mawde's record was 6 and 4 respectively and William Walker 6 and 3. Tempest Pollard managed 11 appearances in 1688/9 as against only 3 the previous year: John Speight 5 times against one, Samuel Thornes 8 against 4, and Robert Bradford, who appeared 7 times in 1688/9, failed to appear at all the previous year.

Men on regular call as jurors at the Court Baron were often serving as graves. Bradford was grave of Ossett. John Clarkson was grave of Alverthorpe. John Haigh was grave of Horbury as well as deputy grave for Wakefield, Thornes and Alverthorpe. William Garlicke was grave of Rastrick and John Hinchliffe was grave of

Holme as well as a sworn man for Cartworth. John Harrison was one of the sworn men for Walton, while George Hebdon was a sworn man for Stanley. Other jurors at the Court Baron included Robert Hare, constable for Emley, Thomas Shillitoe, constable for Crigglestone, and William Walker, constable for Midgley. This probably means no more than that they were of local standing. Anthony Bland, a regular signatory to presentments for the Wakefield Court Leet of 6 April 1689, had been one of the two affearers for fines at Wakefield to be elected on 1 October 1687.

Graves were selected on the basis of possession of specific copyhold lands. Where the holders were of superior social standing, such as Roger Nowell, esq, for Stanley, or the governors of the poor of Wakefield for Thornes in 1688, a substitute was found. The presentation of graves was made at the Great Court, held on 12 October in 1688 but confusingly on 30 September 1687. (Obviously the Great Court was held on the court day next after Michaelmas.) It is therefore surprising to find the relevant documentation carefully filed after the business of Courts Baron held on 2 and 23 November, and 4 and 25 January 1689, particularly after the last court. The presentment for Sowerby graveship was signed by John Hargreaves, deputy grave from the previous year, that for Hipperholme by John Brearcliffe, that for Holme by John Hinchliffe, and that for Thornes by Thomas Harrison, each of the latter three being graves from the previous year. The qualifying land is different in each case. Two of the individuals who were co-signatories with the outgoing grave of Sowerby had signed the previous nomination, but this not the case with the others (pp 14, 17, 24, 27-9).

The Court Baron was presided over by Francis Whyte, esq, high steward of the manor and also a justice of the peace.[2] The actual work

---

2 National Archives, Kew, C/93/12/5. This contains a list of West Riding JPs for 1685. In addition to Francis Whyte it includes Thomas Armitage, bart, and John Gill, who were listed as free tenants of the manor, due to appear at the Great Court. I am grateful to Mr G.C.F. Forster for this information.

was done by John Scott, deputy steward, assisted by John Hargreaves senior of Halifax, an attorney who also filled in as deputy grave of Hipperholme and Sowerby. By custom, when a conveyance of land was made involving the consent of a wife, the high steward was required to examine her to confirm that she gave her assent to the transaction.[3] The roll notes that this examination was normally done by Scott, although special appointments of another to perform the duty were made by Whyte on three occasions. Francis Whyte affixed his wax seal between paper to these documents, and the same signet was apparently loaned to seal other court documents including the fictitious leases used to provide cause for seizure of copyhold land where the possessor wished to alter the details of his title.

As for the Court Leet, consideration of the panels to whom the township constables and four sworn men made their half-yearly reports shows various differences of procedure. While the numbers on the panel varied between twelve and fourteen, the numbers who signed the presentments, authorising the amount of fines (which are sometimes written over an earlier sum, usually reducing it) vary considerably. In the Wakefield Court Leet, while the first name on the list, presumably the chairman, usually signed each, his co-signatories often changed. Panellists were fairly stable. John Leake,

---

3 A rather unkempt scrap of paper appended to the record of the court held on 15 February 1689 purports to authorise a family trust on behalf of the wife of Thomas Kent, warranted by the delivery of a straw to Richard Harrison and William Moxon, who endorsed the paper (p 33). It is so illiterate one feels she should have been given the benefit of the doubt, but John Scott primly endorsed the fact that it was void as she had not been examined. It probably relates to conveyance no 36, (pp 30-1) where Thomas Kent, his son John and daughter Elizabeth, with John Bromley of Wakefield, gen, transferred land to Joseph Armitage of Outwoodside, Wakefield. There was no suggestion that Mrs Kent had any part in transaction. Could she have been the second wife, anxious to ensure provision for her own child, her two sisters, and their mother? While Harrison's standing is unclear Moxon was one of the panel of jurors at that court.

who served in October 1687, appeared in October 1688 and April 1689. William Robinson served in October 1687 and April 1689. George Waring served in October 1687 and October 1688. William Bateman served in April and October 1688. John Gupwell, Thomas Harris, Gideon Mawde, Jeremy Milner, Thomas Pasley, Samuel Peaker and Thomas Totty all did the same. Harris carried on to April 1689.

The picture was different in the other leet jurisdictions. At Halifax there was an inner core of five. Jonathan Kighley held the chair in October 1687, and signed most presentments, but Richard Scarborough totalled one more and William Redman one less. In April 1688 Edmund Deane held the chair and signed 15 bills, supported by the same Jonathan Kighley and John Farrer, with John Batley in addition. He continued in the chair in October 1688 with Kighley and Scarborough, supported to a lesser extent by George Towne and John Lockwood. In April 1689 it was Scarborough's turn to take the chair. The others stood down, but the committee system was widened with Abraham Brigge, Joshua Dearden, Michael Oldfield, Richard Patchett and Joshua Whitehead sharing the load.

At Brighouse the committee system also worked to some extent. The chairman signed most presentments, and in October 1687 the work was shared with four others, another six appending the occasional signature. Only Geoffrey Ramsden carried on to the April session, when the chairman was William Wilton, gen. Five panellists failed to sign a single bill, and four signed only once (including Geoffrey Ramsden). Nevertheless, Ramsden was listed in October 1688, when the chairman was Daniel Walker. The next session saw the committee system re-activated with Joseph Lister in the chair, aided by Francis Preistley (chairman in October 1687) and Joseph Wood. Samuel Appleyard was also brought in from October 1687. Jonathan Threapland had been a panellist in October 1687, October 1688 and April 1689, but managed only two signatures during this period.

At Kirkburton the committee system was in full force. In October 1687 John Earnshawe took the chair, supported by John Battye and William Morehouse. He then stood down and was followed in May by William Morehouse, who had the support of Richard Mathewman, John Battye and John Roades. (No one else signed anything.) In October 1688 the chairman was Godfrey Crosland, supported by John Battye, John Rhodes and John Hinchliffe. In April 1689 Richard Morton held the chair, with John Battye still active, but the load was now shared among James Fraunce, Thomas Firth, Thomas Peace, Robert Hare and John Tincker. (One bill was signed by all panellists, perhaps because it was brought up in court by a member. It is couched in the first person and complained of the state of a road leading to a coal pit owned by Robert Hare [p 160].)

The case of Robert Hare is an example of a juror with personal interests in a complaint brought before the court. Was the John Leake, juror at the Court Baron held on 26 April 1689 identical with the John Leake presented at the same court for breaking the pinfold at Stanley and leading a wain with manure on the common balk between Smalley and Harwdfield in Stanley and not keeping to the ancient and usual way? He had been presented previously for a similar offence at the Court Leet on 13 October 1688 and been fined 30s, with an additional 3s 4d for failure to cut his hedge (pp 44, 56, 87, 130). At the Halifax Court Leet held on 15 October 1688 Richard Stansfield of Stansfield was charged with going over a close and breaking down its fence. The bill shows that a traverse was entered, and the jury found that he was entitled to such access. He was the constable of Stansfield (pp 91, 92, 103-4). At the Court Leet held at Kirkburton on 17 October 1688 one of the presentments for Cumberworth was to the affect that Thomas Parkin had assaulted William Marsh, who happened to be one of the four sworn men. This was the subject of a special bill, signed by all the panel. This refined the charge to an affray on 4 June, and named Marsh as bringing the charge on oath, together with a separate sworn testimony by him of an affray on 5 July between Joseph Bilcliffe of Cumberworth and William Richy. In both cases a fine of 10s was imposed (pp 111, 119, 126). Could the Richard Morton, presented by Flockton for breaking down a stile and blocking the usual footway over a close leading to Nether Flockton, be identical with the constable for Holme and chairman for Kirkburton Court Leet the following April? Certainly the presentment was deleted (pp 112, 120, 156). In contradistinction, George Roebucke, a juror at the same court and also a co-constable for Kirkburton, put in a claim against any making a path over Hinchclife croft in Fulstone. Offenders were to be fined a shilling (pp 111, 122). Similarly James Hinchliffe, a juror, put in a claim against any driving sheep or cattle into his close called Goodbentclough in Austonley on pain of 10s (pp 111, 125). At the Court Leet at Kirkburton held on 10 April 1689 John Brooke may well have used his position as one of the sworn men to complain that his close called Boothhousebank was being crossed although there was no usual way there. The proposed fine of 3s 4d was amended to 1s (p 170).

Editorial Method

As in previous volumes the spelling of all proper names of places and persons has been retained. A minimum of punctuation has been added. Deletions have been shown within asterisks. Words inserted above the line are shown within diamond brackets. Marginalia are printed in italics, as are words in Latin inserted after the English translation where the actual words seem worthy of record. Editorial additions are given within square brackets. There are three indexes, of persons, places and subjects. Named closes, fields and shotts are given in the Subject Index, arranged according to graveship. In the index of Places the name is given in its modern form where ascertainable from listing in A.H. Smith, *The Place-Names of the West Riding of Yorkshire, parts II and III* (1961). In a number of cases the modern form breaks the place-name up into its constituent words, such as Booth Stead, Brig Royd, Dick Edge, High Lee, Ing Head, Long Edge, Over Hill House or Tail Small. Names of closes are generally descriptive and one must remember that *inge* represents a meadow by a stream, *pightel* is a small enclosure or croft, and *shutt* is a corner of land or a share of the common land. Each place is identified topographically by township or graveship as indicated by the text. Where no county is shown in the text, the place is located in Yorkshire.

Acknowledgements

It remains for me to express my grateful thanks to the Council of the Yorkshire Archaeological Society for lodging the draft version of the 1688/9 roll within the Tyne and Wear Archives Department at Newcastle upon Tyne for my convenience for transcription, and to Ms E. Rees, Chief Archivist there, for accepting t+his roll for storage while I completed my work. I am obliged to the West Yorkshire Archive Service for supplying me with a microfilm of the engrossed roll, which forms the basis of the text of this volume. Mr Robert Frost, Chief Librarian at Claremont, facilitated the transfer arrangements. Mrs Judith Rushton has coped most patiently with the text as supplied by me on diskette and in hard copy, and dealt with necessary corrections.

C.M. Fraser

MD225/1/414

THE COURT ROLL OF THE MANOR OF WAKEFIELD, 1688/9

membrane 1

Great Court of William Craven, knt, and Edwin Wiat, esq, serjeant at law, lords of the Manor of Wakefield, in fiduciary use for Elizabeth Clapham, widow, held before Francis Whyte, esq, high steward of the Manor Court, at Wakefield on 12 October 4 James [1688].

Free Tenants Present: George, marquis of Halifax, Lyon Pilkington, bart, the heirs of Thomas Savile, esq, Thomas Armitage, bart, the heirs of William Savile, esq, the heirs of Richard Law, gen, George Thornhill, esq, William Farrer, esq, Robert Wrightson, gen, the heirs of Robert Benson, esq, Cyril Arthington, esq, William Horne, gen, Edward Goodwin, gen, John Stanhope, esq, John Gill, gen, by right of his wife, Sarah Brooke, spinster, Benjamin Law, gen, William Potham, gen, Thomas Naylor of Clifton, John Pymont, John Kitson, James Pearson, Richard Liversedge, Thomas Crosland, Thomas Archer, Francis Wilkinson, gen, by right of his wife, James Chadwicke, Richard Swallowe, the heirs of Samuel Fournes, gen, Robert Mitchell, Robert Brigge, the heirs of Robert Johnson, William Dixon, William Hall, Samuel Norton, Thomas Johnson, clerk, and Edward Dixon, for their lands and tenements owed suit of court from three weeks to three weeks by ancient custom, and some made fine with the lord to relax the suit until the next Great Court to be held at Michaelmas next unless something required their presence: which fines were admitted by the steward of the court.
Panel for the lords of the Manor Inquest taken on the oaths of John Harrison, Gideon Mawde, gen, William Hanson, junior, James Wilson, Thomas Paslay, Benjamin Cowpe, Joseph Breare, Joseph Preistley, John Leake, William Dawson of Horbury, John Rowley, Humphrey Roebuck, William Dawson of Rastricke, William Hall, Gervase Sedgwicke, John Walker, and John Mawdsley, jurors, who said that William <12d> Potham, gen, Edward <12d> Goodwin, gen, John <2s 6d> Stanhope, esq, John <12d> Kitson, Thomas<12d> Crosland, and Edward <12d> Dixon owed suit and did not appear nor essoin, so they were in mercy as shown above their heads.
Stanley Item, they presented that Benjamin Clarke, gen, was dead since the last great court, and George Dixon the same.

Hipperholme Item, that Jonathan Hall was dead since the last great court.
Horbury Item, John North the same.
Hipperholme (1) It was attested by John Hargreaves senior, gen and lords' tenant, that John Langley of Northowrome on 10 October instant surrendered into the lords' hands a parcel of land estimated at 20 yards by 10 yards, lately enclosed by the said John Langley and lying above a parcel of land called le Greene between Shibden brooke and Simcarr Inge in Northowrome in the graveship of Hipperholme at an annual lords' rent of ½d, non-compounded: to the use of Joseph Crowther of Northowrome, yeo, his heirs and assigns, for ever. Agreed, to hold by customary service: entry fine [blank].
Holme (2) It was attested by William Turner, gen and lords' tenant, that Richard Tolson of Wath, esq, on 28 September last surrendered into the lords' hands the reversion immediately after the death of himself of the residence (*domus mansional'*) and all structures appurtenant and adjacent at Shaley and the arable close known as Thompson Close in which they stood, and three closes of arable, meadow and pasture with ways, waters, watercourses, easements, profits and commodities appurtaining at Shaley in Wooldale and Scholes in the graveship of Holme, lately held by William Wagstaffe and Robert Wagstaffe or their assigns and now by Thomas Firth or his assigns, with all other customary land of the said Richard Tolson, lately of John Savile, clerk, deceased, at an annual lords' rent of 22d, compounded: to the use of Elizabeth Tolson, eldest daughter of the said Richard Tolson, and the lawful heirs of her body, for lack of which, to the use of Katherine Tolson, second daughter, etc, for lack of which, to the use of Anne Tolson, third daughter, etc, for lack of which to Wilfrid Tolson, third son of Richard Tolson, etc, for lack of which to Edward Tolson, fourth son, etc, for lack of which to Richard Tolson, second son of Richard Tolson, etc, for lack of which to the heirs of Richard Tolson the father for ever, and not otherwise, to hold by the customary service to the manor. Elizabeth Tolson gave 2s 9d as entry fine.
- (3) William Roberts, now or lately of the parish of Stepney, co Middlesex, gen, and Mary his wife, she examined separately by the steward of the manor court by John Scott, gen, deputy steward, outside the court, on 28 September last surrendered into the lords' hands a new house adjoining an old messuage called Burn Lee, two bays of a barn or *lathe*, lately built adjoining an old barn at the east end, an 'outshutt' thereto adjoining, a bay of a *mistall* beside the old barn, with all ways and easements between the new house and new barn and the fold around the said house and as mentioned more fully in the articles of agreement between George Dixon and William Gleidhill, a close

of arable called Crimble Close, another close of arable called Hirst, a close of arable called Lathcroft, another called le Springewood, another beside the highway called Banckwood, a little meadow called le Broad Lane Close at the upper end of the said ground (*fundorum*), half of a little croft under the house on the west end, the east end of a meadow called Knacker, a meadow called Greatbothome, a parcel of ground called a lane, previously fenced at the upper end of a close at Burnlee called Long Close, leading to Springwood, previously occupied by George Dixon, five yards of land to build on the west of the new house, with rights appurtaining in the graveship of Holme, with all ways, watercourses, profits, easements and commodities, these being parcel of an ancient messuage at Burnlee estimated at 8 acres in the occupation of John Gleidhill and previously of Henry Greene, deceased, at an annual lords' rent of 3s 5d, compounded, and also an annuity of 26s 8d payable at Whitsun and Martinmas in equal portions, deriving from a messuage called Whickleden and 19½ acres with buildings in Scholes in the graveship of Holme now occupied by John Greene or his assigns, with all title, interest, etc of the said William Roberts therein: to the use of David Dixon of Burnlee in the parish of Almonbury, salter, his heirs and assigns for ever. Agreed, by customary service: entry fine, 10s 3d.

Alverthorpe (4) It was attested by Thomas Harrison, lords' tenant, that Richard Thornton of Wakefeld, esq, Obediah Lee, clerk, vicar of Wakefeld, John Waterhouse, senior, Thomas Chirrieholme, Charles Naylor, Richard Ellis, Daniel Mawde, Francis Whyte, esq, John Scott, George Redshawe, William Turner, and William Haward, all of Wakefeld, gentlemen, Joseph Watkinson of Flanshawe in the parish of Wakefeld, gen, and Francis Nevile of Chevett, esq, governors of Queen Elizabeth's Free Grammar School at Wakefeld, on 8 October instant surrendered into the lords' hands a parcel of land with all ways, easements and liberties appurtaining in the graveship of Alverthorpe lately occupied by Widow Scott and Widow Kighley or their assigns at an annual lords' rent of 1d, non-compounded: to the use of John Oldroyd of Alverthorpe, clothier, and his executors, administrators, and assigns for the term of 200 years, rendering annually to the Governors, their heirs, successors, and assigns 12d a year at the feast of St Matthew the apostle [21 September], even if not asked. Should the rent fall into arrears by eight days after the date due, the Governors, their heirs, successors and assigns might re-enter and enjoy the lands as before. Granted, by customary service. Entry fine [blank].

Ossett (5) It was attested by William Harrupp, lords' tenant, that Elizabeth Peace of Ossett in the parish of Dewsbury, spinster, on 13 August 1687 surrendered into the lords' hands the reversion after her death of an estimated rood of arable land in the north field of Ossett on the shott called Storgate or Cherrytree shutt, abutting on le New Parke pale to the north and Storgate syke on the south, also a selion and butt in Ossett in the north field on the shott called Ryecroft, estimated at a half acre, lying between the land of Richard Grice, gen, and of John Hopkinson, gen, on the south and west, now occupied by the said Elizabeth Peace, within the graveship of Ossett, with all ways, etc, at an annual lords' rent of 1½d, compounded: to the use of John Peace of Ossett, yeo, his heirs and assigns for ever. Agreed, by customary service: entry fine, 2¼d.

membrane 1 dorse

(6) It was attested by John Mitchell, lords' tenant, that Anne Oates of Dodworth in the parish of Silkston, spinster, on 14 August last surrendered into the lords' hands all the close and parcel of land in the township and graveship of Ossett estimated at 3 acres, commonly called Adcuckroyd, now in the possession of Josiah Oates of Chickingley, yeo, and lately of the inheritance of John Halleley of Earlsheaton, abutting on a vennel leading from Chickingley to Ossett on the north and on the close called le Adcuckroyd to the south and on another close called Adcuckroyd on the west and on two closes called les Pildarse to the east, at an annual lords' rent of 6d, compounded: to the use of Josiah Oates, his heirs and assigns for ever. Agreed: entry fine, 18d.

Horbury (6) (*sic*) It was attested by Samuel Thornes, lords' tenant, that Richard Stephenson of Horbury, cardmaker, on 7 May last surrendered into the lords' hands a rood of arable land in le Milnefield of Horbury on a shott called le Holmes shutt between the land of Robert Leeke, gen, on the north, and of John Wadsworth on the south, and abutting on a close called Wees Pitt close of John Rhodes, gen, on the east, with common pasture and all other rights appurtaining to the said rood in the graveship of Horbury, now occupied by Matthew Stephenson or his assigns at an annual lords' rent of ½d, compounded, to the absolute use of John Batley, his heirs and assigns for ever. Agreed: entry fine, 1½d.

Stanley (7) It was attested by William Midlebrooke, lords' tenant, that Benjamin Clarke, gen, on 14 May last surrendered in court into the lords' hands all messuages, cottages, closes, lands, and tenements with rights appurtaining in the Manor of Wakefeld held by copy of court roll, to such uses as Benjamin Clarke might specify in his last will and testament in writing and not otherwise.

Wakefeld (8) It was attested by William Midlebrooke, lords' tenant, that George Chipchase of Wakefeld, pewterer, and Elizabeth his wife, she examined separately, and John Chipchase of the same, cloth-worker, on 25

September last surrendered into the lords' hands the reversion after the death of Anne, now wife of Anthony Bland of Wakefeld, cloth-worker, mother of the said George and John, of all that messuage and all houses, buildings, barns, structures, folds, yards (*atria*), gardens, orchards, easements and hereditaments appurtaining in Wakefeld in the street called Northgate, now occupied by the said Anthony Bland or his assigns at an annual lords' rent of 1d, compounded, with all title, interest, etc, for the use of the said Anthony Bland, his heirs, and assigns for ever. Agreed: entry fine, 1½d.

Wakefeld The heirs of John Walker were elected as grave for a close called Hodgson Close and Little Fallyng or Fall Lane Close, and deputed John Briggs, who was received and sworn.

Stanley Roger Nowell, esq, was elected grave for lands in Stanley, and had the aid of Lyon Pilkington, bart, for lands late of Saviles, and deputed Joseph Armitage, who was received and sworn.

Alverthorpe John Clarkson was elected grave for lands in Newton previously of Leonard Wilson. He was received and sworn.

Thornes The Governors of the Poor of Wakefeld were elected grave for lands in Thornes. They deputed John Haigh, who was received and sworn.

Sandall Thomas Johnson of Painthorpe, clerk, was elected grave for lands previously of John Haigh and Oliver Haigh, and the said Thomas Johnson was received and sworn.

Horbury George Naylor of the city of London, gen, was elected grave for lands in Ossett, and deputed John Haigh, who was received and sworn.

Ossett Robert Bradford was elected grave for lands in the graveship. He was received and sworn.

Holme Richard Brooke of Lepton was elected grave for a messuage or tenement called Nabb, with lands appurtaining, and had the aid of Luke Firth for lands in Overthwonge, of John Dearniley for lands in Overthwonge lately of Robert Swallowe, of Michael Midgley for lands lately of Anthony Swallowe, of Godfrey Crosland for lands lately of Andrew Swallowe, of the heirs of Josiah Broadhead for a close called Overbinfield, of Sarah Thewlis for 3 acres at Dickedge, of John Armitage for 3 acres in Austonley lately of Richard Broadhead, of James Haigh for a close lately Swallows, of James France for Wheelsbrooke lately Swallows, of Simeon Hirst for two closes lately of Andrew Swallowe, of Thomas Cuttell for a cottage and garden lately appurtaining to the said messuage called Nabb, and of Edmund Broadhead for a parcel of land lately Swallows. He deputed Jonathan Wilson, who was received and sworn.

Sowerby George Holgate was elected grave for a messuage called Wheatley royd and three other messuages with lands appurtenant in Blackwood. He

had the aid of the heirs of Abraham Hitchon of [blank] Brooke, of Job Sutcliffe for a messuage called Inghead, of Thomas Ibbettson for the messuage in Blackwood near Boy Mill, lately of James Dobson, of Richard Midgley for lands at Brearley bridge called Milnehill, lately land of John Farrer, and of John Wilkinson for a messuage in Blackwood called Handcarr, lately of Samuel Haldsworth, with all land appurtenant. He deputed John Hargreaves, gen, who was received and sworn.
Hipperholme Thomas Preistley and Francis Preistley were elected grave for a messuage in Preistley Greene and all land appurtenant in Hipperholme, and Jonathan Preistley for the messuage and land called Winteredge, and the said Thomas and Francis for another messuage at Preistley Greene now occupied by Joseph Halliday with appurtenances, and they deputed John Hargreaves, gen, who was received and sworn.
Rastricke William Garlicke was elected grave for land called Heys lands, and was received and sworn.
Scammonden Thomas Denton was elected grave for two messuages called Crofthouse, and was received and sworn.

[in draft, Wakefield Court Roll MD225/1/414lA after membrance 7]

A
Panel of jurors 12 October 1688
John Harrison
Gideon Mawde, gen
John Mawdsley
William Hanson jr
James Wilson
Thomas Pasley
Benjamin Cowpe
Joseph Breare
Joseph Preistley
John Leake
William Dawson of Horbury
John Rowley
Humphrey Roebuck
William Dawson of Rastrick
William Hall
Gervase Sedgwick
John Walker
John Mawdsley

B

Wakefield At the Great Court holden there the 12th day of October 1688 wee present as followeth:

In primis wee present All Noble men for defalt of non appearaunce each per pole	0 - 6 - 8
Item wee present Knights for the like per pole	0 - 3 - 4
Item wee present Esquiers for the like per pole	0 - 2 - 6
Item wee present Gentlemen for the like per pole	0 - 1 - 0
Item wee present all other sutors for the like per pole	0 - 0 - 6

Stanley Item wee finde that Mr Beniamin Clarke is dead since the last great Court and Beniamin his sonn is the next heire.

Item wee finde that Georg Dixon is dead since the last Court.

Hipperholme Item <Mr> Jonathan Hall is dead since the last Court.

Horbury Item John North is dead since the last Court.

Item wee present all those that essoyne the last Court and not appeard this per pole 0 - 1 - 0

[signed]	John Harrison	William Dawson
	Gideon Maude	John Rowley (did not appear)
	William Hanson	Humphrey Roebuck (did not appear)
	James Willson	William Dawsonn
	Thomas Paslay	William Hall
	Benjamin Coupe	Gervas Sedgeworth
	Joseph Preistley	John Walker
	Joseph Breare	John Maudsley
	John Leake	

C

Copyhold Rents paid by the Heirs of George Thornhill, esq, late of Fixby, deceased:

	l s d
For the demaine of Fixby per annum	1 - 8 - 4
For lower Strangsly & Osburnes	0 - 4 - 0
For Salmon Croft	0 - 0 - 4
For the farme called Knoles in Fixby	0 - 0 - 4
For the farme called the Wood in Fixby	0 - 1 - 1
For parte of John Hirst Farme	0 - 2 - 3
	1 -16 - 4

Copyhold Rents paid by the Tenants of Madam Thornhill the elder as followes:

	l s d
Charles Farrer	0 - 8 - 0
Edward Berry	0 - 9 – 6½
Jonas Preston	0 - 6 - 6
John Hoyle	0 - 1 – 8¼
William Garlicke	0 - 8 - 1
Joshua Lumme	0 - 0 - 3
Isaac Bates	0 - 0 – 9½
Parte of John Hirst Farme about	0 - 8 – 0

membrane 1 dorse continued

Court Baron held on 2 November 1688

Panel for the lords of the Manor Inquest taken on the oaths of Daniel Mawde, gen, Joseph White, Percival Terry, John Walker, John Sunderland, Tempest Pollard, Thomas Totty, Robert Cusworth, Thomas Shillitoe, John Haigh, James Scrivener and Michael Parker, jurors.

Alverthorpe / Thornes They testified that Thomas Mawde of Doncaster, gen, son of John Mawde late of Wakefeld, gen, deceased, by indenture of 13 October last leased to a John Haigh of Horbury, yeo, the two closes of land, meadow or pasture with appurtenances in a field of Alverthorpe called Humble Jumble Field, one in the occupation of Richard Ellis, and the other of William Totty or their assigns (except for a selion in the close of William Totty held of the heirs of William Savile, esq), also the close estimated at 2 acres, lying by le Broadfore, occupied by William Totty or his assigns, also another selion of arable estimated at a half acre in an unenclosed field called Cliffe Field between the lands lately of William Savile, esq, on the north and south, and abutting on the way to le Windywell on the east, with all ways, waters, watercourses, etc, all lying in the graveships of Alverthorpe and Thornes at an annual lords' rent of 2s 8d, compounded: to have and to hold to John Haigh, his executors, administrators, and assigns from that date for 21 years following, without licence of court, to the lords' contempt, etc. Order to the graves of Alverthorpe and Thornes to seize the land into the lords' hands before the next court.

Sandall The same testified that Edward Thomas of Waukcliffe, tanner, and Elizabeth Thomas of Kirke Fenton, widow, mother of the said Edward, Thomas Barber of Wintersett, yeo, and John Walker of Horbury, yeo, by indenture of 9 October last leased to a Joseph Hall of Sandallmagna, yeo, that

messuage with barns, structures, folds, yards, etc, in Humleyroyd now occupied by George Fairbarne or his assigns, also a close called Syke Inge, occupied by Samuel Norton of Kettlethorpe, gen, these lying / **membrane 2** / in the townships of Sandall and Criglestone in the graveship of Sandall, at an annual lords' rent of 13d, compounded, with reversions: to the use of Joseph Hall, his executors, administrators, and assigns for 21 years, without licence of the court, etc. Order to the grave of Sandall to seize the lands.
Item, they testified that John Ashley of Dewsbury fenced, enclosed and dug a parcel of ground lying by the house of John Hemmingway in Dewsbury within the jurisdiction of the court. *amerced 39s 11d*
Ossett (9) It was attested by Joseph White, lords' tenant, that John Hileley of Earlesheaton, yeo, and Elizabeth his wife, she examined separately, on 17 August last surrendered into the lords' hands 5 roods of arable on a shott in the field called Arundell Field at Arrlesheaton, with all ways, etc, in the graveship of Ossett, now occupied by the said John Hileley or his assigns at an annual lords' rent of 2d, compounded: to the use of Richard White, son of the said Joseph, his executors, administrators, and assigns from 29 September 1689 for 10 years at an annual rent to John Hileley, his heirs and assigns of a red rose at the time of roses, if asked. Agreed: entry fine, 3d.
Hipperholme (10) It was attested by John Hargreaves senior, gen, lords' tenant, that Joseph Wood senior of Fould in Northowrome and Joseph Wood junior of the same, son and heir apparent, on 19 October last surrendered into the lords' hands 2 closes of land and pasture, one called Mainroyde, estimated at 2½ acres, and the other called Anthonywell Close adjoining and estimated at 1½ acres, with their appurtenances in Northowrome in the graveship of Hipperholme, now occupied with the messuage called Willroyde House by Daniel Pellington and Nathaniel Pellington or their assigns, with all ways, etc, at an annual lords' rent of 16d, compounded: to the use of James Cawbert of Eland Hall in Eland, yeo, his heirs and assigns for ever, under conditions expressed in indentures of contract of sale of the date of the surrender between Joseph Wood senior and junior and the said James Cawbert. Agreed: entry fine, 4s.
Wakefield (11) Thomas Bargh of Wakefeld, grocer, by John Scott, gen, deputy steward of the court, outside of court on 29 November 1686, surrendered into the lords' hands the reversion immediately after his death of that messuage near le Bitchhill in Wakefield in Northgate, also all shops, cellars, frontages, 'penthouses' (*imbricamenta*), privileges, liberties, etc, at a lords' rent of [blank], compounded, now occupied by Thomas Bargh or his assigns: to the use of William Bargh, youngest son of the said Thomas, his heirs and assigns for ever, provided that if Joseph, son and heir apparent of

Thomas Bargh, his heirs, executors, and assigns paid to William Bargh, his executors, administrators, and assigns £100 within 12 months after the decease of Thomas, without fraud or delay, the surrender became void. Also if Thomas Bargh during his lifetime wished to revoke the surrender he might offer to William Bargh and John Scott or any other representative 6d in the presence of two or more credible witnesses, and declare that he had changed his mind. As Thomas was dead, it was agreed that William Bargh, his heirs and assigns have the property for ever, under the conditions, by customary service. Entry fine of [blank].

Holme (12) Martha Howitt, widow, cousin and next heir of John Hadfield, the son of John Hadfield and Elizabeth his wife, she being sister and next heir of John Roberts late of Staleywood, co Cheshire, wheelwright, deceased, appeared before the steward of the court and gave 12s 6d for leave to inherit a new house adjoining an old messuage called Burn Lee, with all houses, buildings, barns, structures, folds, gardens, orchards, closes, lands, tenements and hereditaments, etc, in the graveship of Holme, now occupied by John Gleidhill or his assigns at an annual lords' rent of 3s 5d, compounded, with an annuity of 26s 8d payable at Whitsun and Martinmas in equal parts, derived from a messuage called Whickleden and 19½ acres and all structures built thereon in Scholes in the graveship of Holme, previously occupied by Joseph Mosley and John Tincker or their assigns, following the decease of John Hadfield the son, whose cousin and next heir was the said Martha Howitt. Agreed, Martha Howitt, her heirs and assigns to hold for ever, by customary service.

Rastricke / Hipperholme (13) Brian Thornhill, son and next heir of George Thornhill lately of Fixby, esq, deceased, came before the steward of the manor and gave [blank] for leave to inherit all those messuages, lands and tenements commonly called le Demesne of Fixby, and all lands called Lower Strangstye and Osburnes, and all that close or parcel of land called Salmon Crofte, and all that land called Knowles, and all that land called le Wood in Fixby, also all that land now occupied by John Hirst, with appurtenances in the graveship of Rastricke, also all other customary messuages, cottages, closes, land, tenements, mills, and hereditaments of which George Thornhill died so seised in the graveships of Rastricke and Hipperholme or elsewhere in the Manor of Wakefield, by whomsoever occupied, at an annual lords' rent of [blank], compounded. After the death of George, Brian was son and next heir. Agreed that he should hold by customary service, to him, his heirs and assigns for ever.

Sandall (14) It was testified by Daniel Mawde, gen, lords' tenant, that Joseph Oley senior of Heath in the parish of Warmfield on 12 September last surrendered into the lords' hands the reversion after the death of Joseph of a close of land, meadow or pasture called Roundynge, estimated at a half acre, and another close of land, meadow or pasture called Carsom Inge, estimated at 2½ acres, lying as three units in the graveship of Sandall, at an annual lords' rent of 12d, compounded: to the use of Deborah Rouse, Frances Oley and Elizabeth Oley, daughters of the said Joseph Oley, their heirs and assigns for ever. A fourth unit should go to Frances Oley for the use of Anne Oley *alias* Penny, for a term of 8 years, then to Edith Hartley, another daughter of the said Joseph, her heirs and assigns for ever. The reversion was agreed, namely, three units to Deborah Rouse, Frances Oley and Elizabeth Oley, their heirs and assigns for ever, and a fourth unit to Frances Oley for the use of Anne *alias* Penny for a term of 8 years and thereafter to Edith Hartley, her heirs and assigns for ever, to hold by customary service. Deborah, Frances and Elizabeth gave an entry fine of 13½d, and Frances fined 2¼d, and Edith Hartley fined 2¼d.

Rastrick / Hipperholme (15)Mary Thornhill, widow, lately wife of George Thornhill late of Fixby, esq, deceased, came before the steward and fined 12d for leave to have custody of Brian Thornhill, son and heir of George, with all his customary land and appurtenances in the several graveships of Rastricke and Hipperholme or elsewhere in the Manor during his minority. Agreed, until Brian reached the age of 21 years, she giving an account of her stewardship to Brian when he came of age.

Sum of court [blank]

[in draft, after membrane 11]

A

Panel: Daniel Mawde gen

Joseph White	Tempest Pollard	John Haigh
Percival Terry	Thomas Totty	James Scrivener
John Walker	Robert Cusworth	Michael Parker
John Sunderland	Thomas Shillitoe	

B

Indenture of 13 October 1688 between Thomas Mawde of Doncaster, co York, gen, son of John Mawde late of Wakefield, gen, deceased, of the one part, and John Haigh of Horbury, yeo, of the other, to the intent to give a voluntary cause of forfeiture and seizure of the land ... 'and to cutt off and destroy all remainders estates intaile and all other supposed and surmised rights... to reduce the same into a perfect state of inheritance in fee simple ... hath devised ... unto the said John Haigh ... all those two closes of land ... in

Humble Jumble Field [as above, p 8] for a term of 21 years at a rent of 5s a year in equal portions at Whitsun and Martinmas if lawfully demanded'. Sealed and delivered in the presence of Jo[hn] Scott and Robert Scott. Sealed by Thomas Maude.

2 Nov 1688 The Jury doe present and say that the lands and premisses above mencioned are devised contrary to the Custome of the Manour of Wakefield and therefore are forfeited and ought to be seised into the Lords of the said Manour hands.

[signed] Daniel Mawde John Haighe
John Walker John Sunderland
Record'

[endorsed] Mr Mawde of Doncaster Seisour

C

This Indenture made the Ninth day of October 1688 betweene Edward Thomas of Waukcliffe, co York, tanner, and Elizabeth Thomas of Kirk Fenton, widow, mother of the said Edward, Thomas Barber of Wintersett, yeo, and John Walker of Horbury, yeo, of the one party, and Joseph Hall of Sandall Magna, yeo, of the other party [as above, p 8]. The former have leased to the latter that messuage at Humleyroyd for 21 years at an annual rent of 20s, payable at Martinmas and Whitsun in equal portions, if demanded.

Sealed and delivered in the presence of
Thomas Johnson
Jo[hn] Scott
Robert Scott

Seals of Edward Thomas
Elizabeth Thomas her mark
Thomas Barber
John Walker

2nd Novembris 1688

The Jury doe present and say that the Lands and Tenements abovemencioned are devised contrary to the Custome of the Manour of Wakefield and therefore are forfeited and ought to bee seised.

[signed] Daniel Mawde John Haighe
John Walker Tempest Pollard Record'

[endorsed] Edward & Elizabeth Thomas Indenture & Warrant to give cause of Seisour'

D

2 November 1668

Wee the Jury there sworne for the lords of the Mannour doe present John Ashley of Dewsbury for encroaching, incloseing, ditching and digging upp one parcell of ground lyeing neare, adjoyneing and belonging to the now

dwellinghouse of John Hemmingway scituate in Dewsbury aforesaid within the Jurisdiction of this Court in xxxix^{s} xj^{d}.
[signed] Daniel Mawde / John Walker / John Haighe / Tempest Pollard

E
[Calendared]Whereas Thomas Mawde of Doncaster, gen, son of John Maude late of Wakefield, gen, deceased, had by Indenture given cause of forfeiture of those two closes of land, meadow or pasture with appurtenances in the field of Alverthorpe called Humble Jumble Field, one now or late in the occupation of Richard Ellis and the other by William Totty or by their assigns, except one selion of land in the close of William Totty now belonging to the heirs of William Savile, esq, deceased, and also that close of land, meadow and pasture estimated at 2 acres near the Broadfore with appurtenances, occupied by the said William Totty or his assigns, another selion of arable estimated at a half acre in the unenclosed field called Cliffefield, between the land of the late William Savile, esq, on the north and south, abutting on the way leading to Windywell on the east, with all ways, etc, in the graveships of Alverthorpe and Thornes at a yearly lords' rent of 2s 8d, compounded, as soon as three proclamations should be made, the lands were to be regranted, except the exceptions, to the same Thomas Mawde, his heirs and assigns for ever. This would be a sufficient warrant. Dated 13 October 4 James II, 1688.

Sealed and delivered before Signed: Thomas Maude [armorial seal]
Jo[hn] Scott / Robert Scott

F
A similar indenture whereby [Edward Thomas of Waukcliffe, tanner], Elizabeth Thomas of Kirkfenton, widow, Thomas Barber of Wintersett, yeo, and John Walker of Horbury, yeo, having given cause for forfeiture of the messuage in Humley royd, occupied by George Faireburne, and a close called Syke Ing Close, occupied by Samuel Norton of Kettlethorpe, gen, in the graveship of Sandall, being copyhold, having given cause for forfeiture, etc, authorized the regrant of the same to the same Samuel Norton. Witnessed 9 October 1688.

Sealed and delivered before [signed and sealed] Edward Thomas
Thomas Johnson Elizabeth * Thomas
Robert Scott Thomas Barber
John Walker

G
Wee whose names are underwritten doe present Thomas Johnson of Painethorpe, Clarke, this 27th of October 1688 Grave for Sandall for certaine lands formerly John Haighs and Oliver Haighs within the Graveshippe of Sandall, for the ensieing year.

[signed] Samuell Norton / Edward Illott / Joseph Hall / John <his mark> Leake

membrane 2 dorse

Court Baron held on 23 November 4 James II [1688]

Panel Inquest taken on the oaths of Daniel Mawde, gen, Gideon Mawde, gen, Robert Mansfield, Thomas Totty, Thomas Dodgson, Edmund Wood, Tempest Pollard, Francis Hatfield, John Clarkson, Robert Cusworth, Samuel Thornes, and John Leake, jurors.
Alverthorpe Certificate by the grave of Alverthorpe of the seizure of two closes, etc in the field of Alverthorpe called Humble Jumble Field (as above, p. 8). First proclamation.
Sandal Certificate by the grave of Sandall of the seizure of a messuage, etc at Humleyroyd, etc, in the townships of Sandall and Criglestone in the graveship of Sandall at a lords' rent of 13d, compounded. First proclamation.
Horbury (16) John North, son and next heir of John North, late of Horbury, yeo, deceased, came before the steward and gave the lords 9d for leave to inherit a messuage with appurtenances in Horbury and two crofts made into one in the graveship of Horbury, now occupied by Mary North, widow, or her assigns at an annual lords' rent of 3d, compounded, after the death of John North, his father. Agreed: to hold for ever by due service.
Sowerby (17) It was attested by John Hargreaves, senior, gen, lords' tenant, that Nathan Kirshaw of Soyland, yeo, on 17 November instant surrendered into the lords' hands two messuages with barns and structures at Redieshaw in Soyland in the graveship of Sowerby, and an estimated 9 acres 1 rood of land, meadow and pasture appurtenant, and another parcel of land from the lords' waste in Soyland, now enclosed in a close called le Halfeacre, containing 4 perches, occupied by Sarah Holroyd and Martha Hoyle or their assigns, with ways, waters, turbary, easements and emoluments in Soyland in the graveship of Sowerby at an annual lords' rent of 2s 7d, compounded: to the use of Joseph Kirshaw of Soyland in Sowerby, yeo, nephew of Nathan, his heirs and assigns for ever. Agreed, to hold by due service. Entry fine: 7s 9d.

Wakefield (18) William Hall of Wakefeld, barber, and Margaret his wife, she examined separately before the steward by John Scott, gen, deputy steward, surrendered outside court on 24 April past into the lords' hands a little house, cottage or tenement in Wakefeld at the lower end of the street in Wakefield called Rattonrow or Breadboothes, 4 yards in length and 4 yards in breadth, occupied by the said William Hall or his assigns at an annual lords' rent of 6d, compounded: to the use of Benjamin Clarke of Stanley, gen, his heirs and assigns for ever, on condition that if William Hall and Margaret his wife, their heirs, executors, administrators or assigns paid without fraud or delay to the said Benjamin Clarke or his certain attorneys, executors or administrators the sum of £5 with consideration on 24 April 1689 at the residence of Benjamin Clarke at Stanley, the surrender would become void. Because the said Benjamin was dead, it was agreed that Benjamin his son and heir and his assigns hold the house on the same conditions. Benjamin Clarke the son paid an entry fine of 18d.

Ossett (19) Richard Liversedge of Boothroyd in the parish of Dewsbury, yeo, by John Scott, gen, deputy steward, on 2 November instant surrendered outside court into the lords' hands three little closes or pighells of land in Ossett commonly called Burdleys, leading to Riplin Syke, estimated at 3 acres, also 6 acres of arable on several shotts in the east, west and north fields of Ossett with all ways etc in the graveship of Ossett, occupied by James Wilson and John Peace of Ossett, farmers (*agricol'*) or their assigns at an annual lords' rent of [blank], compounded: to the use of the said John Peace, his heirs and assigns for ever, on condition that if Richard Liversedge, his heirs, executors, administrators or assigns paid without fraud or delay to John Mann of Liversedge Lodge in the parish of Birstall, clothier, his executors, administrators or assigns £60 with consideration on 3 February next, also if Richard Liversedge, his heirs, etc indemnified John Peace, his heirs, etc for an obligation of the same date, whereby John Peace was obligated with Richard Liversedge in a debt to John Mann in the sum of £120, conditional on payment of the said sum of £60 with consideration on 3 February, and would indemnify John Peace, his heirs, etc, for any suits, disputes, costs, damages and expense etc arising from the obligation, then the surrender became void. Entry fine: [blank].

Sowerby (20) Richard Boyes, now or lately of Halifax, clerk, by John Scott, gen, deputy steward, on 9 November instant surrendered out of court into the lords' hands that messuage called Over long bothom, and all houses, edifices, barns, structures, lands, tenements and hereditaments in Warley in the graveship of Sowerby, now occupied by John Haigh or his assigns at an annual lords' rent of 10d, compounded: to the use of John Chesman of Leeds,

flax-dresser, 'son in law' of the same Richard Boyes, his executors, adminstrators and assigns for the 80 years following, should Richard Boyes live so long, at an annual rent of a red rose in the time of roses, if lawfully required. Agreed: entry fine, 15d.
Alverthorpe (21) William Horne of Wakefeld, gen, came into court and took a parcel of lords' waste land lying near le Humble Jumble brigg in the graveship of Alverthorpe containing 17 yards in breadth and 35 yards in length, abutting a cottage occupied by John Warde and John Robinson, and a close of the same William Horne on the north, and on le Becke on the west. Agreed it be held by him, his heirs and assigns for ever, at the lords' will and 2d new rent, payable at the usual times. Entry fine: 3s.

Sum of Court [blank]

[in draft, after membrane 15]
A
Panel for the lords of the manor and between parties

Daniel Mawde, gen	sworn
Gideon Mawde, gen	sworn
Robert Mansfield	sworn
Thomas Totty	sworn
Thomas Dodgson	sworn
Edmund Wood	sworn
Tempest Pollard	sworn
Francis Hatfield	sworn
John Clarkeson	sworn
Gervase <5s> Harrison	-
Robert Cusworth	sworn
Samuel Thornes	sworn
[diff hand] John Leake	sworn

Thomas Johnson sworn grave of Sandall
[no endorsement]

B
Wakefield Maner' Warrant of Francis Whyte, esq, high steward, to the grave of Alverthorpe and his deputy, to seize into the lords' hands before the next court at Wakefeld two closes of land, meadow or pasture in the field of Alverthorpe called Humble Jumble Field, one occupied by Richard Ellis and the other by William Totty, or their assigns, except etc, also a close estimated at 2 acres near le Broadfore, occupied by William Totty or his assigns, also a

selion estimated at a half acre in Cliffefield between the land late of William Savile, esq, to the north and south, and abutting a way to le Windy well on the east, in the graveships of Alverthorpe and Thornes at a lords' rent of 2s 8d, compounded. Given on 2 November 4 James II [1688]

[signed] Jo[hn] Scott

[endorsed] Wee whose names are here under written Tennants to the Lords of this Mannour of Wakefeild did the nineteenth day of Novembre Anno Regno Regis Jacobi secondi nunc Anglia etc quarto seize the Closes of land meadow and pasture into the hands of the lords of the Mannour contained in this precept. Wittnesse our hands the day and yeare abovesaid.

[signed] Daniel Mawde

Jerr' Spinke / Thomas Tottie / John Haighe grave

C

Wakefeld Maner' Warrant of Francis Whyte, esq, high steward, etc, to the grave of Sandall and his deputy to seize the messuage with all barns, structures, folds, yards, etc in Humleyroyd, occupied by George Fairebarne or his assigns, also the close called Syke Ing, occupied by Samuel Norton of Kettlethorpe, gen, or his assigns in the township of Sandall in the graveship of Sandall at a lords' rent of 13d, compounded.

Given on 2 November 4 James II [1688]. [signed] Jo[hn] Scott

[endorsed] November the 20th 1688

This warrant was executed by us then whose names are underwritten

Edward Illott / Jo. Wood / Joseph Hall / John Kirsell I

Richard Scholey depetty grave

D

Wee whose names are here unto subscribed doe find and present Roger Nowell esq to be grave this yeare: assistant to him Sir Lyon Pilkington Barronet for Savile land.

[signed] Gidion Maude / Francis Hatefield

Jarwis Harison / Thomas Dodgshon

[no endorsement]

membrane 3

Court Baron held on 14 December 4 James II [1688]

Panel Inquest taken on the oaths of Gideon Mawde, gen, Robert Cusworth, Jeremy Milner, Percival Terry, Gervase Harrison, Joseph White, Michael

Parker, Richard Hemmingway, James Scrivener, John Scrivener, Robert Bradford, and John Haigh, jurors.

They testified that William Sutcliffe of Hoohoyle in Erringden, yeo, and Henry Hyleley of Sowerby, yeo, by indenture of 21 November past leased to a William Midgley of Halifax, gen, that messuage called Hileley with all houses, edifices, barns, structures, folds, gardens, tofts, crofts, and closes appurtaining in Sowerby in the graveship of Sowerby, now occupied by Samuel Sutcliffe or his assigns at an annual lords' rent of 2s 5½d, compounded, with reversions and remainders, to William Midgley, his executors, administrators and assigns for 21 years, without fine or leave of the lords of the manor, in contempt and contrary to the custom of the court. Order to the grave of Sowerby to seize the land into the lords' hands before the next court.

Holme Item, they testified that Thomas Morehouse of Ebsonhouse in Fulstone in the parish of Kirkeburton, yeo, by indenture of 10 December instant leased to a Jeremy Kay of Copthurst in the parish of Kirkeburton, yeo, the messuage with appurtenances in Fulstone in the graveship of Holme commonly called Ebsonhouse and all closes known as le Croft under the house, le Parke, Over Ebsonroyds and Nether Ebsonroyds, Coat Close, Well Inge, Newlands Ing, Ebsonroyd Inge, Whitley, Stubbinge, Nookes, Ryebanck, Acre, Acre Inge, Scotroydleys, Great Adamley, Little Adamley, Adamley Inge, Overnewlands and Nethernewlands, with all ways etc, appurtenant in the graveship of Holme in the several occupation of the said Thomas Morehouse and John Turton or their assigns, at an annual lords' rent of 8s 1d, compounded (except part of a close called Whitley, not compounded), with reversions and remainders, to hold by Jeremy Kay, his executors, administrators and assigns for 21 years, without fine with the lords or leave of court, in contempt of the lords and contrary to the custom of the manor. Order to the grave to seize ...

Alverthorpe Second proclamation Appeal for claims to hold two closes from the lord of the manor in the field of Alverthorpe called Humble Jumble Field, one occupied by Richard Ellis and the other by William Totty or their assigns, saving a selion occupied by William Totty belonging to the heirs of William Savile, esq, deceased, and a close estimated at 2 acres near le Broadfore, occupied by William Totty, and a selion of arable estimated at a half acre, unenclosed, in a field called Cliffefield between land late of William Savile esq on the north and south, abutting on the way to le Windywell on the east in the graveship of Alverthorpe at a lords' rent of 2s 8d, compounded.

Sandal *Second proclamation* Appeal for claimants to hold a messuage, etc at Humleyroyd occupied by George Fairbarne or his assigns, and a close called Syke Inge occupied by Samuel Norton of Kettlethorpe, gen, or his assigns in the townships of Sandall and Criglestone in the graveship of Sandall at a lords' rent of 13d, compounded.
Alverthorpe (22) Richard Nayler of Wakefield, clothier, and Mary his wife, she examined separately by John Scott, gen, deputy steward, surrendered outside court on 5 December instant into the lords' hands a cottage in the graveship of Alverthorpe at the upper end of a close lately of John Roades abutting on le Westgate Moore, adjoining a close previously of Cotton Horne, gen, to the north, and a beck (*rivolam*) on the west, with all ways, etc, now occupied by John Warde and John Robinson or their assigns at an annual lords' rent of 1d, compounded: to the use of William Horne of Wakefield, gen, his heirs and assigns for ever. Agreed: entry fine: 3d.
Ossett (23) Jeremy Goodall, now or lately of Gawthorpe, farmer, son of Isabel Fearnley of Gawthorpe, widow, by John Scott, gen, deputy steward, surrendered outside court on 22 November past into the lords' hands the reversion after the death of Isabel Fearnley of the close of arable, meadow or pasture called New Close or Coalpitt Closse in Gawthorpe, now occupied by John Bradley of Gawthorpe, cardboard maker, or his assigns, estimated at six acres, with all ways, etc, at an annual lords' rent of 12d, compounded: to the use of the said John Bradley, his heirs and assigns, forever. Agreed: entry fine, 18d.

Sum of court [blank]

[in draft, after membrane 17]
A
Pannell pro Dominis Manerij inter partes

Gideon Mawde gen	sworn	Robert Cusworth	sworn
Jeremy Milner	sworn	Percival Terry	sworn
Gervase Harrison	sworn	Joseph White	sworn
Michael Parker	sworn	Richard Hemmingway	sworn
James Scrivener	sworn	John Scrivener	sworn
Robert Bradford	sworn	John Haigh	sworn
Joseph Armitage	sworn	deputy grave of Stanley	

[no endorsement]

B
Indenture of 21 November 4 James, 1688, between William Sutcliffe of Hoohoyle in Erringden, yeo, and Henry Hyleley of Sowerby, yeo, of the one

part, and William Midgley of Hallifax, gen, of the other part, whereby to give cause of forfeiture, etc, Sutcliffe and Hyleley leased to William Midgley that messuage commonly called Hileleigh and all houses, edifices, barns, buildings, folds, gardens, tofts, crofts, closes, lands, tenements and hereditaments thereto belonging, lying in Sowerby in the graveship of Sowerby, now occupied by Samuel Sutcliffe or his assigns at a lords' rent of 2s 5½d, compounded, with all reversions and remainders, for a term of 21 years at a yearly rent of 40s payable at the feasts of Pentecost and Martinmas by equal portions. Witnessed

Sealed and delivered
in presence of us [signed and sealed] William Sutcliffe
Henry Hyleley

John Hargreaves jr
Susanna Hargreaves
Jo[hn] Hargreaves

[1]The jury doe present & say that the lands above-mentioned are devised contrary to the Custome of the manner and therefore are forfeited and ought to be seized into the Lords hands

[signed] Gideon Maude / John Haighe / Richard Hemingway / John Scrivener

[no endorsement]

C

Indenture of 10 December 4 James II [1688] between Thomas Morehouse of Ebsonhouse in Fulstone, parish of Kirkeburton, yeo, of the one part, and Jeremy Kay of Copthurst in the said parish, yeo, of the other part, witnessed that Thomas Morehouse to give cause of forfeiture, etc, had demised to Jeremy Kay his executors, administrators and assigns all his tenements in Fulstone in the graveship of Holme commonly called Ebsonhouse, and all closes belonging thereto, called the Croft under the house, the Parke, Over Ebsonroyd and Nether Ebsonroyd, Coat Close, Well Inge, Newlands Ings, Ebsonroyd Inge, Whitley, Stubbing, Nooks, Ryebanck, Acre, Acre Inge, Scotroydleys, Great Adamley, Little Adamley, Adamley Inge, Over Newlands and Nether Newlands, with all ways etc, in the graveship of Holme occupied by Thomas Morehouse and John Turton or their assigns at a lords' rent of 8s 1d, compounded, save the close called Whitley, non-compounded, and reversions and remainders, granted to Jeremy Kay, his executors,

[1] The verdict is written in the same hand as the indenture.

administrators and assigns for the term of 21 years at a yearly rent of 5s, payable at Pentecost and Martimas, in equal portions.

witnessed in presence of John Scott / Robert Scott

[sealed] Thomas Morehouse

14° die Decembris 1688

The Jury doe present and say that the lands and premises abovemencioned are devised contrary to the custome of the Mannour and therefore are forfeited and ought to be seised into the Lords hands.

[signed] Gideon Maude

Record' John Haighe / Richard Hemingway / John Scrivener

[endorsed] Thomas Morehouse of Ebsonhouse Indenture to give cause of Seisour.

D

Whereas wee William Sutcliffe of Hoohoyle in Erringden, yeo, and Henry Hyleley of Sowerby, yeo, have by our Indenture of lease granted to William Midgley of Hallifax for 21 years all that messuage called Hileleigh etc in Sowerby in the graveship of Sowerby, now occupied by Samuel Sutcliffe or his assigns at a lords' rent of 2s 5½d, compounded, with reversions and remainders, to give voluntary cause of forfeiture, the two desire the Lords of the Manor and their Stewards after the third proclamation to regrant the same to the said William Sutcliffe of Hoohoyle in Erringden, yeo, his heirs and assigns forever. Witnessed 21 November 4 James II, 1688.

Sealed & delivered in presence of William Sutcliffe [seal]

John Hargreaves jr Henry Hyleley [seal]

Susanna Hargreaves

Jo[hn] Hargreaves

[no endorsement]

E

14 die xbris 88

Wee the Jury doe present that Abraham Langley of Preistley doth refuse to pay his uncompounded fyne for one Close called Quarlers lying in Lightcliffe, therefore the said Close of land is forfeited and ought to bee seised.

Wee present John Hinchliffe<Grave>of Holme for not appearing att this Court and paying his Copyhold rents for that Graveshippe.

[signed] Gideon Maude John Haighe

Richard Hemingway John Scrivener

membrane 3 dorse

Court Baron held at Wakefield on 4 January 4 James II [1689]

Panel Inquest taken on the oaths of Daniel Mawde, gen, Francis Roades, Joseph White, John Gupwell, William Castlehouse, William Sunderland, Tempest Pollard, William Walker, Samuel Thornes, John Cawthorne, Percival Terry and John Scrivener, jurors, who testified that Henry Beale, gen, who lately held to him and his heirs by copy of the manor roll half a house and 3½ acres of land at le Bothomhouses in the graveship of Stanley at an annual lords' rent of 15d, compounded, died two years passed, and because neither George Beale, his son and heir, nor another had come to make fine with the lords within the space of three great courts after the death, according to custom, the lands were forfeit to the lords of the manor. Order to the grave of Stanley to seize the same into the lords' hands before the next court.

Alverthorpe Third proclamation for claimants for two closes of land, meadow or pasture in the field of Alverthorpe called Humble Jumble Field, one lately occupied by Richard Ellis and the other by William Totty or their assigns, saving etc, etc.

Sandal Third proclamation for claimants for a messuage at Humleyroyd lately occupied by George Fairbarne or his assigns, etc.

Sowerby (24) Richard Boyes, now or lately of Halifax, clerk, and Elizabeth his wife, she examined separately by John Scott, gen, deputy steward, surrendered outside court into the lords' hands on 31 December last all that messuage called Over Longbothom and all houses, edifices, barns, etc, in Warley in the graveship of Sowerby occupied by John Haigh or his assigns at an annual lords' rent of 10d, compounded, with all rights, reversions, remainders, etc, to the use of John Chesman of Leeds, flax-dresser, his heirs and assigns forever. Agreed, by due service. Entry fine: 2s 6d.

Hipperholme (25) Judith Hall, sole daughter and heiress of Jonathan Hall, gen, deceased, came before the steward and gave 17s 7½d for leave to inherit those customary messuages, cottages, closes, lands, tenements and hereditaments in the graveship of Hipperholme, by whomsoever occupied, at an annual lords' rent of 5s 10½d, compounded, whereof Jonathan Hall, her father, died seised. Agreed.

Stanley (26) It was attested by Daniel Mawde, gen, lords' tenant, that Francis Hatfield of Stanley, gen, on 6 December past surrendered into the lords' hands the reversion after the death of Francis of a messuage or new erection, with all 'outhouses', barns, etc, occupied by the said Francis Hatfield or his assigns, and all closes of land, meadow or pasture appurtenant, known as le

Laith Croft, with two closes adjoining, lately 'devised' into three closes estimated at 8 acres, also occupied by the same Francis Hatfield or his assigns, with all ways, etc, in Stanley in the graveship of Stanley at an annual lords' rent of 2s, compounded: to the use of Anne Hatfield, only daughter and heiress of the said Francis Hatfield, her heirs and assigns for ever. Agreed: entry fine: 3s.

Alverthorpe (27) Thomas Maude of Doncaster, gen, son of John Mawde (sic) of Wakefield, gen, deceased, came into court before Francis Whyte, esq, high steward of the manor court, and took from the lords of the manor the two closes in the field of Alverthorpe called Humble Jumble Field, etc, except etc, in the graveship of Alverthorpe at a lords' rent of 2s 8d, compounded, seized into the lords' hands because the said Thomas Maude by indenture / **membrane 4** / dated 13 October past leased the same to a John Haigh of Horbury, yeo, for a term of 21 years without leave of court, etc, and it was seized at the court held at Wakefield on 2 November. Proclamations were made in three courts for claimants, and only Thomas Maude offered himself. Agreed that he, his heirs and assigns hold by the ancient rent and service. Entry fine: 8s.

Sandall (28) Samuel Norton of Kettlethorpe in the parish of Sandallmagna, gen, came into court before Francis Whyte, esq, high steward of the manor court, and with the assent of Edward Thomas of Walkcliffe, tanner, Elizabeth Thomas of Kirke Fenton, widow, mother of the said Edward, Thomas Barber of Wintersett, yeo, and John Walker of Horbury, yeo, took from the lords' hands that messuage with barns etc, at Humleyroyd now occupied by George Fairbarne or his assigns, and a close called Syke Inge now occupied by Samuel Norton or his assigns in the townships of Sandall and Criglestone in the graveship of Sandall at an annual lords' rent of 13d, compounded, with reversions, etc, seized into the lords' hands because the said Edward Thomas, Elizabeth Thomas, Thomas Barber and John Walker by indenture on 9 October past leased the same to a Joseph Hall of Sandall Magna, yeo, his executors, administrators, and assigns for a term of 21 years without leave of court, etc, which was found by enquiry in court on 2 November. Proclamations for claimants were made in three courts at Wakefeld and only Samuel Norton offered himself. Agreed that he, his heirs and assigns hold by ancient rent and custom. Entry fine: 3s 3d.

Sum of court [blank]

[in draft, after membrane 19]
A
Pannell' pro Dominis Manerij

Daniel Maude gen	sworn	Francis Roades	sworn
Joseph White	sworn	John Cupwell	sworn
William Castlehouse	sworn	William Sunderland	sworn
Tempest Pollard	sworn	William Walker	sworn
Samuel Thornes	sworn	John Cawthorne	sworn
Percival Terry	sworn	John Scrivener	sworn

B

Court Baron held on 4 January 1688

The Jury doe present and say that Henry Beale gent who late held to him and his heirs by Copy of Court Roll accordinge to the Custome of the Mannor of Wakefield The moiety or halfe parte of one house and tenement and three acres and a halfe of land lyeing and being att the Bothom houses with their appurtinances within the Graveshippe of Stanley Of the yearly rent to the Lords of the said Mannor of xv^{d} And Compounded for, dyed seised thereof above two yeares agoe. And because neither George Beale son and heire of the said Henry Beale nor any other person comes to claime the same and make Fyne with the Lords for the said premisses as they ought to have done within three Great Courts next after the Decease of the said Henry Beale, according to the Custome of the said Mannour, the said Lands and premisses are forfeited and ought to bee seised into the hands of the Lords of the said Mannour

[signed] Daniel Mawde / Francis Rodes / Tempest Pollard / Samuell Thornes

record'

[no endorsement]

C

The iiij.th day of January 1688

Wee whose names are here under written do present and find that Mr George Naylor of London ought to serve Grave for this yeare now comeinge for the Graveshipp of Horbury for his lands lyinge in Ossett: witnesse our hand

William Wormall / John Rodes / William Issott / John Cawthorne

[no endorsement]

membrane 4 continued

Court Baron held at Wakefield on 25 January 4 James II [1689]

Panel Inquest taken on the oaths of Tempest Pollard, Thomas Shillitoe, Robert Cusworth, George Hebden, John Hinchliffe, John Speight, William

Walker, Thomas Dodsworth, Robert Bradford, John Haigh, John Scrivener, and Richard Terry, jurors.

Holme Certificate by the grave of Holme of seizure into the lords' hands of the message with appurtenances in Fulstone in the graveship of Holme called Ebsonhouse, and all closes and parcels of land appurtenant called le Croft under the house, le Park, Over Ebsonroyds and Nether Ebsonroyds, Coatclose, Well Inge, Newlands Inge, Ebsonroyd Inge, Whitley, Stubb Inge, Nookes, Ryebanck, Acre, Acre Inge, Scotroyd Leys, Great Adamley, Little Adamley, Adamley Inge, Over Newlands and Nether Newlands, with all ways, etc, in the graveship of Holme, now occupied by Thomas Morehouse and John Turton, or their assigns at an annual lords' rent of 8s 1d, compounded, except for the close called Whitley, non-compounded. First proclamation for claimants.

Sowerby (29) It was attested by Edward Denton, lords' tenant, that John Hoyle of Shawe in Soyland in Sowerby, yeo, on 17 December past surrendered into the lords' hands the message called le Shawe and all houses and edifices appurtenant, and an estimated 5 acres of land, meadow and pasture in Soyland in Sowerby in the graveship of Sowerby, and two closes or parcels of land, meadow and pasture called le Rishhey and le Faugh estimated at 3 acres with appurtenances in Soyland in the graveship of Sowerby, now occupied by the said John Hoyle or his assigns, and all ways, etc, at an annual lords' rent of 21d, compounded: to the use of Elizabeth Neale of Barkisland, spinster, her heirs and assigns, for ever, subject to conditions, limits, provisions, payments and agreements in a pair of indentures of the date of the surrender between Elizabeth and John. Agreed: entry fine, 5s 3d.

membrane 4 dorse

\- (30) It was attested by Edward Denton, lords' tenant, that John Dixon of Bentleyroid, yeo, on 26 March past surrendered into the lords' hands the two capital messuages with appurtenances in Sowerby in the graveship of Sowerby called le Upper Bentleyroyd and le Lower Bentleyroyd, with all houses, edifices, barns, structures, stables, folds, orchards, gardens, yards, tofts, crofts, closes, lands, tenements, meadow, feedings, pasture, ways, passages, etc appurtenant, now occupied by the said John Dixon, Samuel Shepheard, Joseph Stocke and John Dixon junior or their assigns, at an annual lords' rent of 6s 7½d, compounded: to the use of Frances Thornhill of Fenay, spinster, her heirs and assigns, subject to such provisions, conditions and limitations declared in a pair of indentures of the date of the surrender between John and Frances. Agreed, to hold by customary service. Entry fine, 19s 10½d.

Sandall (31) It was attested by Richard Grice, gen, lords' tenant, that Thomas Milner of Kirkeburton, yeo, on 5 October past surrendered into the lords' hands the reversion after the death of Elizabeth Milner, his mother, of 3 roods of meadow at Dawgreene in the township of Criglestone and graveship of Sandall in a place called Armitt Crofts between the land lately of Rebecca Oley on the south and the land lately of John Blacker to the north, also a fourth part of a close called Armitt Crofts, now divided by metes and bounds, estimated at 2 acres 1 rood of land and meadow, also the reversion of another little close of land and meadow called the upper part of the Crofte at Dawgreene, abutting on the land lately of John Barber on the east and on Dawdike on the west, estimated at 1½ acres, with appurtenances in Criglestone in the graveship of Sandall at an annual lords' rent of 18d, compounded, with all ways, etc: to the sole use of Robert Waterhouse of Whitley, gen, his heirs and assigns, for ever. Agreed: entry fine, 2s 3d.
- (32) It was attested by Richard Grice, gen, lords' tenant, that Elizabeth Milner of Cawthorne, widow, on 5 October past surrendered into the lords' hands three roods of meadow at Dawgreene in the township of Criglestone and graveship of Sandall in a place called Armitt Crofts between the land lately of Rebecca Oley on the south, etc as above: to the sole use of Robert Waterhouse of Whitley, gen, etc. Agreed: entry fine, 4s 6d.
Sowerby (33) John Chesman of Leeds, flax-dresser, and Elizabeth his wife, she examined separately before the steward by John Scott, gen, deputy steward, surrendered outside court on 17 January instant, into the hands of the lords of the manor that messuage and all barns, structures, gardens, orchards, folds, yards and crofts appurtenant, commonly called Over Longbothom, and all closes, lands, meadow, feedings, pasture, wood, undergrowth, tenements and hereditaments appurtenant or commonly occupied in Warley in the graveship of Sowerby, now occupied by a John Haigh or his assigns at an annual lords' rent of 10d, compounded: to the use of Elizabeth Scott, wife of the said John Scott, and Alice Scott, daughter of the said John, their heirs and assigns for ever, provided that if John Chesman, his heirs, executors, or administrators pay to Elizabeth and Alice, either, or their certain attorney, executors or administrators, £50 with lawful consideration on 17 January 1689/90 without fraud or delay, then the surrender became void. Agreed: entry fine, 2s 6d.

Sum of court [blank]

[in draft, after membrane 22]
A
Panel for the lords of the manor and between parties

Tempest Pollard	sworn	Thomas Shillitoe	sworn
Robert Cusworth	sworn	George Hebden	sworn
John Hinchliffe	sworn	John Speight	sworn
William Walker	sworn	Thomas Dodsworth	sworn
Robert Bradford	sworn	John Haigh	sworn
John Scrivener	sworn	Richard Terry	sworn

Robert Bradford sworn grave of Ossett
John Haighe sworn deputy grave of Horbury and Thornes
Jonathan Wilson sworn deputy grave of Holme
[no endorsement]

B
Wakefield Manor
Warrant of Francis Whyte, esq, high steward, to the grave of Holme and his deputy, to seize into the lords' hands before the next court at Wakefeld the messuage at Fulstone in the graveship of Holme commonly called Ebsonhouse, and all closes, etc. Given on 4 January 4 James II , 1688
[signed] Jo[hn] Scott.
[endorsed] Executed by me John Hinchliffe, grave of Holme, the 16 day of January 1688 in the presents of Mathew Morehouse / James France / John Robucke / Humphrey Robucke

C
At the Courte <Baron> holden at Wakefeild the 25th day of January 1688
Wee present that George Holgate for a Messuage called Wheatleyroyde with three other Messuages with all the land to them belongeinge in Blackwood ought to bee Heade Greave for the Greaveshipp of Sowerby for this yeare And to have Helpes of the coheires of Abraham Hitchon (to witt) [blank] Brooke and Job Sutcliffe for a Messuage called Ingeheade, Thomas Ibbotson for a Messuage in Blackwood next Boy Mill late James Dobsons, Richard Midgley for lands at Breareley bridge called Milne hill, late the Lands of John Farrer, and John Wilkinson for a Messuage in Blackwood called Handcarr late the lands of Samuell Haldsworth, with all the lands and tenements to the same Messuages belongeinge.
[signed] Jo[hn] Harg[reaves] sworn
Thomas Preistley / William Hollingworth / Benjamin Boyes
[no endorsement]

D
Att the Courte Baron holden at Wakefeild the 25th daye of January 1688

Wee present that Thomas Preistley and Francis Preistley for a Messuage called Preistley Greene with all the lands thereunto belongeinge in Hipperholme *and Jonathan Preistley* *ought to bee Heade Greaves for the Greaveshipp of Hipperholme for this yeare, which lands were late the lands of Richard Kent and now in the occupacion of the said Francis Preistley, And to have Helpes of* and Jonathan Preistley for a *Messuage and lands Called Winteridge* messuage and lands called Winteredge <and the said Thomas and Francis* And of themselves for* another Messuage at Preistley Greene now in the occupacion of Joseph Halliday with all the lands and tenements to the same messuages belongeinge *late the lands of Richard Apleyeard* ought to be Graves for the Graveshipp of Hipperholme [signed] John Brearcliffe
Jere: Rossendall Joseph Preistley
[no endorsement]

E

The twentie first day of January Annoque domini 1688
We whose names are subscribed do present and finde that Richard Brook of Lepton for one messuage or Tenement called Nabb with all the lands and tenements thereto belonging is to serve the Office of Grave for the Graveshipp of Holme, And is to have help of Luke Firth for all his lands and tenements in Overthwong; of John Dearnelie for his lands and tenements in Overthwonge, late the lands of Robert Swallow; of Michael Midgeley for all his lands and tenements late the lands of Anthony Swallow; of Godfrey Crosland for lands late the lands of Andrew Swallow; of the heirs of Josias Brodhead for one Close of land called Overbinfield; of Sara Thewles for three acres of lands lying at Dickedge; of John Armitage for three acres of land lying in Austonley, late the lands of Richard Brodhead; of James Haigh for one Close of land late belonging to Swallows; of James France for Wheelsbrook, late the lands of Swallows; of Simeon Hirst for two Closes of land, late the lands of Andrew Swallow; of Thomas Cuttell for one Cottage and a garden, late belonging to the messuage called Nabb; and of Edmund Brodhead for a parcel of land late of Swallows. We present as abovesaid.
[signed] Jonas Haye / James France / John Hinchliffe / Thomas Booth
[no endorsement]

F

23 January 1688

Wee whose names are here underwritten doe present and find that the Governours of the poore of Wakefield ought to serve Grave for the

Graveshippe of Thornes for this yeare now comeing for Lands lyeing in Thornes. Witnesse our hands
[signed] William Horne / John Stockes / Samell Paker / Thomas Harrison
[no endorsement]

G

Wee whose names are here underwritten doe say that John Clarkson of Newton ought to serve greave this yeare 1689 for lands in Newton late Leonard Wilsons for the Graveshipp of Alverthorpe.
Wittnes our hands
[signed] Daniel Mawde
Thomas Burrow / Samuel Hide / John Rose
[no endorsement]

membrane 4 dorse continued

Court Baron held at Wakefield on 15 February 1688 [Old Style]

Panel Inquest taken on the oaths of Daniel Mawde, Gideon Mawde, Robert Mansfield, Thomas Totty, Thomas Shillitoe, Thomas Hunt, John Taylor, Robert Cusworth, Samuel Thornes, William Walker, William Moxon, and Joseph White, jurors.
Alverthorpe They said on oath that John Cromacke of Morley, rope-maker, and Dorothy his wife, she examined separately by the steward, by indenture of 15 February instant leased to a Joseph Hall of Sandallmagna, yeo, a parcel of land taken from the lords' waste in the graveship of Alverthorpe containing 20 yards in length and 7 yards in breadth, with a cottage thereon, / **membrane 5** / at an annual lords' rent of 4d, compounded, to have and hold to Joseph Hall, his executors, administrators, and assigns from the date of the indenture for 21 years, without fine to the lords or leave of court, to their contempt and contrary etc. Order to the grave of Alverthorpe to seize the land into the lords' hands before the next court.
Holme Second proclamation for claimants for a messuage in Fulstone in the graveship of Holme called Ebsonhouse and all closes .. called le Croft under the house, etc with all ways etc in the graveship of Holme, now occupied severally by Thomas Morehouse and John Turton or their assigns at an annual lords' rent of 8s 1d, compounded, except the close called Whitley which was non-compounded.
Ossett / Horbury (34) Appearance of Joseph Naylor, son and heir of Richard Naylor, in court before the steward to give 2s 6d for leave to inherit the reversion after the death of Anne Naylor, lately wife of George Naylor,

deceased, of a messuage and all land appurtenant lately of George Naylor, 'grandfather' of Joseph, with appurtenances in the graveships of Ossett and Horbury, now occupied by the said Anne or her assigns at an annual lords' rent of 10d, compounded, following the death of Richard Naylor. Reversion agreed, that Joseph Naylor, his heirs and assigns hold for ever by due service.

Stanley (35) Appearance of Elizabeth, wife of William Hall, and Sarah Greene, spinster, sisters and coheiresses of Mary Kent, deceased, lately wife of Thomas Kent of Stanley, yeo. They gave the lords [blank] for leave to inherit the reversion after the death of Thomas Kent of all messuages, cottages, closes, lands and tenements whereof Mary died seised, with appurtenances, in the graveship of Stanley, by whomsoever occupied, at an annual lords' rent of [blank] non-compounded after the death of Mary, whose sisters and coheiresses the said Elizabeth Hall and Sarah Greene were. Reversion agreed that Elizabeth and Sarah, their heirs and assigns hold for ever by due service.

- (36) Thomas Kent, now or late of Stanley in the parish of Wakefield, yeo, and John Kent, son and heir apparent of Thomas, and Elizabeth Kent, daughter of Thomas, and John Bromley of Wakefield, gen, by John Scott, gen, deputy steward of the manor court, outside court on 1 February instant surrendered into the lords' hands a parcel of land called Cuttyeard estimated at a rood, with all structures built thereon, now occupied by John Thompson or his assigns, also one of the closes of land, arable, meadow or pasture called Woodside Closes, now occupied by Thomas Scatchard or his assigns, at an annual lords' rent of 8d, compounded, also two closes called Dewceroyds, and another close called Threenooked Close, lately of John Savile, gen, now occupied by Richard Halliday and the said Thomas Kent or their assigns at an annual lords' rent of 22d, non-compounded, lying in the graveship of Stanley, with all rights, reversions, etc, held by Thomas Kent, John Kent, Elizabeth Kent and John Bromley or any of them: to the use of Joseph Armitage of Outwoodside in the parish of Wakefield, gen, his heirs and assigns for ever. Agreed: entry fine of 2s for the compounded land, and [blank] for that non-compounded.

- (37) William Hall of Woodhouse Lane in the parish of Ardsley, shoemaker, and Elizabeth his wife, she examined separately by the steward, surrendered by John Scott, gen, deputy steward, outside court on 25 January past into the lords' hands the reversion after the death of Thomas Kent, now or late of Stanley, yeo, of a parcel of land called Cuttyeard, estimated at a rood, with all edifices built thereon, now occupied by John Thompson or his assigns, also one of the closes of arable, meadow or pasture called Woodside Closes, now occupied by Thomas Scatchard or his assigns at an annual lords' rent of 8d, compounded, also two closes called Dewceroyds and another close called Threenooked Close, lately of John Savile, gen, now occupied by Richard Halliday and the said Thomas Kent or their assigns at an annual lords' rent of 22d, non-compounded, all in the graveship of Stanley, with all rights, reversions, etc, held by William Hall and Elizabeth his wife: to the use of Joseph Armitage of Outwoodside in the parish of Wakefield, gen, his heirs and assigns for ever. Agreed: entry fine of 12d for the compounded land and [blank] for that non-compounded.

Sandall (38) It was attested by Joseph Hall, lords' tenant, that John Hall of Wakefield, tanner, Sarah Hall of Thornes in the parish of Wakefield, widow, mother of John, Thomas Walker of Wakefield, tailor, and John Cliffe of Carleton in the parish of Rothwell, yeo, and Elizabeth his wife, she examined separately before the steward, on 23 November last surrendered into the lords' hands all that part of a close of arable land, meadow and pasture called Kilnehill with all ways, etc, in the graveship of Sandall now occupied by the said Joseph Hall or his assigns at an annual lords' rent of 2s, compounded, being customary land held by copy of the court roll: to the use of John Dalston of Heathhall, knt and baronet, his heirs and assigns for ever by due service. Agreed: entry fine, 6s.

Sowerby (39) It was attested by Henry Naylor, lords' tenant, that Richard Thomas of Reddicarr in Wadsworth, yeo, on 25 October past surrendered into the lords' hands the reversion after the death of the said Richard of the whole messuage, structures, closes, etc in Soyland in the graveship of Sowerby, now occupied by James Bilsbury or his assigns at an annual lords' rent of 2s 4d, compounded: to the use of William Thomas of Reddicarr, his 'son in law' (*generi*) to the intent that / **membrane 5 dorse** / William remain in seisin, subject to conditions in the last will and testament of the said Richard Thomas, provided that if Richard in his lifetime paid to William or another 6d in the presence and hearing of two or more witnesses, and declared his intention to void the surrender, it would become void. Since Richard was now dead, it was agreed that William hold, subject to the uses mentioned in Richard's will. Entry fine, 7s.

Ossett (40) Richard Liversedge of Boothroyd in the parish of Dewsbury, yeo, by John Scott, gen, deputy steward, outside court, surrendered on 4 June 1686 into the hands of the lords those two messuages at Boothroyde with 'outhouses', barns, structures, stables, orchards, gardens, folds, tofts and crofts appurtenant, also a close called Upper Inge, another called Nether Inge, another called Upperhealds, another called Netherhealds, another called Wheat Close, another called Hill Close, and another called Kittroyde, all in the graveship of Ossett, now occupied by the said Richard Liversedge or his assigns or subtenants, with all ways, etc, at an annual lords' rent of 4s 9d, compounded: to the use of Anne Belton of Mount Sorrill, co Leics, widow, her heirs and assigns for ever, provided that if Richard, his heirs, executors, administrators, or assigns or any of them paid Anne, her certain attorney, executors or administrators or any of them within three years following the surrender £250 with consideration, without fraud or delay, giving twelve months notice before payment, the surrender would become void. Agreed: entry fine, 14s 3d.

Sum of court [blank]

[in draft, after membrane 26]
A
Panel for lords of the Manor

Daniel Mawde, gen	sworn				
Gideon Mawde, gen	sworn	Thomas Hunt	sworn	William Walker	sworn
Robert Mansfeld	sworn	John Taylor	sworn	William Moxon	sworn
Thomas Totty	sworn	Robert Cusworth	sworn	Joseph White	sworn
Thomas Shillitoe	sworn	Samuel Thornes	sworn		

B
Indenture of 15 February 5 James II, 1688, between John Cromacke of Morley, rope-maker, and Dorothy his wife of the one part, and Joseph Hall of Sandallmagna, yeo, of the other witnessed that John Cromacke and Dorothy his wife to give a voluntary cause of forfeiture .. to cut off and destroy all remainders, etc, granted, leased, etc, to the said Joseph Hall, his executors, administrators and assigns a parcel of land from the lords' waste in the graveship of Alverthorpe 20 yards by 7 yards with a cottage built thereon at a yearly lords' rent of 4s, compounded, for a term of 21 years at a rent of 5s, payable at Martinmas if lawfully demanded. Witnessed on the above date.

Sealed and delivered in presence of John $^{\text{the mark of}}$ Cromacke
Robert Scott Dorothy $^{\text{the mark of}}$ Cromacke [two paper seals]
Jo: Scott 15° die Februarij 1688/9 (*sic*)

The Jury do present and say that the lands and premisses abovemencioned are demised contrary to the Custome of the Manour and therefore are forfeited and ought to bee seised.

[signed] Daniel Maude / Gideon Maude / Thomas Tottie / Robert Mansfield
Die et anno supradictis predicta Dorothea sola confessa examinata fuit

Jo: Scott

[no endorsement]

C

Whereas I John Cromack of Morley and Dorothy my wife have given cause of forfeiture and seisure ... in the tenure or occupacion of Robert Kirkman and Thomas Foster, now, I the said John Cromack and Dorothy my wife do hereby desire the said Lords and their stewards that so soone as three proclamacions shall bee thereof made and past, as in such cases are used, to Regrant the said Cottage or Tenement with appertinunc' to mee the said John Cromack, my heirs and assignes for ever, and this shalbee their and everye of their sufficient warrant. Witnesse my hand and seal the Five and twentieth day of Aprill, Anno domini 1689.

Sealed and delivered in the presence of the marke of John I Cormacke

[paper seals]

Jo: Scott the marke of Dorothy O Cromacke

26° April' 1689 predicta Dorothea sola confessa and examinata fuit

Jo: Scott

[no endorsement]

D

Thomas Kent wife past a stra in to the hand of Richard Harison and me for thease usages, first to hir husbond for life and to hir child after his desease, and if child die bout isow to hir tow sisters, and they are to pay Joney Kent and Elizabeth Kent eather of them ten pound, and hir mother is to have forte shilinges in the yeare out of it for hir life.

Vacat quia non examinata

[endorsed] William Moxon and Richard Harrison jurors

These are void, she being under Covert and not examined

Jo: Scott

membrane 5 dorse continued

Wakefield Court Baron held at Wakefield on 8 March, William and Mary I [1689]

Panel Inquest taken on the oaths of Michael Parker, John Clarkson, James Wilson, Joseph White, Gervase Harrison, John Mawdsley, Robert Cusworth, John Speight, Joshua Kaye, Samuel Peaker, Samuel Thornes, and Robert Bradford, jurors.

Sowerby Certificate of the grave of Sowerby of seizure of the messuage called Hileleigh with all houses, edifices, barns, structures, folds, gardens, tofts, crofts, closes, etc, in Sowerby in the graveship of Sowerby, now

occupied by Samuel Sutcliffe or his assigns at an annual lords' rent of 2s 5d, compounded. First proclamation.
Alverthorpe Certificate of the grave of Alverthorpe of seizure of a parcel of land taken from the lords' waste in the graveship of Alverthorpe, estimated at 20 yards by 7 yards, with the cottage thereon, at an annual lords' rent of 4d, compounded. First proclamation.
Holme Third proclamation for claims for a messuage with appurtenances in Fulstone in the graveship of Holme called Ebsonhouse, and the closes thereto belonging called le Croft under the house, etc, with all ways, etc, in the graveship of Holme, now occupied by Thomas Morehouse and John Turton or their assigns at an annual lords' rent of 8s 1d, compounded, except for the close called Whitley, non-compounded.
Wakefield (41) Appearance of Joseph Bargh, son and heir of Thomas Bargh late of Wakefield, grocer, deceased, before the steward of the court, who gave the lords 6s for leave to inherit the messuage near le Bitchill in Wakefield in Northgate, and all shops, cellars, frontages, penthouses (*imbricament'*), privileges, liberties, tenements and hereditaments thereto belonging, now occupied by the said Joseph Bargh or his assigns at an annual lords' rent of 2s, compounded, following the death of Thomas Bargh, whose son and heir he was. Agreed for ever, by due service.
- (42) William Bargh of Wakefeld, grocer, youngest son of Thomas Bargh late of Wakefield, grocer, deceased, in consideration of £100 advanced by Joseph Bargh of Wakefield, grocer, eldest son of the said Thomas, surrendered into the lords' hands by John Scott, gen, deputy steward, outside court on 25 January past and quit-claimed all right, etc to the messuage near le Bitchill in Wakefield in Northgate, and to all shops, etc, thereto belonging, now occupied by the said Joseph or his assigns at an annual lords' rent of 2s, compounded: to the use of the said Joseph, his heirs and assigns for ever. Agreed, to hold by due service. He gave 6d for entry of the quitclaim.

membrane 6

Sowerby (43) It was attested by Isaac Nayler, lords' tenant, that John Dickson senior of Sowerby, yeo, on 28 November past surrendered into the lords' hands a third part of a messuage with a barn called Lower Bentleyroyd, also a third part of all several closes called le Longbanck, le Littlebanck, le Banck above the House, and le Bent Inge, as divided from the other two parts, with appurtenances in Sowerby in the graveship of Sowerby, now occupied by John Dickson, junior, or his assigns at an annual lords' rent of 17d, compounded: to the use of John Dickson junior of Sowerby, yeo, his heirs and assigns for ever, provided that if the said John Dickson senior, his heirs, executors, or administrators paid the said John Dickson junior, his

executors, administrators or assigns in full the sum of £40 5s with consideration within five years from the date of surrender on 28 November 1693 the surrender became void. Agreed, by due service. Entry fine, 4s 3d.
Thornes (44) It was attested by Henry Birkhead, lords' tenant, that Matthew Bingley of Norwich city, whitesmith, and Mary his wife, she examined separately by the said Henry Birkhead, specially deputed by Francis Whyte, esq, high steward, on 11 January past surrendered into the lords' hands a messuage or cottage with a barn and a croft estimated at 2 acres, also 1½ acres by estimate in separate fields of Thornes, with all ways, etc, in the graveship of Thornes, now occupied by James Ellis or his assigns at an annual lords' rent of [blank], compounded: to the use of Mary Jackson of Alverthorpe in the parish of Wakefield, widow, her heirs and assigns for ever. Agreed, by customary service. Entry fine [blank].
Wakefield (45) It was attested by Thomas Wilson, lords' tenant, that Mary Naylor of Wakefield, widow, on 4 February past surrendered into the lords' hands the messuage in Kirkegate in Wakefeld called le Pinfold house, with all appurtenances, now occupied by John Nunnes, gen, and Mary Stead, widow, or others whomsoever, also all the messuage in which she now lived, with appurtenances, which two messages owed an annual lords' rent of [blank], compounded: to the use of the last will of Mary Naylor, namely, the messuage called le Pinfold house in Kirkegate in Wakefield to pass to Mercy Brooke, daughter of Mary Naylor, for her term of life, and after her death to Mary Brooke, the 'grandchild' of Mary Naylor, for her and her legitimate issue, and for want of such to the heirs of the body of Mercy Brooke, and for want of such to the right heirs of Thomas Brooke, husband of Mercy, for ever. The other messuage, where Mary Naylor lately lived, should pass to the said Mercy Brooke and Thomas her husband for life, and after their deaths, to the legitimate issue of Mercy Brooke, and for want of such to the right heirs of Thomas Brooke for ever, by due service. Mercy Brooke gave 6d as fine for entry for the term of her life, and Mary Brooke gave 6d for the remainder. Mercy and Thomas Brooke fined for entry 6s 6d.
- (46) In the name of God, amen. I Mary Naylor of Wakefield in the County of Yorke, widdowe, being sick and weak in body but of sound and perfect memory, praised be God, doe make and ordaine this my last Will and Testament in manner and forme followinge. First I committ my soul into the hands of Almighty God, hopeing through the death and passion of our Saviour Jesus Christ to have free pardon and forgivenesse of all my sins; and my body I committ to the earth to be decently buried att the discretion of my Executrix hereafter named. And as for my reall and personal estate wherewith it hath pleased God to blesse me, I give, devise and bequeath as

followeth. First I give and devise all that my messuage or tenement scituate, lyeing and being in Kirkegate in Wakefield aforesaid called the Pinfold house, with all and singuler the appertenaunces to the same belonging or in anywise appertaineing, now in the tenures or occupacions of John Nunnes, gen, and Mary Stead, widdow, or in whose tenure or occupacion soever the same be: to have and to hold the same unto Mercy Brooke my daughter for and dureing the tearme of her naturall life, and after her decease I give and devise the same unto Mary Brooke my Grand-daughter and to the heirs of her body lawfully begotten, and for want of such yssue I give and devise the same unto the heirs of the body of my said daughter Mercy Brooke, and for want of such yssue to the right heirs of Thomas Brooke, her husband, for ever. Also I give and devise all that my messuage or tenement wherein I now live, with all and singuler the appertaunces to the same belonging unto my said daughter Mercy Brooke and her said husband Thomas Brooke for and dureing the tearm of their naturall lives, and after their decease to the heirs of the body of the said Mercy Brooke lawfully begotten; and for want of such yssue to the right heirs of the said Thomas Brooke for ever, which said messuages or tenements are of the nature of copyhold and holden of the Mannour of Wakefield aforesaid, and for which composicion is made for the certainety of the fyne of which said messuages and premisses I have passed a surrender to limmitt to such use as this my said Will does appoint. Also I doe give and bequeath to my servant John Tilson <the summe of> fourty shillings as a legacy. And I doe make and ordaine my said daughter Mercy Brooke sole Executrix of this my last Will and Testament, revoakeing all other Will or Wills by mee formerly made. In witnesse whereof I have hereunto set to my hand and seal the fourth day of February in the yeare of our Lord One thousand six hundred eighty and eight. Mary Naylor the Testator. Sealed, signed, published and declared in the presence of Thomas Wilson, Samuel Hide, William Baynes.

Holme (47) Thomas Morehuse of Ebsonhouse in Fulstone in the parish of Kirkeburton, yeo, appeared in court before Francis Whyte, esq, high steward, and took from the lords of the Manor of Wakefield the messuage with appurtenances in Fulstone in the graveship of Holme called Ebsonhouse, and all closes belonging called le Croft under the house, etc, in the graveship of Holme, which were seized on account of an indenture of 10 December last leasing the same to a Jeremy Kay of Copthirst in the parish of Kirkeburton, yeo, / **membrane 6 dorse** / for 21 years etc, as found in court on 14 December last. Claimants were sought at the three courts afterwards, as required, and only the said Thomas Morehouse offered himself. It was agreed that the part of the messuage and appurtenant buildings occupied by

Thomas Morehouse, together with the closes called Croft under the house, le Acre, le Acre inge, Nookes, Scotroyd leys, le halfe of Whitley, Parke, Over Newlands, Nether Newlands, Coatclose and Well inge, with all ways, waters and hereditaments occupied by him should be held for ever by the same, and the residue be held by Thomas Morehouse and the heirs of his body legitimately procreated, for lack of which heirs it should pass to Elizabeth Morehouse, his sister, wife of John Morehouse, and the legitimate heirs of her body, for lack of which it should pass to the uses mentioned in a surrender made by William Morehouse, father of Thomas, dated 16 May 19 Charles II [1667], recorded at the Great Court held at Wakefield on 10 April 20 Charles II [1668], to hold by the ancient rent and service, saving the right of Elizabeth, now wife of John Turton, to hold as jointure for life, by virtue of a copy of the rolls of the court held at Burton on 16 October 13 Charles II [1661]. Thomas gave the lords 24s 3d as entry fine.

Sandall (48) Daniel Beatson of Humley Mooreside in the parish of Sandall, clothier, and Dorothy Crosland of the same, widow, by John Scott, gen, deputy steward, outside court on 4 May 1683 surrendered into the lords' hands a cottage in Humley Mooreside, with a garden and croft now occupied by the same two or their assigns, with appurtenances, in the graveship of Sandall at an annual lords' rent of 12d, non-compounded: to the use of Thomas Morkill of Newbigginhill in the parish of Sandall, yeo, his heirs and assigns for ever, provided that if Daniel and Dorothy, either of them, or their heirs, executors, administrators or assigns paid to Thomas or his certain attorney etc the sum of 12s annually for four years on 5 May, starting on 5 May 1684, and pay a sum of £10 12s on 5 May 1687 at the residence of Thomas Morkill at Newbigginhill without fraud or delay, the surrender would become void. Agreed: entry fine [blank].

Sum of court [blank]

[in draft, after membrane 32]
A
Panel for lords and between parties
Michael Parker (written above a cancelled Daniel Maude, gen] sworn

John Clarkeson	sworn	James Wilson	sworn
Joseph White	sworn	Gervase Harrison	sworn
John Mawdsley	sworn	Robert Cusworth	sworn
John Speight	sworn	Joshua Kay	sworn
Samuel Peaker	sworn	Samuel Thornes	sworn
		Robert Bradford	sworn

John Walker fined 10s for bad behaviour

[no endorsement]

B

Warrant of Francis Whyte, esq, high steward, to the grave of Alverthorpe and his deputy to seize before the next court a parcel of land taken from the lords' waste in the graveship of Alverthorpe containing 20 yards by 7 yards, with a cottage built thereon, at an annual lords' rent of 4d, compounded. Given on 15 February 1688.

[signed] Jo: Scott

[endorsed]

27° die Februarij 1688.

This precept was executed accordinge to the tenor thereof

[signed] John Haighe grave D[aniel] Maude

Thomas Harrison John + Oldroy his marke

C

Warrant of Francis Whyte, esq, high steward, to the grave of Sowerby and his deputy to seize before the next court the messuage called Hileleigh and all houses, etc, belonging thereto in Sowerby in the graveship of Sowerby now occupied by Samuel Sutcliffe or his assigns at an annual lords' rent of 2s 5d, compounded. Given on 14 December 1688.

[signed] Jo: Scott.

[endorsed in Latin]

21 December 1688

Lands and tenements within mentioned were seized in prescribed form by me

[signed] Jo: Hargreaves In presence of W. Midgley / Richard Thomas / R. Midgley / John Greenwood.

D

Know all men by these presents that I Francis Whyte, esq, High Steward of the Courts of this Mannour of Wakefield in the County of Yorke at the speciall instance and request of John Scott of Wakefield aforesaid, gent, understeward of the Courts of the said Mannour, doe hereby authorise and depute Henry Birkhead of Lightcliffe in the Towneshippe of Hipperholme cum Brighouse in the said County, yeom', to take the examinacion of Mary now wife of Mathew Bingley of the City of Norwich, whitesmith, for the passing of one surrender made from the said Mathew Bingley and Mary his wife <and Daniel Mawde> of one messuage, cottage or tenement, one barne and one croft to the same belonging containeing by estimacion two acres (bee

the same more or lesse) and also of one acre and a halfe of land (more or lesse) lyeing and being in the severall fields of Thornes, with all singuler their appertenances scituate and being within the graveshippe of Thornes and now in the tenure or occupacion of one James Ellis or his assignes of the yearly rent to the Lords of the said Mannor of [blank] and compounded for: to the use and behoofe of Mary Jackson of Alverthorpe in the parish of Wakefield aforesaid, widdowe, and of her heirs and assignes for ever by rents and services accordinge to the Custome of the said Mannour. Given under my hand and seale this eleaventh day of January Anno domini 1688.
Sealed and delivered in the presence of
Robert Scott [signed] Francis Whyte seneschalus [armorial seal]
[no endosement]

membrane 6 dorse continued
Great Court held at Wakefield on 5 April 1 William and Mary [1689]

Free Tenants The noble lord George, marquis of Halifax, Lyon Pilkington, bart, the heirs of Thomas Savile, esq, Thomas Armitage, bart, the heirs of William Savile, esq, the heirs of Richard Law, gen, the heirs of George Thornhill, esq, William Farrer, esq, Robert Wrightson, gen, the heirs of Robert Benson, esq, Cyril Arthington, esq, William Horne, gen, Edward Goodwin, gen, John Stanhope, esq, John Gill, gen, in right of his wife, Sarah Brooke, spinster, Benjamin Law, gen, William Potham, gen, Thomas Naylor of Clifton, John Pyemont, John Kitson, James Pearson, Richard Liversedge, Thomas Crosland, Thomas Archer, Francis Wilkinson, gen, by right of his wife, James Chadwicke, Richard Swallow, the heirs of Samuel Fournes, gen, Robert Mitchell, Robert Brigge, the heirs of Robert Johnson, William Dixon, William Hall, Samuel Norton, Thomas Johnson, clerk, and Edward Dixon for their free lands and tenements owed suit of court from three weeks to three weeks by ancient custom, and some made fine for relaxation until the next Great Court, namely at Michaelmas, unless something required their presence in the meantime. The fines were admitted by the steward.
Panel Inquest taken on the oaths of Thomas Taylor, gen, William Moxon, William Hanson, John Mawdsley, Samuel Glover, Samuel Peaker, George Hebden, Tempest Pollard, John Sugden, John Forrest, Thomas Morehouse, Edward Denton, Samuel Turner, and William Dawson, jurors. They said that William Potham <2s 6d> gen, Edward Goodwin <2s 6d> gen, John Stanhope <6s 8d> esq, John Kitson <6d>, Thomas Crosland <6d> and Edward Dixon <6d> owed suit but did not appear, nor sent an essoin. In mercy as above their names. [These sums are not, in fact, in the engrossed roll.]

Item, they said that Robert Pickard of Ossett had died since the last court.
Sowerby Second proclamation for claimants for the messuage called Hileleigh with houses, etc appurtenant in Sowerby in the graveship of Sowerby, now occupied by Samuel Sutcliffe or his assigns at an annual lords' rent of 2s 5d, compounded
Alverthorpe Second proclamation for claimants for a parcel of land taken from the lords' waste in the graveship of Alverthorpe 20 yards by 7 yards, with a cottage built thereon, at an annual lords' rent of 4d, compounded.
Sandal (49) It was attested by Joseph Hall, lords' tenant, that Thomas Shillitoe of Dirtcarr in the parish of Sandallmagna, fellmonger, and Faith his wife, she examined separately by the steward, on 8 March last surrendered into the lords' hands 3 roods of arable land in a field at Dirtcarr called Bothom Field on the shott called Whinny Moores, with all ways etc appurtenant in the graveship of Sandall, now / **membrane 7** / occupied by the said Thomas Shillitoe or his assigns at an annual lords' rent of [blank], compounded: to the use of Samuel Norton of Kettlethorpe in the parish of Sandallmagna, gen, his heirs and assigns for ever. Agreed: entry fine [blank].
- (50) It was attested by Edward Allott, gen, lords' tenant, that Richard Naylor of Wakefeld, clothier, on 12 November 1686 surrendered into the lords' hands a cottage with 'gardenstead' thereto belonging, adjoining another 'gardenstead' belonging to Deborah Awdsley on the west in Criglestone in the graveship of Sandall, now occupied by Anthony Bedford of Criglestone, blacksmith, or his assigns at an annual lords' rent of [blank], compounded: to the use of the said Anthony Bedford, his heirs and assigns for ever. Agreed: entry fine [blank].
- (51) It was attested by Edward Allott, lords' tenant, that William Womersley of Criglestone, card-board maker, on 11 October 1687 surrendered into the lords' hands a half rood of land on the north end of a close in Criglestone adjoining Criglestone cliffe on the west and a vennel on the north, with all houses and buildings thereon, at an annual lords' rent of ½d, compounded, also a little parcel of land lately taken from the lords' waste in a place called le Cliffe adjoining, with buildings thereon, containing 21 yards by 6 yards with appurtenances in the township of Criglestone in the graveship of Sandall at an annual lords' rent of 1d, non-compounded, now occupied by the said William Womersley or his assigns: to the use of Judith Womersley of High Hoyland, spinster, her heirs and assigns for ever, provided that if William Womersley, his heirs, executors, etc, paid Judith, her executors, etc, the sum of £14 with consideration on 11 October 1688 without fraud or delay the surrender would become void. Agreed: entry fine of 1½d for the compounded land and [blank] for that non-compounded.

Ossett (52) It was attested by Josiah Oates, lords' tenant, that William Hargreaves of Brey in Gomersall, yeo, and Sarah, now his wife, she being a daughter and coheiress of William Birkhead of Great Gomersall, yeo, deceased, she having been examined separately by the steward, on 29 March last past surrendered into the lords' hands and quitclaimed all rights etc in a third part of three several closes of land, meadow or pasture near Ossett called Great Maplewell or Neare Maplewell, Farr Maplewell and Maplewell Inge, estimated at 15 acres, abutting le Towne Field of Ossettt on the north, and a parcel of common or waste on the south called les Lights, with appurtenances in the graveship of Ossett, now occupied by James Wilson of Ossett, cordwainer, or his assigns: to the use of the said James Wilson, his heirs and assigns for ever. Fine for enrolment of quitclaim, 6d.
Wakefield (53) It was attested by Richard Shaw, lords' tenant, that Timothy Roote of Howden, clerk, on 11 February 1687 [1688] surrendered into the lords' hands the messuage in Wakefield in Northgate near Bitch-hill and all houses, structures, shops, cellars, yards, profits, liberties, easements and hereditaments thereto appurtenant in the graveship of Wakefeld, now occupied by John Croft or his assigns at an annual lords' rent of 21d, compounded: to the sole use of John Pollard of Northbyerley in the parish of Bradford, yeo, his heirs and assigns for ever, provided that if the said Timothy Roote, his heirs or assigns paid John Pollard, his executors etc, the sum of £100 with consideration on 10 February next after the date of the surrender, this would become void. Agreed: entry fine, 5s 3d.
Stanley (54) It was attested by William Hanson, lords' tenant, that Francis Aiskell, gen, and Elizabeth his wife, she examined separately by the steward, on 20 October last surrendered into the lords' hands two closes of arable, meadow and pasture known as Brigg Close and Horse Close, with appurtenances in the graveship of Stanley at an annual lords' rent of [blank], compounded, with all claims etc: to the use of Oswald Hatfield, gen, his heirs and assigns, for ever. Agreed: entry fine [blank].
- (55) It was attested by William Hanson, lords' tenant, that Gervase Hatfield senior, gen, on 29 June past surrendered into the lords' hands all claims, reversions, etc, after the death of the same in a messuage in Stanley occupied by William Troughton, with all structures thereon, with two crofts and two closes of arable, meadow or pasture known severally as les Penny yards and Bullacre, another close called le Cowpasture, another called le Harry Carr, two closes called les Grith Fields, a close called le Moldroyd, a close called le Edd Croft, another called le Brigg Close, together with all other customary land in the several fields of Stanley or elsewhere in the Manor [at a lords' rent

of 2s 8d][1]: to the use of Oswald Hatfield, gen, son of the said Gervase, his heirs and assigns for ever, provided that Oswald, his heirs, executors or administrators pay sums hereafter expressed on the days and times specified. / **membrane 7 dorse** / These terms were that Gervase Hatfield, son of the said Gervase Hatfield senior, should be paid £100 within 12 months after his father's death, should he live so long, also Thomas Hatfield, son of Gervase Hatfield senior, should be paid £50 within a year of his father's death, should he live so long, also Savile Hatfield, son of the said Gervase Hatfield senior, should be paid £30 within the year, should he live so long and reach the full age of 21, also Elizabeth Hatfield, daughter of the said Gervase Hatfield senior, should be paid annually £4 at Pentecost and Martinmas in equal portions, the first payment to be made on the Pentecost after the death, and thereafter during the term of her natural life, also Mary Hatfield and Martha Hatfield, daughters of the said Gervase Hatfield senior, each of them be paid £30 when they reached 21 years, if still alive, also Elizabeth Hanson, daughter of William Hanson of Stanley, should be paid £10 when she attained 21 years, should she live so long, and if there should be default in payment, then the land would pass to the use of the said Gervase Hatfield, junior, Thomas Hatfield, Savile Hatfield, Elizabeth Hatfield, Mary Hatfield, Martha Hatfield, and Elizabeth Hanson and each of them for so long as the money remain unpaid. Agreed: entry fine of [4s][2].

Alverthorpe (sic) (56) Matthew Clayton of Wakefeld, cloth-worker, and Sarah his wife, she examined separately by John Scott, gen, deputy steward, outside court, on 29 March past surrendered into the lords' hands and quitclaimed all rights in a messuage, cottage or tenement, and a barn and croft appurtenant, estimated at 2 acres, also in an estimated 1½ acres in the several fields of Thornes, with all ways, etc, in the graveship of Thornes, now occupied by James Ellis or his assigns at an annual lords' rent of [blank], compounded, to the absolute use of Mary Jackson of Alverthorpe in the parish of Wakefield, widow, her heirs and assigns for ever. Fine to enrol, 6d.

Sum of court [blank]

[in draft, after membrane 37]

A

Great Court held on 5 April 1689 Panel for the Lords of the Manor

Thomas Tayler, gen sworn
William Moxon
William Hanson

---

[1] This is in the draft version only.

[2] In draft version only.

John Mawdsley sworn
Ferdinand Smith
Samuel Glover
Samuel Peaker
George Hebden sworn
Tempest Pollard
John Sugden
John Forest
Thomas Morehouse sworn
Edward Denton
Samuel Turner
Jeremy Bairstowe <10s for not coming>
William Dawson sworn
[no endorsement]

B
Att the Great Court Baron of Sir William Craven, Knight, and Edwin Wiat, Esq, Lords of the Mannor of Wakefeld, holden there the fifth day of April anno domini 1689.

Wee the Jury there sworne for the Lords of the said Mannour doe present all Earls and Lords for not appeareing att the said court per pole xs
Item wee present all Knights and Esqrs for the like per pole vjs viijd
Item wee present all gentlemen for the like per pole ijs vjd
Item wee present all other suteors for the like per pole vjd
Item wee present all those Copyholders that essoind last Great Court and did neither essoine nor appeare this court per pole xijd
Item wee find that Robert Pickard of Ossett is dead since last Great Court and Edward Pickard is his son and next heire.
[Signed] Thomas Taylor / William Moxon / William Hanson / John Maudsley / Samuell Glover / Samuel S Peaker / George H Hebden / Tempest Pollard / John Sugden / John Forrest / Thomas Morehouse / Edward E Denton / Samuell Turner / William Dawson
[no endorsement]

membrane 7 dorse continued
Court Baron held at Wakefeld on 26 April 1 William and Mary

Panel Inquest taken on the oaths of Gideon Mawde, gen, John Harrison, Thomas Totty, Tempest Pollard, John Forrest, William Moxon, Thomas

Kent, Robert Cusworth, William Preston, Gervase Harrison, John Leake and Robert Mansfield, jurors, who testified that:

Sowerby John Helliwell of Sowerby, yeo, by indenture of 23 April instant leased to a John Wilman of Sowerby, yeo, that messuage called Longedge, a garden and the north-east end of the barn, lately divided from the south-west part, also all the several closes of land, meadow and pasture known as le Great Inge, le Little Inge, le Field on the backside of the laith, le Littlehey, le Faugh and Cattayles, on the north-east of lands late of Jonas Helliwell, with their appurtenances in Sowerby in the graveship of Sowerby, now occupied by the said John Helliwell or his assigns at an annual lords' rent of 18d, compounded, with reversions, to have and hold to the same John Wilman, his executors, administrators and assigns immediately from the date of the indenture for 21 years, without fine with the lords, leave of court, in contempt and contrary to custom. Order to the grave of Sowerby to seize the same into the lords' hands.

Holme They presented that Joshua Kay of Barneside in Hepworth in the parish of Kirkeburton, yeo, by an indenture of 19 April instant leased to a John Haigh of Horbury, yeo, that messuage, house, close of land, meadow and wood called le Inge adjacent to the house, and another close called Nether Hilltopp, with appurtenances in Wooldale, and another little close of land and meadow called Barneside Lane Inge, with appurtenances in Hepworth, and the south part of a fold previously belonging to John Lindley of Barneside as measured from a stone marked with a cross in the wall of the orchard of Joshua Kay at Barneside to 'the partition wall' between the new barn of the said John Lindley and the new barn *lath*[3] of Joshua Kay, also the parcel of land whereon the new barn of Joshua Kay stood, from 'the partition wall', also a parcel of land west of the new barn of Joshua Kay from the partition wall to the 'dearne or meare' fenced there, the said Joshua Kay and his heirs being responsible for the fence for ever; also a way for carts and carriage for Joshua Kay and his heirs for ever across the ground (*fund'*) of John Lindley and from the land south of the said new barn, saving to John Lindley and his heirs all necessary ways and passages in and over the folds of Joshua Kay; also all liberties to use a furnace in the new furnace-house of John Lindley, Joshua Kay paying half the cost of repair and maintenance; also liberty for Joshua Kay and his heirs to lay timber (*jacere lignum*) to sustain their 'wainhouse' above le gavel end wall of the new furnace house, with all liberties, easements, emoluments and hereditaments pertaining to the said messuage and lands in the graveship of Holme, now occupied by Joshua

[3] In draft version only.

Kay and George Charlesworth or their assigns at an annual lords' rent of 12¾d, compounded, with reversions, these being customary land held by copy of court roll: to hold to the same John Haigh, his executors, administrators and assigns from the date of the indenture for a term of 21 years, without fine, leave of court, in contempt and contrary to custom. Order to the grave of Holme to seize the same into the lords' hands.

membrane 8

Stanley Item, they presented that John Leake made a way and led 'manure' with wains on the common apportioned between Smalley and Harwoodfield in Stanley, within the jurisdiction of the court, and not on the ancient, accustomed way. *amerced 39s 11d*

Item, they presented that Elizabeth Leake, widow, or the occupier of a close in Stanley called Fallsyke Close, encroached on the way between Smalley and Harwood field in Stanley and put a hedge (*sepem*) at the east end of the said close. *amerced 39s 11d*

Sowerby Third proclamation for claimants for the messuage commonly called Hileleigh and the houses, etc in Sowerby in the graveship of Sowerby now occupied by Samuel Sutcliffe or his assigns at an annual lords' rent of 2s 5d, compounded.

Alverthorpe Third proclamation for claims for a parcel of land taken from the lords' waste in the graveship of Alverthorpe, estimated at 20 yards by 7 yards, with the cottage thereon, at an annual lords' rent of 4d, compounded.

Wakefeld (57) It was attested by John Wilkinson, gen, lords' tenant, that Joseph Armitage of Dudmanstone in the township of Almonbury, gen, on 6 October 1686 surrendered into the lords' hands all that messuage in Wakefeld commonly known as Cock or Golden Cock, and all houses, barns, structures, folds, yards, shops, cellars, frontages, stalls (*stationes*), liberties, privileges, easements, hereditaments and appurtenances now occupied by Charles Yoward or his assigns in copyhold at an annual lords' rent of 4s, compounded; to the use of Joseph Armitage of Wakefeld, clothier, nephew (*nepotis*) of the same, his heirs and assigns for ever. Agreed: entry fine, 12s.

Horbury (58) It was attested by Robert Mansfield, lords' tenant, that John Walker of Horbury, yeo, on 26 April last surrendered into the lords' hands all customary land held of the lords of the Manor of Wakefield, namely, 1 rood of arable lying in le West Field of Horbury beyond a close called Crosse Close on the shott called Littsbanck shutt, between land of the heirs of Gervase Leeke, gen, on the east and of Thomas Hunt on the west, with common 'of Cowpasture' and all appurtenances in the graveship of Horbury, now occupied by John Walker or his assigns at an annual lords' rent of 1d,

compounded: to the absolute use of the said Thomas Hunt, his heirs and assigns for ever. Agreed: entry fine, 3d.
Ossett (59) Jonas Tommis of Wibsey, parish of Bradford, stapler, and Anne his wife (lately wife of Peter Belton, deceased), she examined separately by John Scott, gen, deputy steward, outside court on 29 March past surrendered into the lords' hands those two messuages, 'outhouses', barns, structures, stables, orchards, gardens, folds, tofts and crofts appurtenant, also a close called Upper Inge, another called Nether Inge, another called Upperhealds, another called Netherhealds, another called Wheat Close, another called Hill Close, and another called Kittroyde, with appurtenances, at Boothroyd in the graveship of Ossett, now occupied by Richard Liversedge, his assigns or subtenants, at an annual lords' rent of 4s 9d compounded, with all rights, etc: to the use of the same Jonas Tommis, his heirs, executors, administators and assigns for ever. Agreed: entry fine, 14s 3d.
- (60) Richard Liversedge of Boothroyd in the parish of Dewsbury, yeo, and Lydia his wife, she examined separately by the steward of the court, and John Peace junior of Ossett, parish of Dewsbury, farmer, by John Scott, gen, deputy steward, out of court, on 23 March last, surrendered into the lords' hands that messuage with appurtenances in Ossett with 'outhouses', barns, structures, orchards, gardens, folds, yards, tofts and crofts appurtenant, and those closes commonly called les Longlands, les Broadroyds, le Overhaygate, le Netherhaygate, and les Honnleys, also a little close or 'pighell' estimated at 3 roods leading to Riplinsyke, a rood on the shott called Sowdell abutting on Mapplewelltree on the east in the East field of Ossett, 2 butts estimated at a rood lying on Sowdell abutting on a croft now occupied by Thomas Barke, three lands in the said field lying on the shott called Wheatley, estimated at 1½ roods, abutting on le Broadroyds, half a land lying on Wheatley on the north side of the road and adjoining 'a common balke' on the east, 4 butts of land in the same field, estimated at a half acre, on the shott called Haggsbutts and abutting a close called Haggsclose, also a half rood in the said field lying on the shott called Hanging butts, abutting on the said pighell of land leading to Riplinsyke, 3 roods in the North field of Ossett on the shott called Storgate and abutting on le Parkewall *Pale* [in draft], a half rood in the said North field lying on Cherrytree shutt abutting on Dobroid Steel, 2 butts in the North field, lying on Tealsmall and abutting on the two lands of Josiah Hepworth, now occupied by Joshua Wilson, two half-roods on Tealsmall part lying in a close of William Heron, now occupied by John Land, a rood under Hounley hedge, 5 roods of land in the said North field on a shott called Oldfield, abutting on a pighell to the north and somewhat to the west of 'a common balke', another rood on Oldfield, abutting on the upper end of the pighell and

joining the lower end, an acre in the West field of Ossett on the shott called Kirkestye under Kirkestye Close hedge, an estimated 1½ roods lying on Kirkestye, abutting on Kirkstye butts, a rood in the said West field on Runtingebutts and abutting at the lower end on the close of John Peace and at the upper end on the close of Anthony Cooper, clerk, now occupied by Robert Nettleton or his assigns, also a cottage with appurtenances in Ossett, all being in the graveship of Ossett and now occupied by John Peace junior and Josiah Claughton or their assigns at an annual lords' rent of 3s 1d, compounded, and all other land held by Richard Liversedge in copyhold in the township of Ossett by whomsoever occupied (saving the copyhold of the said Richard Liversedge now occupied by James Wilson of Ossett, cordwainer, or his assigns): to the absolute use of John Haigh of Whitley in the parish of Thornhill, yeo, his heirs and assigns for ever. Agreed: entry fine, 9s 3d [corrected from 9s 10½d][4]

Hipperholme (61) It was attested by John Hargreaves senior, gen, lords' tenant, that Robert Ramsden of Siddall Hall, yeo, on 19 July last surrendered into the lords' hands the reversion after the death of the same Robert of 1½ acres with all structures thereon with appurtenances in Hipperholme and in a house called Bothomhouse, / **membrane 8 dorse** / a garden, a croft called le Parrocke and 3 closes of land, meadow and pasture called Stoneheap, Scarrbancke, Well Croft and Scale Inge or Sacle Inge, estimated at 2 acres, with appurtenances in the graveship of Hipperholme at an annual lords' rent of 14½d, also two other closes of land and pasture in Bryan Scholes with appurtenances in Northowrome in the said graveship, estimated at 2 acres, at an annual lords' rent of 8d, with all ways, waters, watercourses, etc, now occupied by Abraham Sowood, also two cottages or residences nearby, now occupied by Mary Whyte and [blank] Booth, widow, all compounded: to the use of Robert Ramsden of Quarlers in Northowrome, yeo, younger son of the said Robert, his heirs and assigns for ever, provided that if Robert the father were living on 2 February 1689/90 the surrender would be void. Because Robert was dead, it was agreed that Robert the son etc. Entry fine 5s 7½d.

- (62) It was attested by John Hargreaves senior, gen, lords' tenant, that Robert Ramsden of Siddal Hall in Southowrome, yeo, on 6 April instant surrendered into the lords' hands the reversion after his death of all the messuage called Lane ends with appurtenances in Hipperholme in the graveship of Hipperholme and all houses, structures, folds, gardens, land, tenements, closes, ways, etc now occupied by Samuel Saltonstall or his assigns at an annual lords' rent of 3s, compounded: to the use of John

[4] In draft version only.

Stancliffe of Bayleyhall in Southowrome and Robert Ramsden of Quarlers in Northowrome, yeo, and their heirs in trust that they, their heirs and either of these successors, and their heirs be seised of the same to fulfil the will of the said Robert Ramsden of Siddellhall, and for no other use. Robert now being dead, it was agreed that John Stancliffe and Robert Ramsden of Quarlers stand seised according to the terms of the will. Entry fine, 9s.

- (63) It was attested by John Wilkinson, gen, lords' tenant, that Mary Mawde of Halifax, widow, on 28 July last surrendered into the lords' hands all that messuage called Blackerhouse and all houses, barns, structures, folds, gardens, lands, closes, and grounds appurtenant in Northowrome in the graveship of Hipperholme at an annual lords' rent of 4s, compounded: to the use of such persons as Mary would name in her will. Agreed that Richard Witton of Wakefield, esq, and Thomas Dobson of Vicaridge in the parish of Bingley, gen, their heirs and assigns would hold the same to such uses as declared in the same will: entry fine, 12s.

Sowerby (64) William Sutcliffe of Hoohoyle in Erringden, yeo, came into court before Francis Whyte, esq, high steward of the Manor of Wakefeld, and with the agreement of Henry Hyleley of Sowerby, yeo, took from the lords that messuage called Hileleigh and all houses, edifices, barns, structures, folds, gardens, tofts, crofts, closes, lands, tenements and hereditaments appurtenant in Sowerby in the graveship of Sowerby, now occupied by Samuel Sutcliffe or his assigns at an annual lords' rent of 2s 5½d, compounded, and the reversions of the same, lately seized into the lords' hands because William Sutcliffe and Henry Hyleley by an indenture dated 21 November last leased the same to a William Midgley of Halifax, gen, to have and hold to William Midgley, his executors, administrators and assigns for a term of 21 years, without leave of court, to the contempt of the lords and contrary to custom, as shown at the court held at Wakefeld on 14 December past and presented by enquiry. After three proclamations in court for claimants none but William Sutcliffe presented himself. Agreed that he, his heirs and assigns hold for ever by ancient service. Entry fine, 7s 4½d.

Alverthorpe (65) John Cromacke of Morley, rope-maker, came into court before Francis Whyte, esq, high steward, and with the consent of Dorothy his wife, she examined separately by the steward, took from the lords of the manor a parcel of land taken from the lords' waste in the graveship of Alverthorpe containing 20 yards by 7 yards with a cottage built thereon, now occupied by Robert Kirkeman and Thomas Foster or their assigns at an annual lords' rent of 4d, compounded, lately seized into the lords' hands because John Cromacke and Dorothy his wife, she examined by the steward, by an indenture of 15 February last leased the same to a Joseph Hall of

Sandallmagna, yeo, his executors, administrators and assigns for a term of 21 years without leave of court, to the contempt of the lords, and contrary to the custom of the manor, as shown in court at Wakefeld on 15 February by enquiry. Proclamation was made at three courts for claimants and only John Cromacke appeared. Agreed etc. Entry fine, 12d.

- (66) Brian Scawberd of Alverthorpe and Dorothy his wife and William Foster of Alverthorpe, cordwainer, and Ellen his wife came into court before the steward and took from the lords a cottage previously built on the lords' waste in Alverthorpe, now occupied by the said Brian Scawberd or his assigns, lately in two tenements. It was agreed that Brian and Dorothy hold to them and their assigns for their natural lives and the life of the longer liver, / **membrane 9** / and then to William Foster and Ellen his wife for their natural lives and the longer liver, then to the heirs of their two bodies lawfully procreated, for lack of which, to the right heirs of William Foster for ever, rendering the annual lords' rent of 6d new rent at the usual times. Brian and Dorothy gave the lords an entry fine of 2s 6d for the term of their lives, and William and Ellen gave 2s 6d for the reversion.

- (67) In the name of God Amen, the twenty eight day of July in the fourth yeare of the Raigne of our Soveraigne Lord King James the second by the grace of God King of England, Scotland, France and Ireland, Defender of the Faith etc Annoque Domini 1688, I Mary Mawde of Halifax in the County of Yorke Widdowe being somewhat infirme of body but of good and perfect memory (praised be God for the same), and calling to mind the certainety of Death and the incertainety of the time thereof, and being mindfull to be in readinesse when it shall please God to call me, doe make and ordaine this my last will and testament in forme followinge. First I comitt my soule to God that gave it me and my body to the earth from whence it came, in stedfast hope of a joyfull resurrection att the last day, and as for all such worldly estate as it hath pleased God to blesse me withall, my will and mind is and I doe hereby give and dispose of the same as followeth. And first for my lands, my will and mind is that soe much of all my true and lawfull debts as my personall state will not extend to pay shall be paid and satisfied out of the same, and whereas I have by my writeing of surrender bearing date with this my last will and testament surrendered into the hands of the Lords of the Mannour of Wakefield according to the custome thereof all that messuage or tenement called Blackerhouse and all the houses barnes buildings lands closes and grounds whatsoever to the same belonging with their appertinunces in Northowrome in the graveshippe of Hipperholme of intent to make courting thereof to the use and behoofe of such person and persons as I the said Mary Mawde shall in and by my last will and testament give and devise the same unto, as by the said surrender may more att large appeare. Now my will and mind is and I doe hereby give devise and bequeath all the said messuage or tenement called Blackerhouse and the lands closes and premisses thereunto belonging and also the moiety or half parte of all that mannor or lordshippe of Cromwellbothom and Southowrome and either of them in the said county of Yorke, with all the rights, members and appertinunces thereunto belonging, and all the free rents and annuityes yssueing and payable forth of and within the said Mannour, and also the moiety or halfe parte of all that capitall messuage or tenement called Cromwellbothom and all the lands, tenements, meadowes, woods, pastures, closes, grounds and hereditaments to the same belonging with their appertinunces in Southowrome aforesaid, all those two messuages or tenements called Upperbinns and Netherbinns and all the houses, barnes, buildings, lands, closes and grounds to the same belonging with their appertinunces in Southowrome aforesaid, now in the tenure or occupacions of James Scholefield or John Scholefield or their assignes, and also all that messuage or tenement scituate att the chappell of Breares in Southowrome aforesaid and all the houses, barnes, buildings, lands, closes and grounds to the same belonging now in the tenure or occupacion of Joseph Crowther or his assignes; and also all those two messuages or tenements with thappertinunces in Southowrome aforesaid and all lands closes and grounds thereunto belonging now in the occupacions of John Ambler and Widdowe Ambler or their assigns and also two dwellinghouses newly built and a barne and the moiety of all these severall closes of land called by the name of Lawhillcloses scituate and lyeing in Southowrome aforesaid and the moiety of two cottages scituate att Barraclough Lanehead in Southowrome aforesaid; and also all that capitall messuage or tenement with thappertinunces in Halifax aforesaid wherein I now dwell, and the lands closes and grounds thereunto belonging unto Richard Witton of Wakefield esquire and Thomas Dobson of Vicaridge in the parish of Bingley gent' and their heirs for ever; to have and to hold the said moiety or halfe parte of the said mannor or lordshipp and of the said capitall messuage, severall other messuages, moity of the said closes and cottages lands closes and all other the premisses beforementioned with their appertinunces unto the said Richard Witton and Thomas Dobson and their heirs for ever; in trust and confidence nevertheless and to the intent and purpose that they the said Richard Witton and Thomas Dobson and their heirs and the survivour of them and his heirs shall forth of the rents and profitts of all the said premisses beforemencioned by them to be received give and allow unto John Mawde and Jonathan Mawde my Grandchildren yearly and every yeare for and dureing the <tearme of> twelve yeares now next comeing sufficient maintenance and education accordinge to their degree and quality, and with the residue of the said rents and profitts that shall remaine after maintenance deducted as aforesaid shall yearly and every yeare dureing the said tearme pay and satisfie all my legacyes and the remainder of my said debts, and what shall further remaine of the rents and profitts of my said reall estate after legacies and debts be paid my will is the same shall be paid to the said John and Jonathan Mawde, and after the end and expiracion of the said tearme of twelve yeares then in trust and confidence that they the said Richard Witton and Thomas Dobson and their heirs and the survivour of them and his heirs shall stand and be seised of all the said premisses beforemencioned to and for the proper use and behoofe of the said John Mawde and Jonathan Mawde and of their heirs and assigns for ever, equally to be divided betwixt them: subjett and lyable neverthelesse to the proviso or condicion hereafter mencioned (that is to say) Provided allwayes and it is my will and mind that if the said John Mawde and Jonathan Mawde shall att any time after they shall enter into and possess themselves of all the said premisses beforemencioned give or allow any summe or summes of money for the maintenance forth of the said reall estate or any parte thereof unto Sarah Mawde their Mother or suffer her to dwell with them or have any releife livelyhood or succour from them or either of them during her naturall life: that then the said Richard Witton and Thomas Dobson and their heirs shall stand and be seised of all the said premisses beforemencioned to the use and behoofe of them the said Richard Witton and Thomas Dobson and of their heirs and assigns for ever. And as for my personall estate, my will and mind is that my debts and funerall expenses shall be paid out of the same soe farr as the same will extend, which being done, I give and bequeath unto James Hoile and Martha Riddlesden my servants either of them five pounds apeice: also I give unto Mary daughter of Joseph Mawde of Sowerby five pounds: and I doe hereby nominate make and appoint the said Richard Witton and Thomas Dobson executors of my said last will and testament, hopeing they will be carefull in the management of my estate accordinge to my trust in them reposed, and my will and mind is that they my said trustees shall have all their charges and expences borne and allowed them which they shall in anywise lay out and expend in the management of my said estate: and I give unto the said Richard Witton and Thomas Dobson either of them tenn pounds apeice as a legacy for their paines. In testimony whereof to this my present last will and testament containeing foure sheets of paper I have hereunto set my hand and seale the day and yeare abovesaid: Mary Mawd. Sealed, signed, read, published and declared to be her last will and testament in the presence of us, James Hoile, Anne Maxwell, John Croyser, Thomas Preistley, James Fleeming.

membrane 9 dorse

In the name of God Amen, the seaventeenth day of October in the yeare of our Lord 1688, I Mary Mawde of Halifax in the County of Yorke, widdowe, haveing heretofore made and published my last will and testament bearing date the twenty eight day of July last past before the date hereof and being now weake in body but of good disposeing memory and understanding, and haveing a desire to make an addition to my said will, do by this present codicill ratify and confirme my said will made and published as aforesaid with this addition and alteracion followinge (that is to say) I do give and devise my messuage or tenement called Blackerhouse scituate in Northowrome and a close of land called Coalpitt Close and a square close lyeing on the southside of the said Coalpitt Close and adjoyneing upon the same, and the two parcells of ground lyeing on the eastside of the said messuage called the Over Paddocke and the Lower Paddocke, all of them belonging to the farme called Blackerhouse Farme, and also one farme in Southowrome and all the lands thereunto belonging or therewithall letten in the occupacion of Thomas Ambler or his assignes, and one other farme in Southowrome and all the lands thereunto belonging and therewithall letten, now in the occupacion of Sarah Ambler, widdowe, or her assignes, to Richard Witton of Wakefield esquire and Thomas Dobson of Vicaridge in the parish of Bingley gent, and their heirs and assignes, to have and to hold unto them the said Richard Witton and Thomas Dobson, their heirs and assignes, for ever, in trust that they the said Richard Witton and Thomas Dobson and the survivour of them or his heirs shall, with all the convenient speed that can be, sell the same and dispose of the money raised by such sale and the rents and profitts which shall be made of the same in the meane time for and towards the payment of my just debts and the legacyes in my said will given and bequeathed which my personall estate will not extend to pay, and pay the overplus if any be (their owne charges and expences about the trust hereby reposed in them being first allowed and deducted) to my Grandchildren John Mawde and Jonathan Mawde when they come of age; but my will and mind is that my said trustees shall upon their sale except and reserve soe much ground out of the farme in the occupacion of Sarah Ambler as shall be a good and sufficient way through the said farme to my coalpitts and to all the rest of my lands for horses, draughts, carts and all other caridges. And whereas I have in and by my said will devised all my messuages and lands to the said Richard Witton and Thomas Dobson and their heirs in trust that they, after the determinacion of the tearme of twelve yeares which I have devised to them for the payment of my debts and legacies, shall stand seised of the same to the use of my Grandchildren John Mawde and Jonathan Mawde, to be equally divided betwixt them, now my will and mind further is that to prevent disputes and controversies which may arise about divideing the houses, that the said Richard Witton and Thomas Dobson and their heirs shall stand seised of my messuage and tenement in Northgate in Halifax wherein I now dwell, and all the buildings outhouses gardens and appertinences thereunto belonging, to the use of the said John Mawde and his heirs after the twelve yeares expired, and of the moiety of the messuage called Cromwellbothom after the said twelve yeares expired to the use of the said Jonathan Mawde and his heirs. And I doe further will and devise that my said Grandchildren John and Jonathan shall within a yeare after the expiracion of the said tearme of tweve yeares limmitted to my said trustees pay unto their sister Mary Mawde the summe of one hundred pounds of lawfull money of Engand out of the estates which I have devised to them or in trust for them (that is to say) each of them the summe of fifty pounds, and it is my desire that this legacy be kept private by my trustees till the same become payable. And I doe will and desire that my trustees after my decease shall surrender all those six closes called the Bancks, [being copyhold lands][5], being parte of the Blackerhouse farme which is not devised to be sold, to my servants Martha Riddlesden and James Hoyle under the yearly rent of foure pounds for the tearme of eleaven yeares. And I doe will and declare that this codicill shall be annexed to my said will and shall be accounted and allowed as part of the same. In Witnesse whereof I have to this codicill set my hand and seale the day and yeare first abovewritten: Mary Mawde. Sealed, signed and published in the presence of us, the whole will being also now published in our presence, 'Mary' being put in by a razure. Thomas Preistley, Anne Maxwell, John Croyser, James Fleeming.

Sum of court [blank]

[in draft, after membrane 47]
A
Panel for the Lords and between parties

Gideon Mawde gen	sworn
John Harrison	sworn
Thomas Totty	sworn
Tempest Pollard	sworn
John Forrest	sworn
William Moxon	sworn

[5] In draft version only.

Thomas Kent sworn
Robert Cusworth sworn
William Preston sworn
Gervase Harrison sworn
John Leake sworn
Robert Mansfield sworn
Richard Greene sworn pinder for Dewsbury

B

Indenture of 23 April 1 William and Mary, 1689, between John Helliwell of Sowerby, yeo, and John Willman of Sowerby, yeo, for the purpose that John Helliwell provide cause of forfeiture of the messuage and cut off estates of entail, being a lease to the said John Helliwell (sic) of all that messuage called Longedge, a garden and the north-east end of the barn as lately divided, all the several closes commonly known as the Greate Inge, the Litle Inge, the Feild on the Backside of the Laith, the Litle Hey, the Faugh and Cattayles, as they lie on the north-east of other lands <late> of Jonas Helliwell in Sowerby and in the graveship of Sowerby, and now occupied by John Helliwell or his assigns, at a lords' rent of 18d compounded, with reversions, to have to the said John Willman, his executors, administrators and assigns for the term of 21 years, on payment of a yearly rent of 40s at Pentecost and Martinmas in equal portions. Witnessed in the presence of Jo. Hargreaves and John Hargreaves junior. Signed John I Helliwell his marke

The Jury doe present and saye that the lands above mencioned are demised contrary to the Custome of the mannor and therefore are forfeited and ought to bee seized into the Lords' hands.

[Signed] Gideon Maude
John Harrison
Thomas Tottie
Robert Mansfield

Record' ad Curiam Baron' tent' apud Wakefeld 26° die Aprilis Anno Domini 1689

[no endorsement]

C

Indenture of 19 April 1 William and Mary, 1689, between Joshua Kay of Barnside in Hepworth in the parish of Kirkburton, yeo, and John Haigh of Horbury, yeo, for the purpose etc, being a lease to John Haigh of all that messuage, house, close of land, meadow and pasture called the Inge adjoining the house, and another close called Netherhill topp with appurtenances in Wooldale, and another little close of land and meadow called Barnesidelane Ing in Hepworth, and the south part of the fold, previously belonging to John Linley of Barneside as the same was meted and divided 'from one stone with a cross thereupon in the orchard wall of the said Joshua Kay at Barneside to the partition wall betweene the new barne or lath of the said John Lindley and the new lath of the said Joshua Kay, and also a parcel of land on which part of the new lath of Joshua Kay now stands, from the partition wall between the said new laithe or barne and all one parcel of land as the same lies on the west side of the said new barn of Joshua Kay from the said partition wall to the dearne or meare in the fence there, the said Joshua Kay and his heirs making the fences here for ever; also a way for cart and carriage for the said Joshua Kay and his heirs forever over the ground of the said John Linley and out of the said land on the south side of the said new lath or barne (always excepted to the said John Linley and his heirs for ever all necessary ways and passages in, through, and over the folds of the said Joshua Kay), and also free liberty for using one oven in the new ovenhouse of John Linley, the said Joshua Kay bearing the charge of maintaining and repairing the said oven, and also liberty for Joshua Kay and his heirs to lay the bearing timber of their wainhouse on the gavel-end wall of the said new ovenhouse, with all liberties, easements ... appurtenant to the said messuage in the graveship of Holme', occupied by Joshua Kay and George Charlesworth or their assigns at a yearly rent of 12½d compounded, all being copyhold land held of the manor of Wakefield: the same being leased to the said John Haigh for a term of 21 years at an annual rent of 20s, payable in equal portions at Pentecost and Martinmas. Witnessed by Jo. Scott and Robert Scott.

26° die April 1689

The Jury doe present and say that the lands and premisses abovementioned are demised contrary to the Custome of the Mannor and therefore are forfeited and ought to be seised.

[Signed] Gideon Maude
John Harrison
Robert Mansfield
Thomas Tottie

Record' Joshua Kaye [Seal on tag appended]

[endorsed] Mr Jos Kay indenture to give cause of seisour.

D

Wakefeld Att the Court Baron holden there the xxvj[th] day of Aprill 1689

Wee the Jury there sworne for the Lords of the Mannour doe present John Leake for makeing a way and leading Manure with a Waine upon the Common balke betwixt Smalley and Harwoodfield in Stanley within the Jurisdiction of this Court and for not keeping the ancient and usuall way

xxxix^{s} xj^{d}

Also wee present Elizabeth Leake, widdowe <or the occupyers of Fallsyke close> for encroachinge upon the way lyeing betwixt Smalley and Harwoodfield in Stanley aforesaid by makeing a Hedge att the Eastend of a close called Fallsyke close. xxxix^{s} xj^{d}

[Signed] Gideon Maude
William Moxon
Thomas Kent
Thomas Tottie Record'

[no endorsement]

membrane 9 dorse continued

Court Baron held at Wakefield on 17 May 1 William and Mary

Panel for Lords of the Manor Inquest taken on the oaths of Tempest Pollard, Thomas Totty, Robert Bradford, Robert Firth, Robert Dickinson, Edmund Wood, James Scrivener, Robert Thornes, John Milner, John Crosland, Jonas Burnett and John Mawdsley, jurors, who said that John Kirke of Alverthorpe refused to pay an uncompounded fine due to the lords of the manor for a close called Doggcroft in Alverthorpe, so the close to be forfeit and seized into the lords' hands.

Sowerby It was certified by the grave of Sowerby that he had seized into the lords' hands that messuage called Longedge, a garden, the north-east end of a barn as divided south by west, also all several closes of land, meadow and pasture known as le Great Inge, le Little Inge, le Field 'on the backside of the Lath', le Littlehey, le Faugh and le Cattayles, as they lie to the north east of lands lately of Jonas Helliwell with their appurtenances in Sowerby in the graveship of Sowerby, now occupied by John Helliwell or his assigns at an annual lords' rent of 18d, compounded, as ordered at the last court. First proclamation for claimants.

Holme It was certified by the grave of Holme that he had seized into the lords' hands that messuage, a house, a close of land, meadow and wood called le Inge adjoining the house, and a close called le Netherhilltopp with appurtenances in Wooldale, and another close of land and meadow called

Barneside Lane Inge in Hepworth and the south part of a fold previously of John Lindley of Barneside adjoining, as bounded from a stone marked with a cross in the orchard wall of Joshua Kay at Barneside as far as 'the partition wall' between the new barn of John Lindley and the new 'lath' of the said Joshua; also a parcel of land on which the new lath stands, from the partition wall between the new barn; also a parcel of land on the west side of the new barn of Joshua to the 'dearne or meare' in the fence, which Joshua and his heirs must maintain for ever; also a cartway for the use of Joshua and his heirs for ever to cross the ground of John Lindley on the south side of the new barn, saving the right of John Lindley and his heirs to cross the fold of John Kay, also freedom to use an oven in the new ovenhouse (*domus fornac'*), Joshua Kaye paying a half part / **membrane 10**/ of costs of repair and maintenance, also freedom for Joshua Kay and his heirs to lay 'the bearing timber of their wainehouse' on the gavel-end of the new ovenhouse, with all other liberties etc in the graveship of Holme, now occupied by Joshua Kaye and George Charlesworth or their assigns at an annual lords' rent of 12¾d compounded, as ordered at the last court. First proclamation for claimants.

Ossett (68) Richard Liversedge of Boothroyd in the parish of Dewsbury, yeo, by John Scott, gen, deputy steward of the manor court, outside court on 11 May instant surrendered into the lords' hands all that messuage and all houses, edifices, barns, structures, folds, yards, orchards and gardens and two crofts belonging thereto called le Over Croft and le Nether Croft, and two little closes or pighells called Burdleys leading to Riplinsyke, also four butts of arable land and meadow or pasture in le East field of Ossett adjoining the pighell on the north and a way leading to Ossett Leights on the south, with all ways etc, all being within the graveship of Ossett, now occupied by James Wilson of Ossett, cordwainer, or his assigns, at an annual lords' rent of 6½d, compounded, also all other customary land of the said Richard Liversedge situated in the graveship of Ossett occupied by the said James Wilson: to the use of Richard Brooke of Lepton in the parish of Kirkeheaton, yeo, and William Bingley of the same, yeo, and their heirs, with the intent that Richard Brooke and William Bingley, their heirs and survivor and their heirs stand enfeoffed of the said messuage and closes to specified uses, namely, to Richard Liversedge and Lydia now his wife and their assigns for the term of their natural lives and the longer liver, after which to the heirs of their two bodies legitimately procreated, for lack of which, to the right heirs of Richard Liversedge for ever. Agreed that Richard Brooke and William Bingley and their heirs hold according to the prescribed form by due service. Entry fine, 19½d.

Sum of court [blank]

[in draft, after membrane 49]

A

Panel for Lords and between parties

Tempest Pollard / *Robert Beckwith* / Thomas Totty / Robert Bradford / Robert Firth / Robert Dickinson / Edmund Wood / James Scrivener / Robert Thornes / John Milner / John Crosland / Jonas Burnett / John Mawdsley [all sworn]

John Haigh grave of Horbury

Thomas Hunt sworn pinder of Sandall

[no endorsement]

B

Verdict of jury at the Court Baron held on 17 May 1 William and Mary

Wee the Jury there sworne for the Lords of the Mannour doe present and say that John Kirke of Alverthorpe doth refuse and neglect to pay an uncompounded Fyne due to the Lords of the said Mannor for one Close of Land called Doggcroft <also Dodg crosse> lyeing in Alverthorpe aforesaid, Therefore the said Close of land is forfeited and ought to be seized into the said Lords' hands.

[signed] Tempest Pollard / Thomas Tottie / Robert Dickinson / Edmond Wood

Record'

[no endorsement]

C

Wakefeld at the Court Baron [as above]

Wee the Jury there sworne for the Lords of the Mannour doe present John Haigh, Deputy Grave of Wakefeld, Thornes and Horbury, for not appeareing att the said Court xxxix^{s} xj^{d}

Item Mr Joseph Armitage, Grave of Stanley, for the like xxxix^{s} xj^{d}

[signed] Tempest Pollard / Robert Dickinson / Edmond Wood / John Maudesley / Thomas Tottie

[no endorsement]

D

Warrant of Francis Whyte, esq, high steward, to the grave of Sowerby and his deputy to seize into the lords' hands before the next court held at Wakefeld the messuage called Longedge, a garden and the north by east end

of a barn, divided south by west, also all the closes called le Great Inge, le Little Inge, le Field 'on the backside of the Laith', le Littlehey, le Faugh and Cattayles, as they lie north by east of the land lately of Jonas Helliwell in Sowerby in the graveship of Sowerby, now occupied by the said John Helliwell or his assigns at an annual lords' rent of 18d compounded. Dated 26 April 1 William and Mary, 1689.
[signed] Jo: Scott
[endorsed, in Latin] Nono die May 1689
Lands and tenements within mentioned were seized by me into the lord's hand as ordered:
[signed] John Hargreaves, in the presence of
Isaacke Farrar / John J Hitchin [mark] / Jeremie Waddington / Thomas Swaine

E

Warrant of Francis Whyte, etc, to the grave of Holme and his deputy to seize into the lords' hands etc a messuage, house, a close called le Inge adjacent thereto, and a close called Netherhilltopp in Wooldale, and another close called Barneside lane Inge in Hepworth, and that south part of a fold belonging to John Lindley of Barneside as delimited etc, now occupied by Joshua Kay and George Charlesworth or their assigns at a lords' rent of 12¾d, compounded. Dated 26 April 1 William and Mary. [sealed with Whyte's armorial seal]
[signed] Jo: Scott

[endorsed] May the 13th 89
All that is mencioned in this Coppy was taken up and seased by mee Jonathan Wilson as according to the Custom of the Mannor of Wakefield in the presence of those persons whose names are here under written.
[signed] William W Beevor his mark
Henry Besten / Philip Wray / Godfrey + Beevor his mark

membrane 10 continued

Court Baron held at Wakefield on 7 June 1 William and Mary

Panel for Lords of the Manor Inquest taken on the oaths of Matthew Morehouse, Francis Rhodes, William Moxon, Samuel Thornes, Gervase Harrison, Francis Blacker, Robert Cusworth, Edward Denton, Robert Thornes, John Speight, James Scrivener and Daniel Lindley, jurors.

Thornes They testified that Dorothy Armitage late of Heath, widow, deceased, lately held to her and her heirs in copyhold a parcel of land taken from the lords' waste, estimated at 1 rood, in the graveship of Thornes, previously occupied by William Read or his assigns at an annual lords' rent of 2d, not compounded. She died so seised about four years previously, and no one offered to fine with the lords within the space of three great courts after her death. Order to the grave of Thornes to seize the land before the next court.
Sowerby Second proclamation for the messuage called Longedge, etc.
Holme Second proclamation for the messuage etc, including the close called Netherhilltopp in Wooldale etc.
Alverthorpe (69) It was attested by Thomas Brooke, gen, lords' tenant, that William Horne of Wakefeld, gen, on 30 April last surrendered into the lords' hands two closes of arable, meadow or pasture estimated at 6 acres abutting and adjoining le Broadforebeck, with all ways, etc, in the graveship of Alverthorpe, now occupied by Obediah Lupton of Wakefeld, gen, or his assigns, at an annual lords' rent of [blank] compounded: to the use of the said Obediah Lupton, his executors, administrators and assigns from 2 February past for 21 years at an annual rent of £5 payable to William Horne, his heirs and assigns at Pentecost and Martinmas in equal portions under such terms as were contained in a pair of indentures dated with the surrender. Agreed, to hold by due service. Entry fine [blank].
Stanley (70) It was attested by William Moxon, lords' tenant, that Joshua Hanson of Leeds, cloth-worker, and Mary now his wife, she examined separately by the steward of the court, on 20 May last surrendered into the lords' hands 3 roods / **membrane 10 dorse** / of arable land in the field of Stanley called le Heathfield in a place called Gledallrood, also 2 other roods of arable in the same field near le Parkepale, also a selion on a 'headland' in le Kirkefield of Stanley estimated at 1½ roods, another selion in the same Kirkefield abutting on a headland, and another selion estimated at 1½ roods in le Kirkefield abutting on le Stammersyke on the south, all within the graveship of Stanley, now occupied by William Hanson junior of Stanley, yeo, brother of the said Joshua, or his assigns, at an annual lords' rent of 7d, compounded: to the use of the said William Hanson, his heirs and assigns for ever. Agreed: entry fine, 21d.
- (71) George Beale, gen, son and heir of Henry Beale, gen, deceased, came into court before the steward and gave the lords 3s 9d for leave to inherit half a house, tenement and lands at le Bothomhouses in the graveship of Stanley, now occupied by Richard Smerthwaite or his assigns at an annual lords' rent

of 15d compounded, after the death of Henry his father. Agreed, to hold by due service.

Sowerby (72) It was attested by Edward Denton, lords' tenant, that Simeon Dyson of Swiftplace in Stanningden in the graveship of Sowerby, yeo, and Jane now his wife, she examined separately by Henry Ellistones, gen, acting as deputy for Francis Whyte, esq, high steward, on 22 May last surrendered into the lords' hands a messuage and 10 acres of land, meadow or pasture in Stanningden in the graveship of Sowerby called Swiftplace, and 1 rood lately taken from the lords' waste in the graveship of Sowerby, now occupied by the said Simeon Dyson or his assigns, also a half rood in Stanningden in the graveship of Sowerby, previously of Jane Dyson and William Roades, with all houses and structures built thereon, now also occupied by the said Simeon Dyson or his assigns, also a watercourse descending into the said half rood from a close of a George Firth called Swiftcroft, with the buildings thereon, all owing an annual rent to the lords of 3s 6d, compounded, with all houses, edifices, barns, structures, folds, gardens, orchards, closes, etc, appurtenant: to the use of James Ryley of Barkisland, yeo, his heirs and assigns for ever, under the conditions specified in a pair of indentures of the same date as the surrender. Agreed: entry fine, 10s 6d.

- (73) It was attested by Edward Denton, lords' tenant, that Robert Preistley of Baiteings in Sowerby, yeo, and Phoebe now his wife, she examined separately by Henry Ellistones, gen, acting as deputy for Francis Whyte, esq, high steward, on 22 May last surrendered into the lords' hands that capital messuage called le Baitings now occupied by the said Robert Preistley and Henry Preistley, his son and heir, or their assigns, and all houses, edifices, barns, structures, stables, folds, orchards, gardens, lands etc appurtenant to the same, and all that great parcel of 'mooreground' (*fund'*) or common stretching from Baitinges yate to Little Manshead *alias* Manshead, thence to Blackstone edge and so by the highway to Stockforthbrooke, with appurtenances, lying in Soyland in Sowerby in the graveship of Sowerby, now occupied by the said Robert Preistley and Henry Preistley or their assigns at an annual lords' rent of 20s, compounded, with reversions, saving a parcel of land at the upper end of a close of pasture called Horsehey, estimated at 8 days labour with a plough, divided from the other parcels by a ditch, and also saving common of pasture and turbary on the common for Robert Preistley, his heirs and assigns for ever in respect of four messuages called le Clayclough, le Baitingsyate and Manshead, now occupied by Henry Marsden, George Clegg and Charles Clegg or their assigns: to the use of the said Henry Preistley, son and heir of the said Robert Preistley, his heirs and assigns for ever, and for no other use. Agreed, saving the exception, to hold by due service. Entry fine, £3.

- (74) It was attested by John Hargreaves senior, gen, lords' tenant, that Isaac Farrer of Feildhouse in Sowerby, yeo, and Isaac Farrer junior of Ballgreene in Sowerby, yeo, on 15 May last surrendered into the lords' hands a messuage called Ballgreene with a barn and all 'outhouses' and all closes appurtenant with all ways, passage, watercourses, etc, in Sowerby in the graveship of Sowerby, now occupied by the said Isaac Farrer junior or his assigns at an annual lords' rent of 3s 4d, compounded: to the use of Thomas Buckley of Little Haworth, Lancashire, gen, and William Midgley of Halifax, gen, and their heirs for ever, to such intentions as expressed in the surrender, namely to the use of Isaac Farrer junior and Patience now his wife and their assigns for the term of their natural lives and the longer liver, as jointure for Patience should she be the surviver of her husband, and after their deaths to the use of the male heirs of the bodies of the said Isaac and Patience, for the lack of which to the use of the female issue of the same, for the lack of which to the use of the right heirs of Isaac Farrer senior for ever. Agreed, to hold by due service. Entry fine, 10s.

- (75) It was attested by Edward Denton, lords' tenant, that Joshua Crosley of Cromwellbothom in Southowrome, yeo, on 14 May last surrendered into the lords' hands 4 acres 3 roods of land, meadow and pasture with all edifices built thereon, with appurtenances, in Crawwellshawes in Sowerby in the graveship of Sowerby, with the 12 closes in Sowerby commonly called les two Parkes, le Crofte in which the house (*domus*) stands, le Upper Roughhey, le Lathfield, le Nether Roughhey, le Great Inge, le Little Inge, le Coyte Field, le Bents, le Furrfield, and le Faugh, being customary land held by copy of the court roll, with all ways, passage, water, watercourses, common of pasture and turbary, etc, in the graveship of Sowerby, now occupied by Jeremy Crosley or his assigns at an annual lords' rent of 19d, compounded: to the use of William Horton of Barkisland, gen, his heirs and assigns for ever. Agreed: entry fine, 4s 9d.

membrane 11

Rastrick (76) It was attested by Thomas Taylor, gen, lords' tenant, that Robert Ramsden of Rastricke, yeo, on 6 April 1688 surrendered into the lords' hands those four closes of land, meadow or pasture with appurtenances in Rastricke in the graveship of Rastricke commonly known as Great Inge, le Inge Tongue, le Middle Inge and le Lowermost Inge, estimated at 16 acres, now occupied by the said Robert Ramsden and Timothy Tayler of Rastricke or their assigns, with all ways, etc, appurtenant at an annual lords' rent of 4s, compounded: to the use of John Kaye, bart, Thomas Wivill and Thomas

Horton, esqs, and their heirs, being feoffees under the will of George Thornhill late of Fixby, esq, deceased, under the condition that if Robert Ramsden, his heirs, executors or administrators paid or caused to be paid to the said John Kay,Thomas Wivill and Thomas Horton, any of each, or their certain attorney or the heirs of any the sum of £230 with lawful consideration on 6 April 1789 at Fixbyhall, the surrender became void. Agreed, to hold by due service. Entry fine, 12s.

Horbury (77) Whereas at the Great Court at Wakefield on 24 April 1 James II [1685] it was attested by Lawrence Horrocks, lords' tenant, that John Radcliffe of Topcliffe, clerk, on the previous 18 December surrendered into the lords' hands all the customary messuages, cottages, closes, land, tenements and hereditaments of the same John Radcliffe, with appurtenances, in Horbury in the graveship of Horbury or elsewhere in the Manor at an annual lords' rent of [4s 8½d][1], compounded and for [blank] for the remaining parcels non-compounded: to the use of such persons as John Radcliffe named in his last will and further to a codicil thereto annexed, to be granted to Elizabeth, late wife of the said John Radcliffe, for her lifetime and afterwards to Mary Radcliffe, daughter of the said John Radcliffe, to her and her lawfully procreated heirs, for lack of which to John Liversedge, nephew (*nepoti*) of John Radcliffe, to him and his heirs for ever: Elizabeth Radcliffe paid [7s 0¾d] as entry fine for her life interest in the compounded land and [blank] for the non-compounded land, and Mary Radcliffe paid [7s 0¾d.] and [blank] for the non-compounded land for the remainder.

- (78) Whereas I John Radclife late vicar of Topcliffe have passed a surrender in the Copyhold Court of Wakefield of all my Copyhold Lands in Horbury within the Mannour of Wakefield aforesaid to the uses and as I shall dispose the same by my last Will and Testament, I doe hereby give and bequeath all my said Copyhold Lands in Horbury aforesaid unto Elizabeth my wife dureing her naturall life, and after her decease to my Daughter Mary Radcliffe and to the heirs of her body lawfully to be begotten, and for want of such <yssue> then I doe give the said lands to John Liversedge my Nephew and to his heirs for ever. Witnesse my hand the Eight and Twentieth day of January in the third yeare of our soveraigne Lord King James the second Annoque Domini 1687 John Radcliffe. Sealed and Delivered in the presence of John Kettlewell, Thomas Harris, Henry Hall.

Sum of this court [blank]

---

[1] Item 7 was entered on draft roll and the amounts of the fines entered in the margin. The item was then cancelled and replaced by an identical record, with the annual lords' rent left blank.

[in draft, after membrane 55]
A
Pannell pro dominis Manerij ac inter partes
Matthew Morehouse sworn
Francis Rhodes / William Moxon / Samuel Thornes / Gervase Harrison / Francis Blacker / Robert Cusworth / Edward Denton / Robert Thornes / John Speight / James Scrivener / *William Walker* / *John Haigh* / <Daniel Linley> [all sworn]

B
Wakefeld At the Court Baron of William Craven knt and Edwin Wiat esq, serjeant at law, lords of the manor of Wakefeld in trust for Elizabeth Clapham, widow, on 7 June 1689
Wee the Jury there sworne for the Lords of the Mannour doe present and say that Dorothy Armitage late of Heath, widdowe, deceased, who late held to her and her heirs by Copy of Court Roll accordinge to the Custome of the said Mannour One parcell of Land heretofore taken of the waste of the Lords containeing by estimacion a Rood (more or lesse) and heretofore in the occupacion of William Read or his Assignes of the yearly rent to the Lords of ij^{d} and not Compounded for, dyed thereof seized above foure yeares ago, and because noe person nor persons came to claime the same and make fyne with the Lords within three Great Courts next after the decease of the said Dorothy Armitage, Therefore the said parcell of Land is forfeited and ought to bee seized into the said Lords hands.
[signed] Mathew Morehouse / Francis Rodes / William Moxon / Daniel Lindley

Record'

[no endorsement]

C
Wakefeld At the Court Baron...
We the Jury there sworne for the Lords of the Mannor doe present and find that the owners and occupyers of one parcell of land containeing six yeards in length and five yeards in breadth with a cottage thereupon built, scituate, lyeing and being on the Brookebancke and abuttinge on this Brooke or river on the North and the house heretofore of Timothy Rawson on the East, within the Graveshippe of Wakefeld and heretofore the Inheritance of Isaac Gascone and Ralph Gascone or th'one of them, do refuse and ought to pay the Copyhold rents due for the same to the Lords of the said Mannour.

Therefore the said parcell of land and cottage are forfeicted and ought to bee seized into the said Lords hands.

Alsoe wee present and say that the owners and occupyers of one house with th'appertenances scituate and being in Wakefeld in a certaine street there called Northgate, betweene a house heretofore of John Sunderland on the East parte and a house heretofore of [blank] Blades now in the occupacion of Daniel (?) Swindon [corrected from Isaac Sugden] or his assignes on the West parte, now or late the Inheritance of Bartholomew Banister, gent, doe refuse and neglect to pay the Copyhold rents due for the same to the Lords of the Mannour abovesaid. Therefore the said house is forfeicted and ought to bee seized into the said Lords hands.
[signed] Mathew Morehouse / Francis Rodes / William Moxon / Daniel Lindley

D

Wakefeld maner' At the Court Baron ...
Wee lay in paine that Judeth Platts of Sowerby Widowe doe before the Twenty fourth daye of this instant June make up and repaire her fences adioyning on the hyewaye in Sowerby aforesaid leadinge from a messuage there called Stubbin to a place called Kebroyd ford, and so keepe the same in suffitient repaire from time to time, upon paine to forfeit for every defalt
xx^{s}
[signed] Mathew Morehouse / Francis Rodes / William Moxon / Daniel Lindley
[no endorsement]

E

Know all men by these presents that I Francis Whyte esq, High Steward of the Courts of the Mannour of Wakefield in the County of Yorke att the request of John Scott, gent, understeward of the Courts of the said Mannour, doe hereby authorize, appointe and depute Henry Ellistones of Howroyd in Barkisland in the said County, gent, to take the examinacion of Jane now wife of Simeon Dyson of Swiftplace in Stanningden in Sowerby in the said County, yeoman, to the passing of one Surrender bearing Date with these presents made from the said Simeon Dyson and Jane his wife of All that one Messuage or Tenement and tenn acres of Lands, meadow or pasture with their appertenances in Stanningden within the Graveshippe of Sowerby aforesaid, called or commonly knowne by the name of Swiftplace, and of one Rood of Land late taken of the waste within the said Graveshippe of

Sowerby, now or late in the tenure or occupacion of the said Simeon Dyson or his assignes, And also of one halfe Rood of Land with th'appertenances in Stanningden aforesaid, heretofore the Lands of one Jane Dyson and William Roades, with all the houses and buildings thereupon builded, now also in the tenure or occupacion of him the said Simeon Dyson or his assignes, And also of one watercourse descending from one Close of one George Firth called Swift Croft into the said halfe Rood of Land with the buildings upon the said halfe Rood of Land builded, All which said premisses are of the yearly rent to the lords of the said Mannour of iij^{s} vj^{d} And Compounded for, and all the houses, edifices, barnes, buildings, folds, gardens, orchards, land, tenements, closes, pastures, feedings, woods, underwoods, wayes, water courses of water, commons, common of pasture and turbary, libertyes, profitts, commodityes, easements, emolluments and hereditaments whatsoever to the said Messuages and Tenements parcels of land and watercourse belonging, or of right appertaineing: To the use and behoofe of James Ryley of Barkisland aforesaid in the said County, yeoman, and of his heirs and assignes for ever (under and upon such Provisoes, Condicions, limmitacions and agreements as are or are to be mencioned, specified and declared in one paire of Indentures or Deeds Indented bearing Date with the said Surrender and made or mentioned to bee made betweene the said Simeon Dyson of th'one parte and the said James Ryley of th'other parte. Given under my hand and Seal the Twenty second day of May in the first yeare of the Raignes of our Soveraigne Lord and Lady William and Mary by the grace of God King and Queen of England etc, Annoque Domini 1689.

Sealed and Delivered in the presence of

Edward Speight Francis Whyte senescallus [paper armorial seal]

[endorsed] Executio istius Commissionis patet in quadam schedula hinc annex'

[signed] Henry Ellistones

F

Commission to Henry Ellistones of Howroyd in Barkisland, gen, to examine Phoebe now wife of Robert Preistley of Bayteings in Sowerby, yeo, concerning the surrender of 'all that messuage or tenement commonly called .. the Bayteings', now occupied by the said Robert Preistley and Henry Preistley, his son and heir apparent, ...and all houses, etc, appurtenant to the said capital messuage .. 'And of all that parcell of Moore-ground or Common extending and reaching from Bayteings yate unto a place called Little Manshead, otherwise Manshead, and soe to a place called Blackstone edge and soe downe by the high way from thence to a place called Stockforth

Brooke, with all and singuler their appertenances, scituate, lyeing and being in Soyland in Sowerby .. in the several tenures of the said Robert and Henry Preistley or their assigns, at the yearly rent to the Lords of 20s compounded', with reversions and remainders (one parcel of land lying in the upper end of one close, pasture or field called Horseley, estimated at 'eight dayes work with a Plow, divided from the other parte thereof with a ditch, allways excepted', and also excepting common of pasture and turbary, 'unto the said Robert Preistley, his heirs and assignes for ever of, in and upon the Common aforesaid for foure Messuages or Tenements with their appertenances called .. the Clayclough, the Bateings yate <and Manshead> [different hand],' now occupied by Henry Marsden, George Clegge and Charles Clegg or their assigns: to the use of the said Henry Preistley and of his heirs and assigns for ever. Given .. 22 May, 1 William and Mary, 1689.

Sealed and Delivered in the presence of Francis Whyte
Edward Speight senescallus [paper armorial seal]
[Endorsed as E]

membrane 11 continued

Court Baron held at Wakefeld on 28 June, 1 William and Mary [1689]

Panel for Lords of Manor Inquest taken on the oaths of Tempest Pollard, Samuel Thornes, John Phillippe, John Cawthorne, Samuel Peaker, John Sugden, Daniel Mawde, gen, John Haigh, Thomas Totty, John Clarkson, Jonas Shauu and John Walker, jurors.

Sowerby Third proclamation for claimants in court for the messuage called Longedge with garden, etc, and several closes called le Great Inge, le Little Inge, le Field on the backside of the laith, le Littlehey, le Faugh, and le Cattayles, as they lay on the north and east of lands late of Jonas Helliwell, with their appurtenances in Sowerby in the graveship of Sowerby, now occupied by the said (sic) John Helliwell or his assigns at a lords' rent of 18d, compounded.

Holme Third proclamation for claimants for the messuage, house, close of land, meadow or wood called le Inge adjoining the house, and a close called le Netherhilltopp in Wooldale, another called Barnesidelane Inge in Hepworth, and the south part of a fold previously of John Lindley of Barneside, etc, now occupied by the said Joshua Kaye and George Charlesworth or their assigns at an annual lords' rent of 12¾d, compounded.

Hipperholme (79) Thomas Roper came into court as the brother and next heir of Judith, late wife of William Pollard of Otley and a daughter of Jeremy Roper, late of Adderishgate in Northowrome, deceased, and gave the lords 9d for leave to inherit half of the two closes known as New Closes, with appurtenances, at or near a messuage called Blakehillend in Northowrome, all now occupied by Edward Gill or his assigns, with all ways, passages, water, watercourses and hereditaments appurtaining to the two closes, at a lords' rent of 3d, compounded, after the death of Judith. Agreed: to hold by due service.

- (80) It was attested by John Hargreaves senior, gen, lords' tenant, that Jonathan Preistley of Westercrofte, yeo, on 25 June last past surrendered into the lords' hands the reversion after his own death of that messuage at Westercrofte in Northowrome in the graveship of Hipperholme, now occupied by the said Jonathan Preistley or his assigns, and all houses, barns, structures, folds, gardens, etc, commonly occupied with them, commonly called Spencer Farme, and two other closes of land lately bought of Joseph Preistley and adjacent, now occupied by Jonathan Preistley or his assigns / **membrane 11 dorse** / at an annual lords' rent of 3s 2d, compounded: to the use of Nathaniel Preistley, a younger son of the said Jonathan Preistley, his heirs and assigns for ever. Agreed, by due service. Entry fine, 4s 9d.

Horbury (81) It was attested by John Walker, lords' tenant, that Thomas Totty and Priscilla his wife, she examined separately before the steward, on 24 June instant surrendered into the lords' hands a rood of arable land in Horbury in le Milne Field on a 'shutt' called le Long south field, between the land of William Wormall on the west and of William Langfield on the east, and abutting the River Calder on the south and the croft called Walker Crofte on the north, with 'common of Cow pasture' and all appurtenances in the graveship of Horbury, now occupied by the said Thomas Totty or his assigns at an annual lords' rent of 2d, compounded: to the absolute use of George Cockill and Elizabeth his wife, their heirs and assigns for ever. Agreed, to hold by due service. Entry fine, 6d.

Sowerby (82) It was attested by John Hargreaves senior, gen, lords' tenant, that Dorothy Wilkinson of Wakefeld, widow, on 20 April last past surrendered into the lords' hands the messuage called Foote in Warley in the graveship of Sowerby and all buildings, etc, appurtenant, now occupied by Joseph Firth or his assigns, also two fulling mills near the messuage called Boymilne and le Milne next the House, with all goytes (*gurgites*), pits (*restagnec'*), stews, attachments to stews, waterwheels (*tympan' circuil'*), wheel races (*tympanorum material' Anglice* 'geares'), ways, waters, and watercourses appurtenant, now occupied by the said Joseph Firth or his assigns at an annual lords' rent of 2s 9d, compounded: to the use of Caleb Gudgeon of Norland, clothier, his executors, administrators and assigns from 2 February last past for 21 years on conditions as to annual rent and repairs expressed in a pair of indentures of the same date as the surrender made between the said Dorothy and Caleb. Agreed, to hold by due service. Entry fine, 4s 1½d.

Holme (83) Joshua Kaye of Barneside in Hepworth in the parish of Kirkeburton, yeo, came into court before Francis Whyte, esq, high steward of the manor, and took from the lords that messuage, house and close of land, meadow and woodland called le Inge adjoining the House and a close called le Netherhilltopp in Wooldale and another close called Barnesidelane Inge in Hepworth, and the south part of a fold previously of John Lindley of Barneside from a stone with a cross in the orchard wall of the said Joshua Kaye at Barneside to the 'partition wall' between the new barn of John Lindley and the new 'lath' of the said Joshua Kaye, also the parcel of land on which the said new lath now stood, from the partition wall on the west to the 'derne' or 'meare' as fenced, the said Joshua Kaye and his heirs to make the fences there for ever, also a carriage way for the said Joshua Kaye and his heirs forever across the ground of John Lindley and from the parcel of land on the south of the new barn - saving to John Lindley and his heirs all necessary ways and passages across the fold of Joshua Kaye, and all liberties to use a 'furnace' in the new ovenhouse of John Lindley, Joshua Kaye paying half the cost of repairs and maintenance of the said furnace, also liberty for Joshua Kaye and his heirs to lay weight-carryng timber for 'their wain house' on the Gavelend wall of the new ovenhouse, with all liberties, easements, emolluments, and hereditaments thereto appurtenant, in the graveship of Holme, now occupied by Joshua Kaye and George Charlesworth or their assigns at a lords' rent of 12¾d, compounded, lately seized into the lords' hands (save the exceptions) because Joshua Kaye, by indenture of 19 April last leased the same to a John Haigh of Horbury, yeo, for him, his executors, administrators and assigns for 21 years, without leave of court, to the contempt of the lords of the manor and against custom, as ascertained by inquest in court at Wakefield on 26 April. Public proclamation was made at the next three courts, as custom required, and only Joshua Kaye came. He, his heirs and assigns were authorised to hold the same at the ancient rent and by due service, and paid an entry fine of 3s 2¼d.

Sowerby (84) John Helliwell of Sowerby, yeo, came before Francis Whyte, esq, high steward, and took from the lords the messuage called Longedge, a garden and the north and somewhat east end of a barn, as divided from the south and somewhat west end, also all the several closes of land, meadow and pasture commonly known as le Great Ynge, le Littleynge, le Field on the backside of the Laith, le Little Hey, le Faugh, and le Cattayles, lying to the north and east of land lately of Jonas Helliwell, with appurtenances in

Sowerby in the graveship of Sowerby, now occupied by the said John Helliwell or his assigns, at an annual lords' rent of 18d, compounded, with reversions and remainders, lately seized into the lords' hands because by an indenture of 23 April last John Helliwell leased the same from the same date to John Wilman of Sowerby, yeo, to have to him, his executors, administrators and assigns for 21 years, without leave of court, etc, as testified by a jury at the court held at Wakefield on 26 April. Proclamation for claimants was made at three courts, and only John Helliwell offered himself. Granted to John, his heirs and assigns on the ancient terms: an entry fine of 4s 6d.

Holme (85) It was attested by Richard Mathewman, gen, lords' tenant, that John Browne of Hepworth and Susan his wife, she examined separately by the steward, on 10 April last surrendered into the lords' hands a messuage or residence where John Browne then lived, a garden, part of a lath as now divided, with a 'folding' adjacent, a croft adjacent, and all several closes, doles and parcels of arable, meadow or pasture, namely half a close called Deinroyds as now divided, half a close called Kemphouse as now divided, two days' work in les West fields, half a close called Mooreyngs as now divided, half a close called Hey as now divided, 5 roods / **membrane 12** / of land in le Berristall Field, half a close called Farrfield as now divided, a little close called Heward carr, and a parcel of meadow in a close called Carre, and half a close called Hanroyde as now divided, lately of John Marshe late of Hepworth, with all ways, waters, watercourses, etc, in Hepworth in the graveship of Holme, now occupied by the said John Browne or his assigns at an annual lords' rent of 2s 3d, compounded, with all their rights: to the sole use of Robert Beever of Hepworth, his heirs and assigns for ever. Agreed: entry fine of 6s 9d.

Sum of court [blank]

[in draft, after membrane 59]

A

28 June 1689 Pannel for Lords of Manor

Tempest Pollard	sworn	John Sugden	
Samuel Thornes		<Daniel Mawde, gen>	
John Phillippe		*Robert Bradford*	sworn
William Curties	sworn	John Haigh	
John Cawthorne		Thomas Totty	
Samuel Peaker			
	John Clarkeson		
Jonas Shauu			sworn
John Walker			

John Briggs, sworn deputy grave of Wakefeld
[no endorsement]

membrane 12 continued

Wakefield Court Baron, held on 19 July 1 William and Mary [1689]

Panel Inquest taken on the oaths of John Rhodes, gen, John Murgatroyd, gen, Tempest Pollard, Thomas Totty, John Speight, James Wilson, George Hebden, Francis Mathewman, Christopher Rapier, James Scrivener, Robert Bradford and Henry Wilson, jurors.

Thornes (86) Susan Paulden of the city of York, spinster, by John Scott, gen, deputy steward of the court, outside court on 11 July instant surrendered into the lords' hands half a close of arable, meadow or pasture commonly called Crosseclose, estimated at 6 acres, abutting on Thornes Moore on the south and the land of John Harris, esq, on the north, with all ways, etc, in the graveship of Thornes, now occupied by John Peaker or his assigns at an annual lords' rent of 10½d, compounded: to the use of Mary Beeston of Wakefield, widow, her heirs and assigns for ever. Agreed: entry fine, 2s 7½d.

Hipperholme (87) Judith, wife of Daniel Hoyle, sole daughter and heir of Anthony Westerman late of Halifax, chapman, deceased, came before the steward and gave 19½d as fine for leave to inherit a messuage and two closes of meadow or pasture with appurtenances in Northowrome in the graveship of Hipperholme, commonly called les Pighells, estimated at 2 acres, now occupied by Richard Jepson or his assigns, at an annual lords' rent of 6½d, compounded: after the death of Anthony Westerman, whose daughter and heir she was. Agreed, to hold by due service.

[*Horbury*] (88) It was attested by John Rhodes, gen, lords' tenant, that John Longley of Horbury, gen, on 8 April last surrendered into the lords' hands all that customary land held by copy of court roll, all messuages, lands, tenements, closes and hereditaments with 'common of Cowpasture' and all ways, etc, in Horbury at an annual lords' rent of 16d, compounded: to the absolute use of the last will of the said John Longley, it being his true intent that George Usher of Adwalton, gen, and Richard Grice of Horbury, gen, and their heirs hold the same to the uses expressed in his last will. Agreed: entry fine, 4s.

Wakefield (89) It was attested by Thomas Burrow, lords' tenant, that Timothy Roote of Howden, clerk, on 10 October last surrendered into the lords' hands all that messuage or tenement in Wakefeld in the street called Northgate on le Bitch-hill, with all houses, structures, shops, cellars, yards,

profits, etc, appurtenant in the graveship of Wakefeld, now occupied by John Crofte or his assigns at an annual lords' rent of 21d, compounded: to such uses as expressed in the last will of Timothy Roote: according to which Timothy Roote granted to William Heaward of Wakefeld, gen, and Richard Shaw of the same, gen, and their heirs for such uses as expressed in that will. Agreed: entry fine of 5s 3d.
- (90) This is parte of the last will and testament of Timothy Roote of Howden, co York, clerke (vizt)

First I give and devise all that messuage and tenement, buildings, fronts, cellars, backsides, hereditaments and appurtenances thereunto belonging, scituate and being att the Bitchhill in Wakefield now in the tenure and occupation of John Crofte his assignes or undertenants, unto William Haward and Richard Shaw, both of Wakefield aforesaid, yeomen, and their heirs upon trust and confidence and to the intent that they shall with all convenient speed after my decease sell the said messuage or tenement, buildings, fronts, cellars, hereditaments with thappertenances aforesaid in Wakefield for soe much as the same will give, bona fide, for the payment of all my just and lawfull debts, and the overplus to be distributed equally amongst my three children Thomas, Anna, and Timothy Roote, and my mind is that the rents and profitts of that my said messuage in Wakefield untill sale be made thereof (that parte of the rents due to John Pollard upon account onely excepted) shall goe towards the maintenance and education of my three children aforesaid.

Sum of court [blank]

[in draft, after membrane 61]
A
Court held on 19 July 1689 Panel for Lords of Manor

John Rhodes, gen	sworn	George Hebden	sworn
<John Murgatroyd>		Frank Mathewman	"
Tempest Pollard	"	Christopher Rapier	"
Thomas Totty	"	James Scrivener	"
John Speight	"	Robert Bradford	"
James Wilson	"	Henry Wilson	"

membrane 12 continued

Wakefield Court Baron held on 9 August 1689.

Panel for the Lords Inquest taken on the oaths of Michael Parker, John Speight, Joseph White, John Phillippe, William Curtice, James Earnshawe,

Richard White, John Taylor, George Hebden, James Scrivener, Thomas Tottye and Robert Bradford, jurors, who testified that Martha Greene of Austonley, widow, Rebecca Greene of the same, widow, and Benjamin Greene of the same, yeo, children of the same Martha put posts (*stoopes*) and hung gates (*pender' januam*) at both ends of a piece of common land or lords' waste called Feildend Banck in Austonley in the graveship of Holme in the jurisdiction of the court, where stoops were never before, nor gates, and 'have encroached' on and enclosed the common and waste. *Fine of 39s 11d.*

Ossett (91) Joseph White junior of Earlesheaton, yeo, and Mary his wife, she examined separately by John Scott, gen, deputy steward, out of court on 15 April 1687 surrendered into the lords' hands the reversion immediately after the death of Thomas Archer of Chickingley, father of Mary, of the undivided half of a close now divided into two and estimated at 4 acres in Gawthorpe at Hardacres, and another close in Ossett called Mooreroyd with their several appurtenances in the graveship of Ossett, now or lately occupied by the said Thomas Archer and a William Gill or their assigns at an annual lords' rent of 17d, compounded: to the use of John Wilks of Outwoodside in Stanley, roper, his heirs and assigns, for ever; on condition that if Joseph White, his heirs, executors and administrators or any of them paid John Wilks or his certain attorney, executor or administrator / **membrane 12 dorse** / 24s on 16 April 1688 and £21 4s on 16 April 1689 without fraud or delay the surrender would be void. Agreed that John Wilks hold the same by due service. Entry fine, 4s 3d.

Ossett (92) Abraham Fletcher of Chickenleybanck in the parish of Dewsbury, clothier, and Susan now his wife, she agreeing separately before John Scott, gen, deputy steward, outside court on 17 January last surrendered into the lords' hands all that west half of a messuage and half of all structures, crofts and appurtenances at Chickenleybanck, also half of all those 10 arable lands (*fund'*) in the field called Quarrell Field, estimated at 4 acres, adjoining the land of Richard Grime on the north and of John Speight on the west, with all appurtenances, in the graveship of Ossett, now occupied by the said Abraham Fletcher or his assigns at an annual lords' rent of 9½d, compounded: to the use of Michael Parker of Dewsbury and John Speight of Ossett and their heirs, to the intent that Michael Parker and John Speight, their heirs and survivers and their heirs be seised of the half messuage and structures, namely a parlour and a chamber, and two bays of the barn on the west of the messuage and structures, with sufficient ways, waters, liberties and convenient access to these 'rooms' and structures, to the use of John Fletcher, son of the said Abraham, and Elizabeth Browne, daughter of James Browne of Chickenley, whom John would soon marry, God willing, and their assigns for the term of their natural lives and the longer liver, and then to the use of the heirs of their bodies, lawfully procreated, and for lack of such, to the heirs of Abraham Fletcher for ever. If John died before Elizabeth, leaving child or children, an annuity of 20s should be paid from the other half of the messuage, etc, during the natural life of Abraham, payable at Whitsun and Martinmas in equal parts, starting from whichever feast fell first after John's death: to the use of Elizabeth for the natural term of Abraham's life. If the annuity were unpaid within 10 days after either feast, Elizabeth and her assigns might enter and distrain. Concerning the other half of the messuage, etc, it would be to the use of Abraham Fletcher and his assigns for his natural life, then to John Fletcher and Elizabeth Browne, his intended wife, and their assigns for the term of their natural lives, and the longer liver, then to their lawfully procreated heirs, for lack of which, to the right heirs of Abraham for ever. Agreed, Michael Parker and John Speight and their heirs to hold according to the said uses and by due service: entry fine [blank].

Sum of court [blank]

[in draft, after membrane 63]

A

Panel	Michael Parker	sworn	James Earnshawe	sworn
	James Scrivener	sworn		
	John Speight	sworn	Richard White	sworn
	Thomas Totty	sworn		
	Joseph White	sworn	John Taylor	sworn
	Robert Bradford	sworn		
	John Phillippe	sworn	George Hebden	sworn
	William Curtice	sworn		

B

Wakefeld Att the Court Baron of Sir William Craven Knt and Edwin Wiat esq Sergeant att Law, lords of the Mannor of Wakefeld, holden there the ninth day of August ... 1689.

Wee the Jury there sworne for the Lords of the said Mannour doe present Martha Greene and Rebecca Greene both of Austonley Widdowes and Benjamin Greene of the same, yeoman, son of the said Martha Greene, for setting Stoopes and hanging yates att both ends of one peice or parcell of Common or wast ground belonginge to the said Lords called Feildendbanck in Austonley within the graveshippe of Holme and Jurisdiccion of this Court where never any Stoopes or Yates were nor ought to bee and thereby incroaching and incloseing the Common and wast of the Lords of the said Mannor xxxixs xjd.

[signed] James I Scrivener Richard R White Robert I Bradford James Earnshaw / Thomas Tottie / Micheall Parkar / John I Speight / John Taylor / Joseph I White / William W Curtice / John I Phillippe / George H Hebden

membrane 12 dorse continued

Wakefield Court Baron, held on 30 August 1 William and Mary [1689]

Panel for the Lords Inquest taken on the oaths of Francis Rhodes, Tempest Pollard, Thomas Shillitoe, Samuel Thornes, John Haigh, William Curtice, George Hebden, John Land, Francis Allen, Robert Bradford, James Scrivener and William Holdsworth, jurors, who attested that John Murgatroyd of Edgend in Warley, yeo, Henry Murgatroyd, and James Murgatroyd, younger sons of the said John, by indenture dated 10 August instant leased to a John Cockcroft of Bradford, gen, all that messuage and houses, structures, closes, lands, tenements and hereditaments thereto appendant at Wainstalls in Warley in the graveship of Sowerby, now severally occupied by John Ryley and a John Bellfield or their assigns at an annual lords' rent of 8d, compounded, with reversions: to be held by John Cockcroft, his executors, administrators and assigns from that date for a term of 21 years, without leave, in contempt, etc. Order to the grave of Sowerby to seize the same into the lords' hands before the next court.

Alverthorpe (93) It was attested by Toby Sill, gen, lords' tenant, that Benjamin Watkinson of the city of London, gen, on 18 April last surrendered into the lords' hands all that capital messuage called Flanshaw Hall and all houses, buildings, barns, structures, dove-cotes, stables, folds, yards, gardens, orchards and crofts appurtenant, also all the several closes of land commonly called les Tofts, le Broad Inge alias Lower Inge, le Great-Gelder Inge, le Little Gelder Inge, le Mean Earley, le Little Earley, le Farr Earley, le Dunston Close, le Broom Royd, le Lyme Garth, le Wowan Close, and three other closes called le Four Lands head, le Thistle Close, and le Througstile Close, lying near Westgate Moore, also another close estimated at 4 acres, previously of Matthew Wentworth, gen, and all other customary lands and tenements lately of Edward Watkinson, late of Wakefield, gen, deceased, father of the said Benjamin, with appurtenances in Flanshawe in the graveship of Alverthorpe, now occupied by Joseph Watkinson of Flanshawe Hall in the parish of Wakefield, gen, his assigns or subtenants at an annual lords' rent of 10s 2d, compounded: to the use of the said Joseph Watkinson, his heirs and assigns for ever, on conditions in an indenture of the date of surrender. Agreed: entry fine of 30s 6d.

Hipperholme (94) It was attested by John Hargreaves, junior, lords' tenant, that Henry Birkhead of Cliffe house in Lightcliffe, yeo, on 16 August 1688 surrendered into the lords' hands all that messuage called Cliffe house with appurtenances in Lightcliffe in the graveship of Hipperholme, a barn, a garden and 7 closes of land, meadow and pasture with appurtenances in Lightcliffe commonly occupied with the same, now occupied by the said Henry or his assigns, and all ways, waters, watercourses, liberties, etc, at an annual lords' rent of 3s 1¾d, non-compounded: to the use of Joseph Crowther of Northowrome, yeo, his heirs and assigns for ever: provided that if Henry, his heirs, executors, administrators or any of them paid or caused to be paid to the said Joseph Crowther or his certain attorney, executor, administrator or assigns or anyone of them the sum of £212 on 17 August 1689 at the residence of the said Joseph Crowther in Northowrome the surrender became void. Agreed: entry fine [blank] [in draft margin: Entry fine £18]

membrane 13

Holme (95) Michael Midgley, son and heir of Jeremy senior, late of Overthwonge, deceased, came before the steward of the court and fined [blank] for leave to inherit all the messuage and houses, buildings, barns, structures, folds, orchards, gardens, crofts, closes, lands, tenements and hereditaments appurtenant in Overthwonge in the graveship of Holme at an annual lords' rent of 2s 1½d, not compounded, of which the said Jeremy Midgley died seised. Agreed, to hold to him, his heirs and assigns by due service. [in draft margin: Entry fine £6].

Alverthorpe (96) It was attested by William Holdsworth, lords' tenant, that John Holdsworth of Alverthorpe in the parish of Wakefeld, clothier, on 1 April 1688 surrendered into the lords' hands a close called le Farwill Lane Close, estimated at 3 acres, and its appurtenances, at an annual lords' rent of 13½d, now occupied by Joseph Holdsworth, son of the said John Holdsworth: to the use of the said Joseph, his heirs and assigns for ever: to the uses expressed in the last will and testament of the said John. Agreed, to hold by due service. Entry fine, 3s 4½d.

Sum of court [blank]

[in draft, after membrane 65]

A

Panel for lords and between parties

Francis Rhodes / Tempest Pollard / Thomas Shillitoe / Samuel Thornes / John Haigh / William Curtice / George Hebden / John Land /

Francis Allen / Robert Bradford / James Scrivener / William Holdsworth [all sworn]

B

Indenture of 10 August 1689 between John Murgatroyd of Edge-end in Warley, yeo, Henry Murgatroyd and James Murgatroyd, younger sons of the said John, AND John Cockcroft of Bradford, gen, to provide cause for seizure of the messuage, lands and tenements hereafter mentioned, and to cut and destroy all estates and entails, leasing to the said John Cockcroft the messuage etc at Wainstalls in Warley in the graveship of Sowerby, now occupied by John Ryley and John Belfield or their assigns, owing a lords' rent of 8d, compounded, with reversions: to have for 21 years at a yearly rent of 40s, payable at Whitsun and Martinmas in equal parts.

Sealed and delivered in the presence of Thomas Cockcroft John Turner John Hargreaves	The Jury doe present and say that the lands above mentioned are demised contrary to the Custome of the Manner and therefore are forfeited and ought to bee seized into the Lords hands

[signed] John M Murgatroyd [seal affixed]
Henry Murgatroyd [seal affixed]
James I Murgatroyd [seal affixed]
his marke

Francis Rodes / Tempest Pollard / John Haighe / Willian (sic) Holdsworth /

Recorded in court at Wakefeld 30 August 1689

C

Whereas wee John Murgatroyd of Edge end in Warley, yeo, Henry Murgatroyd and James Murgatroyd, younger my sounes, have by our Indenture of Lease bearing date with these presents demised, granted and to ferme letten unto John Cockcroft of Bradford .. gent for the terme of Twenty one yeares from the date and makeinge of the said Indenture ALL THAT messuage ... at Wainstalls in Warley .. in the Graveshipp of Sowerby, ... They desire the lords of the Manor, 'the Three proclamacions beinge the[re] made and past as in such cases is used, to regrant the same to John Turner of Midgley, ... fellmonger, and to his heires and assignes for ever. And for soe doeinge this shall bee a sufficient Warrant. Witnes our hands and Seal[es] the Tenth daye of August in the First yeare of the R[aigne] of our Sovereigne

Lord and Lady now Kinge and Queene over [England], etc, anno Domini 1689.

Sealed and delivered in the presence of us	John M Murgatroyd his marke	[seal affixed]
Thomas Cockcroft	Henery Morgatroyd	[seal affixed]
John Hargreaves junior	James I Murgatroyd his marke	[seal affixed]

membrane 13 continued

Court Baron held at Wakefeld on 20 September 1 William and Mary [1689]

Panel for the Lords Inquest taken on the oaths of Robert Mansfield, Samuel Peaker, Francis Hatfield, gen, James Wilson, John Haigh, John Forrest, William Harrupp, Samuel Thornes, Michael Parker, Thomas Shillitoe, John Sugden, Tempest Pollard and Jeremy Milner, jurors, who attested that Peter Sergeant of Wakefeld, William Haigh of the same, and John Binnes of Horbury dug a piece of ground adjacent to the stone wall part of the structure of a messuage of Anthony Bland, situated in Wakefeld Northgate, thereby letting down and baring and undermining the wall and structure to its great ruin. Each was amerced 30s.

Wakefield / Thornes (97) Joseph Hall, brother and next heir of Hannah, lately wife of Barnaby Thompson, deceased, came before the steward of the court and gave the lords 4s 1½d for leave to inherit a messuage with appurtenances in Wakefeld in a street called Westgate, lately occupied by Zachary Moore and now by Thomas Wilson or his assigns, also two closes commonly called Long closes in the graveship of Thornes, now occupied by the said Joseph Hall and a John Baynes or their assigns at an annual lords' rent of [blank], compounded. Hannah Thompson was now dead, and he was her brother and next heir. Agreed that he inherit and hold by due service.

Alverthorpe (98) It was attested by William Turner, gen, lords' tenant, that Toby Sill of Wakefeld, gen, on 16 August last past surrendered into the lords' hands all that parcel of land, meadow or pasture estimated at a half acre, now enclosed on the west side of a close of Toby Sill, lately bought by him from Charles Jackson, gen, deceased, now occupied by Richard Norfolke junior, gen, which parcel adjoined the land of Daniel Mawde junior of Alverthorpe, gen, on the west and abutted on Humble Jumble beck on the south, with its appurtenances in the graveship of Alverthorpe, with all the rights of Toby Sill, at an annual lords' rent of 1d, compounded: to the use of the said Daniel Mawde, his heirs and assigns for ever, in exchange for a similar amount of land of Daniel in the said enclosure near the east side and surrendered by

Daniel to Toby and his heirs. Agreed, to hold by due service: entry fine of 3d.

- (99) It was attested by William Turner, gen, lords' tenant, that Daniel Mawde junior of Alverthorpe, gen, on 16 August last past surrendered into the lords' hands a selion of land, meadow or pasture estimated at a half acre in an enclosure of the inheritance of Charles Jackson, gen, deceased, and now of Toby Sill of Wakefeld, gen, now occupied by Richard Norfolke junior, gen, or his assigns, which lay by the east hedge (*sepem*) of the enclosure abutting on Humble Jumble beck on the south in Alverthorpe with all rights, etc, as now divided, at an annual lords' rent of 1d, compounded: to the use of Toby Sill of Wakefeld, gen, his heirs and assigns for ever, in exchange for a similar amount of land of Toby Sill adjoining on the west side. Agreed: entry fine of 3d.

- (100) It was attested by William Turner, gen, lords' tenant, that Toby Sill of Wakefield, gen, on 16 August last past surrendered into the lords' hands a close of arable, meadow and pasture commonly called Kay Close, lately of Charles Jackson, gen, deceased, estimated at 3 acres, now occupied by Daniel Mawde junior, gen, or his assigns, together with 1 acre 1 rood of land of the same Daniel in the said close abutting on the close of Daniel called Rose Katherine Leys on the west, another close called Katherine Leys to the south, another called Taylors close to the east, and on Long close to the north, with all their appurtenances in Alverthorpe in the graveship of Alverthorpe, at an annual lords' rent of 7½d, compounded: to the use of the said Daniel Mawde, his executors, administrators and assigns, for a term of 21 years after 2 February last past the date of the surrender, at a rent to Toby Sill, his heirs and assigns of 40s a year, payable at Whitsun and Martinmas equally, provided that if the rent remained unpaid for 10 days after either date, Toby Sill, his heirs and assigns might re-enter and repossess. Agreed: entry fine, 11¼d.

Ossett (101) It was attested by William Turner, gen, lords' tenant, that Ruth Terry, spinster, a daughter of Richard Terry, late of Boothroyd in Dewsbury, yeo, deceased, on 5 July last surrendered into the lords' hands, remitted and quitclaimed for ever to Toby Sill of Wakefield, gen, (now in peaceful possession), his heirs and assigns all rights in that messuage and appurtenances at Gawthorpe in Ossett, with houses, buildings, barns, structures, stables, folds, orchards, gardens, tofts and crofts appurtenant and in / **membrane 13 dorse** / those parcels of land appurtenant, commonly called les Two Farther Hartley Fields, les Two Nearer Hartley Fields, le Pighell abutting on Newparke pale and le High Close in Gawthorpe, and all ways, waters, watercourses, liberties, profits, etc, lately occupied by John

Roades and Abraham Fletcher or their assigns at an annual lords' rent of 2s 1½d, compounded: to the sole use of the said Toby Sill, his heirs or assigns for ever. Fine to enrol the quitclaim, 6d.

- (102) It was attested by William Harrupp, lords' tenant, that John Halleley of Earlesheaton, yeo, and Elizabeth his wife, she examined separately by the steward of the court, on 2 February last past surrendered into the lords' hands those 2 closes of arable, meadow and pasture estimated at 6 acres in Earlesheaton in the graveship of Ossett commonly called le Hoylehead and Farr Arrundell Field now in one close, with all ways, watercourses and appurtenances at an annual lords' rent of [blank], compounded: to the use of Josiah Oates of Chickingley, gen, his heirs, executors, administrators and assigns for a term of 10 years from the date of the surrender, without payment of any other rent to John and Elizabeth, who would pay all rates (*assessmenta*) and taxes on the same during this term. Agreed, to hold by due serice. Entry fine [blank].

Holme (103) It was attested by John Walker, lords' tenant, that Thomas Morehouse of Ebsonhouse in Fulstone in the parish of Kirkeburton, yeo, and Isabel, now his wife, she examined separately by the steward of the court, on 22 March last past surrendered into the lords' hands all those two third parts of a messuage and the appurtenances commonly called Ebsonhouse, and all houses, edifices, barns, structures, folds and yards appurtenant in Fulstone, and all closes belonging to the same, commonly called le Croft under the House, le Acre, le Acre Inge, le Nookes, le Scotroydleys, le halfe of Whitley, le Parke, le Over Newlands, le Nether Newlands, le Coatclose, and le Well Inge, with all ways, passages, waters, watercouses, easements and other appurtenances in the graveship of Holme, now occupied by the said Thomas Morehouse or his assigns at an annual lords' rent of 5s 1d, compounded: to the absolute use of Edward Whitley of Cadeby in the parish of Sprodbrough, yeo, his heirs and assigns for ever. Agreed: entry fine, 15s 3d.

Sowerby (104) John Greenwood, son and heir of James Greenwood, late of Pitt in Turvyn in Sowerby, yeo, deceased, appeared in court and paid 2s 6d for leave to inherit all that messuage commonly called le Pitt, and 4 closes of land, meadow and pasture now divided and estimated at 2½ acres, with appurtenances in Turvyn in the graveship of Sowerby, now occupied by John Riddihough or his assigns an an annual lords' rent of 10d, compounded, following the death of the said James Greenwood, whose son and heir he was. Agreed: to hold by due service for ever.

Horbury (105) Following an enquiry sworn for the lords of the manor it was found that John Pollard of Horbury, yeo, about three years previously surrendered by John North, lords' tenant, into the lords' hands all that

messuage and residence with appurtenances in Horbury now occupied by Josiah Wood, also the croft in which it stood, occupied by the said Josiah Wood, also the 2 closes of arable, meadow or pasture in Horbury called Stanner Wells or Stony wells, now occupied by the said John Pollard or his assigns, being customary land held by copy of the court rolls, with all ways, easements, liberties, etc appurtenant at an annual lords' rent of 1d, compounded: to the use of Joshua Pollard, second son of the said John Polland, his heirs and assigns for ever. Agreed: entry fine, 3d.
Sowerby (106) Joseph Flather of Ovenden, farmer, and Susan his wife, she examined separately by Jonathan Wilson, deputed for the occasion by Francis Whyte, esq, high steward of the court, out of court before John Scott, gen, deputy steward, on 21 December last past surrendered into the lords' hands that messuage with houses, barns, structures, closes, lands, tenements and hereditaments appurtenant in Finkell Street in Sowerby in the graveship of Sowerby, now occupied by Isaac Richman or his assigns at an annual lords' rent of 16½d, compounded: to the use of Richard Parkin of North Emsall, farmer, his heirs and assigns for ever, on condititon that if Joseph Flather, his heirs, executors, administrators or assigns paid or caused to be paid to Richard Parkin, his certain attorney, executors or administrators, or one of these, the sum of £40 at any time within two years next, with an annual rent of 40s in consideration of the said £40 on 25 December (*Nativity of the blessed Lord and Saviour Jesus Christ*) and 24 June (*Nativity of St John Baptist*) in equal parts without delay until the £40 was repaid, then the surrender would become void. Agreed: entry fine, 4s 1½d.

Sum of court [blank]

[in draft. after membrane 70]
A
Panel for Lords and between parties

Robert Mansfeld	sworn	Samuel Thornes	sworn	
Samuel Peaker	"	*Joseph Hall*		
Francis Hatfield, gen	"	Michael Parker	"	
James Wilson	"	Thomas Shillitoe	"	
John Haigh	"	John Sugden	"	
John Forrest	"	Tempest Pollard	"	[diff hand]
William Harrupp	"	Jeremy Milner	"	[diff hand]

B

Wakefeld Att the Court Baron of Sir William Craven, knt, and Edwin Wiat, esq, Sergeant att Law, Lords of the Manner of Wakefeld, holden there the Twentieth day of September Anno Dni 1689.

Wee the Jury there sworne for the Lords of the Mannour doe present that Peter Sergeant of Wakefield, William Haigh of the same and John Binnes of Horbury for digging uppone parcell of ground adjoyneing to the Fence, Wall and buildings belonging to one Messuage of Anthony Bland scituate in Wakefield Northgate and thereby letting downe the said Fence, and bareing and undermineing the Foundation of the said Wall and buildings to the great decay of the same in the sum Thirty shillings a piece [*different hand*].

[signed] Robert Mansfield / John Haighe / Tempest Pollard / John Sugden

Membrane 14

View of Frankpledge and Tourn at Wakefield, 13 October 4 James II [1688]

Panel for the King Enquiry taken on the oaths of Thomas Harris, John Harrison, John Croft, Gideon Mawde, gen, Samuel Peaker, John Leake, William Bateman, Thomas Totty, Thomas Pasley, George Wareing, John Gupwell, Alvery Milnes, Robert Casson and Jeremy Milner, jurors.

Kirkegate James Oldroyd, constable, and his fellows presented Thomas Bethell as elected to the office of constable for the year following.

They presented that John Hollingworth did not repair the street. *amerced 2s*

Item, Peter Mason, gen, the same *amerced 2s 6d*

Item, Edward Lancaster, the same *amerced 4d*

Item, Sarah Brooke did not clear her ditch *amerced 4d*

Westgate Thomas Burrow, constable, and their fellows presented Richard Norfolke, junior ...

Item, they presented that John Kighley exposed butter for sale without legal weights *6d*

Northgate William Thorrold, constable, and his fellows presented William Warde ...

Stanley Joseph Wadsworth, constable, and his fellows presented Joseph Smith ...

Item, they presented Caleb Glover, Daniel Glover, Robert Glover, Thomas Glover and Matthew Powell, Robert Rigg and Thomas Willans for digging on the common and making pits in the Leeds Road *10s 6d*

Item, they presented that Francis Allen of Wakefield dug a pit in the highway at Thornes *18d*

Sandall Robert Dickinson, constable, and his fellows presented Robert Beckwith ...

Walton with Bretton William Browne and Gervase Kay, constables, and their fellows presented Joseph Wright and William Brooke ...

Horbury William Castlehouse, constable, and his fellows presented Japhet Heald ...

Ossett William Speight, constable, and his fellows presented John White ...

Item, they presented Anthony Whitley for not making his fence adjoining the King's highway *6d*

Normanton Robert Spinck, constable, and his fellows presented Thomas Broadley ...

Item, they presented Thomas Hepworth for not making his fence at the end of his fold *12d*

Soothill William Gill, constable, and his fellows presented Josiah Clapham ...
Dewsbury Abraham Beardshaw, constable, and his fellows presented Michael Ellis ...
Item, they presented that Widow Chaister did not divert water from the highway into Andrew Inge according to custom *10s*
Item, they presented that Michael Parker of Cawsey did not put a stile (*scalam*) from the highway into Tailer Croft in the customary place *3s 4d*
Item, they presented that Robert Richardson and Henry Richardson his son did not yoke their pigs *5s*
Westardsley Abraham Whiteakers, constable, and his fellows presented Timothy Kitson ...
Criglestone [Thomas Shillitoe], constable, and his fellows presented John Hirst ...
Eccleshill William Hutton, constable, and his fellows presented James Wilson ...

Sum of court [blank]

[in draft, membrane 71]
Kirkegate James Oldroyd, constable, George Whyteley, Henry Armitage, John Draper and Abraham Clegg, sworn men. Thomas Bethell was elected to the office of constable for the year following and sworn.
Westgate Thomas Burrow, constable, John Wainwright his deputy, James Braithwaite, Joseph Armitage, John Stables, Thomas Johnson and John Wainwright, sworn men. Richard Norfolke, junior, was elected constable...
Northgate William Thorrold, constable, William Naylor, Thomas Marshall, George Walton and Mark Winterburne, sworn men. William Warde was elected constable...
Stanley Joseph Wadsworth, constable, Thomas Jaques, William Rodley, George Hebden and Samuel Burgh, sworn men. Joseph Smith was elected constable...
Sandall Robert Dickinson, constable, Anthony Crawshawe, Abraham Roberts, Edward Beckitt and Thomas Kershawe, sworn men. Robert Beckwith was elected constable...

membrane 71 dorse

Walton with Bretton William Browne and Gervase Kay, constables, John Knutton, John Turner, John Harrison, James Chappell, sworn men. Joseph Wright and William Brooke were elected constables...

Horbury William Castlehouse, constable, George Issott, John Haigh, Thomas Hunt and Thomas Bedford, sworn men. Japhet Heald was elected constable...
Ossett William Speight, constable, John Forrest, Francis Marsden, Richard Terry and Samuel Copley, sworn men. John White was elected constable...
Normanton Robert Spincke, constable, William Bluitt, John Standidge, William Ash and Richard Jubb, sworn men. Thomas Broadley was elected constable...
Soothill William Gill, constable, Richard Wood, Robert Roades, Daniel Hargreaves and Samuel Dobson, sworn men. Josiah Clapham was elected constable...
Dewsbury Abraham Beardshaw, constable, Joshua Fell, Isaac Smith, John Thornes and John Dey, sworn men. Michael Ellis was elected constable...
Westardsley Abraham Whiteaker, constable, Anthony Williamson, Daniel Nettleton, sworn men. Timothy Kitson was elected constable...

membrane 72

Crigglestone Thomas Shillitoe, constable, Robert Cooke, Richard Mitchell, Matthew Law and Timothy Milner, sworn men. John Hirst was elected constable...
Eccleshill William Hutton, constable, John Baraclough, sworn. James Wilson was elected constable...

Wakefield John Walker was elected to the office of sealer of hides for the year following and sworn.
Ossett Edward Whitley was elected to the office of pinder for the year following and sworn.

[in draft, after membrane 72]
A
Wakefield, 13 October 1688 Panel for the King

Thomas Harris, sworn		John Leake	
John Harrison		William Bateman	sworn
John Croft	sworn	Thomas Totty	
Gideon Mawde, gent		Thomas Pasley	
Samuel Peaker			

George Warin	
John Gupwell	sworn
Alvery Milnes	
Robert Casson	
Jeremy Milner	sworn

Anthony Bland
Robert Gunson) sworn affearers
Thomas Pitt)
John Walker sworn as sealer of hides

B

Kirgat Bil of presentments

Wee whose names are subscribed doe present as followeth
Imprimis <wee present> John Hollinworth <pro not repairing the street> two shillings.
Item, Mr Peter Mason two shillings six penies for the like.
Item, William Potter for <the like> Wrengate <four pence>
Item, Edward Ainley for <the like in> Wrengate *two <one> shillings*
Item, Widdow Thompson for <the like> Wrenggat <four pence> one Shilling
Item Edward Lancaster <for the like> *one shilling* <four pence>
Item Sarah Brook *one shilling* for not dressing her ditch four pence
*Japhet Thornton for the like *one shilling* four pence*
Item, <for> the causey an pavement before the court or Mote Hall wee present *Christopher [ ]lton or* the Lord of the Mannor or whom it concerns wee present ten shillings
[signed] James Oldrod constable
George W Whyteley his mark / Henry Armitage / John Drapar / Abraham X Clegg his mark sworn men

[signed] Thomas Harris / Gideon Maude / Thomas Paslay / Robert Cason
[signed] Thomas Pitt / Robert Gunson ferrors

Kirkegate

[no endorsement]

C

October the 13th 88 Wakefield court

We present John Kighley for his Butter want of weight the 21st of September 88, We present him *one shilling* six pence
[signed] James Braithwait / Joseph Armitage / John I Stables his marke / Thomas Johnson / J[ohn] Wainwright
[signed] Robert Casson / Thomas Harris / Gideon Maude / Thomas Pasley

Westgate

[endorsed] Thomas Pitt Robert Gunson

D

Wakefield Northgate
Omne bene
Northgate

[no endorsement]

E

Stanley Bill November 2 1688

Traverse Accordinge to a paine laid wee present John Leak for making a way and leadinge mayner with a wayne upon the common balke betwixt Smaley and Harrwoodfeild and for not keepinge the ancient and usuall way

thirty shillinges

Alsoe for not cuttinge his hedge in the Harrowdfeild Laine

three shillinges four pence

Wee present Calib Glover and Daniell Glover and Thomas Glover and Robert Glover and Mathew Powell alsoe Robert Rigg and Thomas Willans for breakinge the swarf and digginge pitts in Leeds Roode, each man

one shilling and six pence

Francis Allan in Waikefeild for digginge of a pitt in the high roode in Thornes

two one shillings six pence

Wee lay in pain that all persons for the time to come hereafter shall keep the ancient and usuall way betwixt Smalley and Harwood Feild and not to come out of itt in pain of thirty nine shillings soe doinge

[signed] Josuah Rayner the constable of Stanley
Thomas Jacks / Gorg Hebding / Samuel Burck / William Roodlay
[signed] Thomas Harris / John Harrison / Gideon Maude / Robert Casson
[signed] Thomas Pitt / Robert Gunson

Stanley

[no endorsement]

F

Sandale Bill
Omne bene

[signed] Anthone Croshey / Abraham Roberts / Edward Beckitt / Thomas Kirshaw
Robert Dickinson

Sandall

[no endorsement]

G

The Constable of Walton cum Brittain bill

There is no presentments to bring in

[signed] Thomas Pitt Constable

Robert Gunson William W Browne

John Knutton / John Turner / John Harrison / James I Chappell four men

Walton cum Bretton

[no endorsement]

H

Horbury bill

Omnia bene

Horbury

[no endorsement]

I

Ossett bill

Item, Mr Richard Nettelton is presented three shillings and four pence for not scowrin his dich att head of Raven Royd.

Anthony Whitley for not makin his fence agenst the Kings high-street is presented six pence

[signed] John White, constable

[signed] Francis F Marsdin / John Forrest / Richard Terry / Samwell S Copley the four sworn men

[signed] Thomas Paslay / Thomas Harris / Gideon Maude / Georg Waring / Thomas Pitt / Robert Gunson

Ossett

[no endorsement]

J

Presentments mayd by the constobel and four men of Normanton

Item, we present Mrs Levet for hir garth being unmayd	0 - 1 - 0
Item we present Thomas Heyworth for his garth end	0 - 1 - 0
Item, we present Mistress Higins for hir swine being onroung	0 - 0 - 4
*Item, we present Thomas Scoley for a land end being unmayd	0 - 0 - 4*
*Item, we present Matthew Ingland for a land end	0 - 0 - 4*

[signed] Robert Spinke, constable

William Bluett / Jonathan Stanadge / John Godson / John Foster 4 Men

[signed] Georg Warin / Gideon Maude / Thomas Harris / Thomas Paslay / Robert Casson

Thomas Pitt / Robert Gunson
Normanton
[no endorsement]

K

Sothill bille for presentments
Omne banne
Soothill
[no endorsement]

L

The Bill for Dewsbry (sic)
Traverse We present Widou Chaster for not taking the water out of the hiway into Androu Ing acording to custum 0 - 10 - 0
We present Micaell Parker <of Cawsey> for not seting a stell out of the hiway into Taler Croft in the acustumed plase 0 - 3 - 4
We present Robard Ritchisan and his sun Henry for not yoking and ringen ther swine 0 - 5 - 0
[signed] Mikell his mark ME Ellis, Cunstabell
Isak his mark I Smith John I Thorns
Joshua I his mark Fell John X his mark Dey sworn men
[signed] Thomas Pitt / Robert Gunson
[signed] Thomas Harris / Thomas Paslay / Robert Casson / Gideon Maude
Dewsbury
[no endorsement]

M

West Ardsley bill
Our high ways are made; our diches scowered. We have noe presentments.
by Robert Casson juryman
West Ardsley
[no endorsement]

N

The constable of Criglestone Bill
As for any person in our towneshipe, We doe not finde them to be presentable but omne bene.
[signed] John Hirst, Constable
Robert Cooke / Richard Michell / Matthew Law / Timothy Milner four men
Criglestone

O

Eccelcell bill 8ber 13th 88

We have no presentments to put in
[signed] William Hutton, constable
[signed] John Barraclough, sworn man

Eccleshill

[no endorsement]

P

[Names of] Constables

Kirkgate Thomas Bethell, sworn
Westgate Richard Norfoke, junior, sworn
Northgate William Warde, sworn
Stanley Joseph Smith, sworn
Sandall Robert Beckitt, sworn
Walton cum Bretton Joseph Wright sworn for Walton / John Barker, deputy / William Brooke, sworn
Horbury Japhet Heald , sworn
Ossett John White, sworn
Normanton Thomas Broadley, sworn
Soothill Josiah Clapham, sworn
Dewsbury Michael Ellis, sworn
Westardsley Timothy Kitson, sworn
Criglestone John Hirst, sworn
Eccleshill James Wilson, sworn

membrane 14 continued

View of Frankpledge and Tourn at Halifax, 15 October 4 James II [1688]

Panel for the King Inquest taken on the oaths of Edmund Deane, gen, Jonathan Kighley, Richard Scarborough, Joshua Stainton, James Bates, Thomas Lister, John Lockwood, Joseph Ramsden, Major Marshall, John Utley, John Sugden, Robert Halstead and George Towne, jurors.

HALIFAX Joseph Drake and Jonas Blaymires, constables, and their fellows presented Isaac Wilkinson and Gabriel Learoyd as constables for the year, and they were sworn.

Item, they presented Abraham Scott for not repairing the way opposite his house at the lower end of the township *2s 6d*

Item, they presented Henry Ramsden for the same *10s*

Item, they presented John Lister of Horton, gen, for the same in Norgate end

3s

Item, they presented John Dodgson for affray and drawing blood from the body of Thomas Sheard *10s*

SOWERBY James Farrer, constable, and his fellows presented John Stansfeld ...

SKIRCOATE Thomas Ramsden, constable, and his fellows presented Joseph Robinson ...

OVENDEN John Wadsworth, constable, and his fellows presented John Firth ...

WARLEY Benjamin Nicholson, constable, and his fellows presented James Chadwicke ...

WADSWORTH Richard Thomas, constable, and his fellows presented William Wilkinson ...

MIDGLEY Samuel Midgley, constable, and his fellows presented William Walker ...

RISHWORTH with NORLAND James Hamer, constable, and his fellows presented Richard Tayler ...

STANSFIELD Joshua Dawson, constable, and his fellows presented Richard Stansfield ...

LANGFIELD Jonas Knowles, constable, and his fellows presented Thomas Walton ...

HEPTONSTALL Joseph Sutcliffe, constable, and his fellows presented William Crabtree ...

ERRINGDEN Edward Sutcliffe, constable, and his fellows presented Isaac Farrer ...

Item, they presented John Varley, senior, and John Varley, junior, of Ogden, within the jurisdiction of the court, for detention of two heifers waived from the lord of the court leet *39s 11d*

Item, they presented that Thomas Greenwood of Mytham in Stansfield, within the court's jurisdiction, detained 'a waife swarm of bees' from the lord of the court leet *39s 11d*

Item, they presented Richard Stansfield of Stansfield for crossing a close called Leys in Stansfield, within the jurisdiction of the court, and overthrowing a fence there *39s 11s*

Sowerby (107) It was attested by Henry Nayler, lords' tenant, that Judith Stell of Halifax, widow, and Benjamin Holroyd of Halifax, mason, son of Judith, on 29 September last surrrendered into the lords' hands a messuage commonly called le Stubinge or Hushehill with barns, structures and two closes of land belonging thereto estimated at 1½ acres with appurtenances in Sowerby in the graveship of Sowerby, now occupied by Richard Thomas of

Stockes in Erringden, yeo, and his assigns at an annual lords' rent of 6d, compounded: to the use of the said Richard Thomas, his heirs and assigns for ever. Agreed: entry fine, 18d.

[in draft, membrane 73 dorse]

Election of constables

Halifax Joseph <*5s*> Drake and Jonas *<5s>* Blaymires constables. Elkanah Gillott, John Wilson, Henry Holmes, Francis Dixon, William Mamond and William Hoyle, sworn men. Isaac Wilkinson and Gabriel Learoyd were elected constables for the following year and sworn.

Sowerby James Farrer, constable, Richard Wadsworth, Daniel Holden, John Crosley, John Currer, sworn men. John Stansfield was elected constable...

Skircoate Thomas <5s> Ramsden, constable, Joseph Mellin, Anthony Milner, sworn men. Joseph Robinson was elected constable...

Ovenden John Wadsworth, constable, Henry Butterfeld and William Crowther, sworn men. John Firth was elected constable and deputed Jonah Deane, who was received and sworn.

Warley Benjamin Nicholson, constable, Isaac Kitching and Charles Wood, sworn men. James Chadwicke was elected constable...

Wadsworth Richard Thomas, constable, William Thornas, Paul Whitwham, John Webster and John Dewhirst, sworn men. William Wilkinson was elected constable...

Midgley Samuel Midgley, constable, Daniel Breare and Thomas Blagbrough, sworn men. William Walker was elected constable...

Rishworth cum Norland James Hamer, constable, Jeremy Bothomley, deputy, Michael Soothill, John Crowther, George Whitley and Isaac Bothomley, sworn men. Richard Taylor was elected constable and deputed James Roper, who was received and sworn.

membrane 74

Stansfield Joshua Dawson, constable, Michael Bentley, Peter Ormeroyd, James Stansfield and John Horsfall, sworn men. Richard Stansfield was elected constable...

Langfield Jonas Knowles, constable, Robert Farrer, John Law, John Ingham and Abraham Clegg, sworn men. Thomas Walton was elected constable...

Heptonstall Joseph Sutcliffe, constable, Ambrose Greenwood, Jonathan Crabtree, John Horsfall, senior, and John Horsfall, junior, sworn men. William Crabtree was elected constable and deputed William Greenwood, who was received and sworn.

Erringden Edward Sutcliffe, constable, John Fletcher, James Ratcliffe, William Crabtree and Abraham Midgley, sworn men. Isaac Farrer was elected constable...
Halifax John Cowlen, Joshua Wilson, Henry Hemmingway and Abraham Hodgson were sworn searchers of hides for the following year.

membrane 14 continued

Sowerby (108) Whereas in a suit in the Court of Chancery of 14 November last in a cause depending between John Thorpe and Susan his wife, Thomas Rigge and Mary his wife, plaintiffs, and Robert Haineworth, Gregory Cockcroft <and John Cockcroft> his son, Martha Gleidhill, widow, <Jeremy and Mary Gleidhill>, infants, Josiah Midgley, Thomas Pickles and Robert Allanson, defendents, <it was decreed that the defendents> surrender customary messuages, lands and tenements mentioned in a surrender dated 16 May 1662 to enforce payment of £430 with interest and costs: IN ACCORDANCE WITH THIS DECREE it was attested on the oath of William Midgley, gen, lords' tenant, that the said Robert Haineworth and Mercy his wife, Gregory Cockcroft, John Cockcroft and Agnes his wife, Martha Gleidhill, widow, Jeremy Gleidhill and Mary Gleadhill, infants, Josiah Midgley, Thomas Pickles and Mary his wife, and Robert Allanson, (the said Mercy, Agnes, and Mary Pickles being examined separately by the said William Midgley, deputed by Francis White, esquire, high steward) on 26 September last surrendered into the lords' hands all that messuage commonly called Upperfieldhouse, and all lands, tenements and hereditaments appurtenant in Sowerby in the graveship of Sowerby, previously occupied by Elizabeth Mitchell, widow, deceased, or her assigns, also another messuage called Littlefield<house>, and a barn, a garden and two closes estimated at one acre appurtenant or usually occupied with it in Sowerby, previously occupied by John Currer or his assigns, also a cottage in Sowerby previously occupied by the said Elizabeth Mitchell or her assigns, all paying an annual lords' rent of 6s 7d, compounded: to the use of the said John Thorpe and Susan his wife, Thomas Rigge and Mary his wife, their heirs and assigns for ever. Agreed: entry fine of 19s 9d.

- (109) It was attested by William Midgley, gen, lords' tenant, that John Wilkinson and Thomas Wilkinson, younger sons of Matthew Wilkinson of Greenhead in Huddersfield, gen, in consideration of £60 2s, paid by their father, surrendered on 10 May last past into the lords' hands all that messuage and 2½ acres in Sowerby in the graveship of Sowerby, and a rood of land in Sowerby between the highway and land called Hollingbanke, lately occupied by Edward Sutcliffe or his assigns and now by / **membrane 14 dorse** /

Thomas Rigge or his assigns and all houses, edifices, barns, structures, gardens, ways, passages, waters, watercourses, liberties, easements, and hereditaments whatsoever at an annual lords' rent of 11½d, compounded: to the use of Thomas Rigge and Robert Allanson junior of Ovenden, yeo, their heirs and assigns for ever. Agreed: entry fine 2s 10½d.

- (110) It was attested by John Hargreaves, senior, gen, lords' tenant, that John Mitchell of Scoute in Northowrome, gen, and Mary now his wife, she being examined separately by the steward, on 19 April last surrendered into the lords' hands all that messuage commonly called Boostead with appurtenances in Warley in the graveship of Sowerby, now occupied by Jonas Boardall or his assigns, also another messuage in Warley commonly called Harrison Farme, now occupied by John Clay or his assigns, also another messuage in Warley commonly called Vicars Farme, now occupied by Richard Illingworth or his assigns, also all houses, edifices, barns, structures, folds, gardens, lands, tenements, meadows, closes, pasture, feedings, ways, etc pertaining to the three several messuages in Warley in the graveship of Sowerby now occupied by the same Jonas Boardall, John Rigge and Richard Illingworth or their assigns at an annual lords' rent of 5s, compounded: to the use of James Oates of Murgatroyd in Warley, gen, his heirs and assigns, for ever. Agreed: entry fine 15s.

- (111) It was attested by George Oldfield, lords' tenant, that Samuel Wood of Pighellstreet in Sowerby, blacksmith, on 27 August last past surrendered into the lords' hands and quitclaimed all rights in the residence or tenement in Pighellstreet in Sowerby in the graveship of Sowerby lately occupied by John Wood, deceased, father of Samuel, and now occupied by himself or his assigns, also a 'smithy shopp' near the aforementioned residence, and a piece of ground at the east end of the said house, with a parlour, a chamber, a cellar, and 'other rooms' pertaining thereto, and all other 'outhouses', structures, folds, yards and waste ground whatsoever, at an annual lords' rent of ½d, compounded: to the use of John Wood of Pighellstreet in Sowerby, blacksmith, elder brother of the said Samuel Wood, his heirs and assigns for ever. Agreed: entry fine 6d.

- (112) It was attested by James Murgatroyde, lords' tenant, that Michael Firth of Height in Barkisland, gen, John Firth of Watergreene in Sowerby, yeo, Joshua Wade of Warley, yeo, and George Clegge of Sowerby, yeo, enfeoffed the said John Firth, Joshua Wade and George Clegge by sale and surrender with a messuage and land, and on 9 June last surrendered into the lords' hands all that messuage with appurtenances at Lighthasles in Sowerby, adjacent to a capital messuage called Lighthasles, lately occupied by a Susan Midgley, deceased, or her assigns and now occupied by Judith Brigge or her assigns, and a barn with all 'outhouses', gardens, orchards and a close called Laith Field, another called Goofe, another called Crosselands, another called Delfe Field at the south end of a wood, and a close called Ingam Holme, another close called Lower Inge, also appurtenant to the messuage, lately occupied by Susan Midgley or her assigns [and now by Judith Brigge or her assigns][1], with liberties of ways and passage to carry grain to the mill in winter time from the messuage by le Mooreyate and Granhamhey lower yate as the road now leads and to return, at an annual lords' rent of 4s 3¾d. compounded: to the use of Judith Brigge of Warley, spinster, her heirs and assigns for ever. Agreed, entry fine 12s 11¼d

- (113) It was attested by Benjamin Boyes, lords' tenant, that Henry Wilson, senior, of Kirkecliffe in Soyland in Sowerby, yeo, on 13 October instant surrendered into the lords' hands that messuage called Kirkecliffe in Soyland in Sowerby and all houses, barns, structures, lands, closes and ground, now occupied by the said Henry or his assigns, and all ways, passage, waters, watercourses, liberties, common pasture, turbary, easements, emoluments and hereditaments whatsoever at an annual lords' rent of 6s 2d, compounded: to the use of James Ryley of Barkisland, yeo, his heirs and assigns, on conditions expressed in a pair of indentures dated as the surrender. Agreed, to hold by due service: entry fine, 18s 6d.

[*Hipperholme*] (114) It was attested by John Hargreaves, senior, gen, lords' tenant, that John Fearnside of Northowrome, yeo, and Mary now his wife, she being examined separately by the steward, on 15 October instant surrendered into the lords' hands a messuage, a little house called 'a smithy' and an estimated 3½ acres of land in Northowrome in the graveship of Hipperholme, now occupied by Abraham Hanson and Abraham Hardistye or their assigns, the messuage being commonly called Thorntree or Jagger Smithy, at an annual lords' rent of 16d, compounded: to the use of Joseph Crowther of Northowrome, yeo, his heirs and assigns for ever. Agreed, to hold by due service. Entry fine, 4s.

- (115) It was attested by John Hargreaves, junior, lords' tenant, that Isaac Hollings of Horton and John Sagar of Allerton in Bradford-dale, gen, on 4 October instant surrendered into the lords' hands and quitclaimed for ever all rights etc in messuages, cottages, houses, etc in Hipperholme in the graveship of Hipperholme by whomsoever occupied, held in copyhold, lately of the inheritance of Jeremy Rosendale, lately of Skircoate, yeo, deceased, compounded: to the use of Jeremy Rossendale of Skircoate, gen, son and

[1] In draft version only.

heir of the said deceased Jeremy Rosendale, his heirs and assigns for ever, by due service. He gave 6d for enrolment of the quitclaim.

Scammonden (116) It was attested by John Hargreaves, junior, lords' tenant, that John Bothomley of Croftehouse in Scammonden, clothier, and Richard Bothomley of the same, clothier, on 13 October instant surrendered into the lords' hands those two eighth parts of that messuage called Crofthouse in Scammonden in the graveship of Scammonden and all houses, edifices, barns, structures, folds, orchards, gardens, lands, tenements, meadow, closes, pasture, feedings, ways, etc, now occupied by Elizabeth Bothomley and Jeremy Bothomley or their assigns, at an annual lords' rent of 9d, compounded: to the use of George Fairbancke of Mouldson place in Stainland, yeo, his heirs and assigns for ever. Agreed, to hold by due service: entry fine, 2s 3d.

- (117) John Denton of Hey Croft in Scamonden came into court as brother and next heir of William Denton, late of the same, yeo, deceased, and gave the lords 4s 6d as fine for leave to inherit that messuage in Scamonden now occupied by the said John Denton, another house with a barn, another house with a 'turfehouse' and a barn appurtenant, and a way from le Hoyle Field and Stubbinge and le / **membrane 15** / Stubbynge Inge with appurtenances in Scammonden, now occupied by the said John Denton or his assigns, and also the several closes of land, meadow and pasture commonly called le Stubbing Inge, le Little Stubbinge, le New Close, and le Overbrinke, with appurtenances in Scammonden in the graveship of Scammonden, now occupied by the said John Denton or his assigns, all at an annual lords' rent of 18d, compounded, following the death of William Denton, his brother. Agreed, to hold by due service.

Sum of court [blank]

[in draft, after membrane 79]

A

Panel for King

Edmund Deane, gen, sworn

Jonathan Kighley	Thomas Lister	John Utley
Richard Scarbrough	John Lockwood	John Sugden
Joshua Stainton	Joseph Ramsden	Robert Halstead
James Bates	Major Marshall	George Towne

[no endorsement]

B

Pained at the Court Leete

	l	*s*	*d*
Robert Gledis for not mending the way at Cabidg Lainend	0	1	0
Dixon doughters for not mending the way before their House	0	2	0
Mr Antrobus or Mr Shaw for not mending the way on boath sides of his House	0	6	8
Daniell Jackson for not mending the way at the Ould Hall	0	2	0
Jeremy Bentley for not mending the way at the Cloath Hall	0	1	0
Nathaniell Halstead for not mending the way at his housing neare the Gibit Laine end	0	3	0

[signed] Edmund Deane
Jonathan Kighley
G[eorge] Towne
John Lockwood

the rest that was payned the last Court Leet are amended

Halifax

[endorsed]

Presentments

Abram Scott for nott mending the gate against his houseinge in the bothom of Towne 0 2 6
Henery Ramsden for nott mending the way against his houseinge in the bothom of Towne 0 2 6
John Broadley for nott mending the way against his houseinge in the Church lane 0 2 6
*Mr Lum for nott mending the way against his lathe by the ..d in the wall 0 5 0
*Mr Longley for nott mending the way near his woolshope near the spoult 5 0
*Joshua Dunne for nott mending the way against his houseing in the back lane 12 0
Mr Lister Horton for nott mending the way against his houseing in near Gate end 3 0
*Mr Robert Atkinson senior for nott mending the way against his houseinge 1 0 0
Mr Ramsden of Crowstone for nott amending the way against his houseinge 13 4
Samuell Newton for nott mending the way against his houseing in Swinemarkett 4 0
Mr Horton of Sourby for nott mending the highway against his houseinge 13 4
*Mr Mitchell for nott mending the way before the House against the Lort end

10 6

John Dodgson for a Blod and a fray against Thomas Sheard 10

Presentors

[signed] Elkanah Gillot
John Wilson
Henrey Holmes
Francis Dixson
William Mamond
William Hoyle

Joseph Drake
Jonas Blaimers Constables

C

October the 15, 88 Sowerby Bill

These are to Sertifie to the Jury of this Cort that wee do not find Any thing Painable or Presentable for the Present, and As for the way that was fined, it is mended according to Content.

Wittness our hands

[signed] Edm: Deane
Jonathan Kighley
Richard Scarbrough
James Bates

James Farrer
Constable

Richard Wadsworth
Daniell D Houldon
his marke
John Crosley
John IC Currer
his marke

Sowerby

[no endorsement]

D

Thomas Ramsden Cunstable Scarcouts Bill

who saith the highways are in good repaire and the stocks and butts and kucke stoole are all in very good repaire, and we have no presentements at all.

The paines was laid upon Nathan: Turner since hee hath repaired it all.

[signed] Edm: Deane
Richard Scarbrough
John Lockwood
Thomas Lister

Thomas Ramsden
Joseph Mellin
Anthony Milner
over serres

Skircoate

[no endorsement]

E

Stockes are in good repayre; Cockstoyle is in good repayre; Buttes are in good repayre; pinfould is in good repayre; sough hoyles are oponed and ditches are well scoured; and all thinges eles in ouor towne are in good repayre to the best of *my* our knowledges.

Paines that wear layd the last court day are amended.

We paine John Hodgshon in thirtey nine shillinges and eleven pence for earth led *out* into shalon<lon> *end*, and we give him 30 dayes to close the rubbeg out of the hi way or othor wayes stand to his fine.

Also wee ley a payne upon John Foirth for a wey leadding betwen Cockhel and Brockhoyles in thertey nine shillinges and leven pence. Wee give him thertey nine dayes to ammend it or elles stand to his fine.

Also we ley a payne upon Jonas Adear and Isack Wilson for a way laing betwen Brockhoyles and Shacking house <in> therty nine shillinges and Alevon pence, and we give 30 dayes to amend it in or eles stand to ther fine.

The paine laid in Hallifax by Ovendon inhabitants is amended.

[signed]	John Wadsworth	ould cunstabl	Edmund Deane
	Henerey Butterfeild	ould overseares	Jonathan Kighley
	William Chrouthour		Richard Scarbrough
	John IF Forth	new constable	James Bates
	Jonathan Ealroyd		
	Daniel Garforth		

F

Warley Bill October 15th 1688

Our Buttes and Stocks and Pinfould and hye wayes are in good repaire, and all other misdemainers wee know none.

Wee doe lay a payne of 39^{s} 4^{d} upon Stocke lane, also the Tuall lane, and the Hand Green leading <to> the Clough in 30^{s} to be amended twixt and Candlemiss next.

[signed]	Edmund Deane	
	Jonathan Kighley	Beniamin Nickalson Constable
	Richard Scarbrough	Isack Cichin presenter
	George Towne	Charles Wadd presenter

Warley

[no endorsement]

G

Wadsworth Bill of presentments October the 15th, anno domini 1688

The say the Stocks Butts and every thinge within the township aforesaid are in good repaire, and they find not any thinge presentable within the township nor any where else. And if any thinge was presented the last court, it is amended.

his marke
William W Thomas
[signed] Edmund Deane
his marke
Richard Scarbrough
Paull W Whitwham
Jonathan Kighley
his marke
John Lockwood
John) Webster
his marke
John D Dewhirst

Wadsworth

[no endorsement]

H

Midgley Bill October 15 1688

These are to Certifie whom it may concern that our butts, stocks and pinfolds are in good repaire; Our highways also. As for blood wipes and frays, we know of none.

All pains that were laid on the last leet are now corrected and amended. All our sows and water courses are open and all right, according to our oaths.

[signed] Edmund Deane Samuell Midgley constable
his mark
Jonathan Kighley Daniell + Broar
Richard Scarbrough Thomas T Blaghbrough
James Bates his marke

Midgley

[endorsed] These are to whom

I

Rishworth cum Norland Bill

These are to sertiefie to the Jury of this Couert that we doe not finde any thinge painable or presentable for the present. Wittnes our handes

[signed] Edmund Deane Michaell Sootell
Jonathan Kighley John Crowther
John Lockwood George X Whitley his marke
Robert Halstead Isacke H Bothomley his marke

Rishworth cum Norland

[no endorsement]

J

Stansfield Bill October 15 Anno Domini 1688

All the high wayes pained in our last [?bill] are welle amended and nowe wee paine one way lyinge in our said towne (that is to say) between the one end of Rowtonstall wood to the other, the same is to be repaired and made good, and also the Busks Swittched before the 15th of December next, in paine of twenty seven shillings; also wee lay a paine of one way in our said towne that is to say between Hartley Clough and Richard Hudsons, the same is to be amended before the 15th of December in paine of 19^{s}.

Our butts, whippstocke, Cuckstoole and all other things given us in charge are in good repaire.

[signed] Michael Bentley — Edmund Deane
Peter X Ormeroyd his marke — Jonathan Kighley
John Lockwood
James Stansfield his marke — John Sugden
John I Horsfall his mark — Joshua Dawson Constable

Stansfield

[no endorsement]

K

October 15th 1688 Langfield Bill

The good men of the Jury this is to inform you that misdemeners pained in our last bill at the last leet court are amended; and now we lay a paine of 10s on a place neare the Parke yate, being a steap place joyning to the high way and very dangerous for travlers, lying in Eringden and belonging to Abraham Sunderland, if it be not amended before Candlemes day next.

As for buts and stocks, they are in good repaire, and for other things given us in charge in charge (*sic*), we know not of aney.

[signed] Robert Farer — Jonas Knolles constable
John Law — Edmund Deane
John Ingham — Jonathan Kighley
Abraham Clegg — G. Towne / John Lockwood

Langfield

[no endorsement]

L

October the 15th

We four with the Constable of Heptonstall

doth inform the Court and the Jury that our Butts, our Stocks, Pinfould, Cookestoole are all in good repaire. Our high wayes in Heptonstall are all in good repaire. What was pained the <last> court is amended. Likewise we lay a paine of 20s upon the high way leading between Jack Bridg and Earneshaw water in Stansfield, if not amended betwixt and Martinmass next.

Also wee lay a paine of twenty shillings upon the high way leading between Earnshaw water and Hartley Clough in Stansfield, if not amended betwixt and Christenmass next.

Also wee lay paine of thirty shillings upon the high way leading between Hartley Clough and Stiperding in Stansfield, if not amended by whome it doth concern between and 11th of November next.

Other misdemainers we know none.

[signed]	Edmund Deane	Joseph Sutcliffe	constable
	Jonathan Kighley	Ambrose Greenwood	
	Richard Scarbrough	Jonathan Crabtree	
	John Lockwood	John Horsfull senior	
		John Horsfull junior	presentours

Heptonstall

[no endorsement]

M

Ayringden Bill of Presentments October the 15th 1688

Wee *They* say that the Stocks, Butts and everythinge within the Township of Ayringden aforesaid are in good repaire, and they find nothinge presentable. And the Way called Jacklane, which was pained the last court is now amended.

All the wayes that was pained the last courte are all amended.

[signed]	Edmund Deane	John Fletcher
	Jonathan Kighley	James Radclef
	George Towne	William Crabtree
	John Lockwood	Abraham Midgley

Erringden

[no endorsement]

N

Halifax ad curiam Let' domini Regis cum turno tentam ibidem Decimo quinto die Octobris Anno Domini 1688

Wee the Jury there sworne for our Soveraigne Lord the King doe present the <present> Searchers and Sealer of leather in Halifax for neglect of their office in xxxix^{s}xj^{d}.

[signed] Edmund Deane / Jonathan Kighley / Richard Scarbrough / George Towne

by enquiry

[no endorsement]

O

Halifax Ad visum Franci Plegii et Curian Let' domini Regis cum turno tentam ibidem decimo quinto die Octobris anno domini 1688.

Wee the Jury there sworne for our Soveraigne Lord the King doe present John Varley the elder and John Varley the younger of Ogden in the Jurisdiccion of this Court for detaineing three waife Heifers from the Lords of this Leet in xxxix^{s} xj^{d}

[signed] Edmund Deane / Jonathan Kighley / Richard Scarbrough / George Towne

by enquiry

[no endorsement]

P

Halifax ad visum franci plegii et curiam Let' domini Regis cum turno tentam ibidem decimo quinto die Octobris Anno Regno Regis Jacobi secondi nunc Anglie etc quarto

Wee the Jury there sworne for our Soveraigne Lord the King doe present Thomas Greenwood of Mytham in Stansfield in the Jurisdiction of this court for detaineing a waife swarme of bees from the Lords of this Leet in xxxix^{s} xj^{d}.

Also wee present Jonas Horsfall of Heptonstall within the Jurisdiction aforesaid for the like in xxx^{s}.

[signed] Edmund Deane / Jonathan Kighley / Richard Scarbrough / John Lockwood

by enquiry

[no endorsement]

Q

Halifax Ad visum franci plegii et curiam etc domini Regis tentam ibidem xv^{o} die Octobris 1688

traverse Wee present Richard Stansfield of Stansfield for going over a close called Leyes in Stansfield in the jurisdiction of this court and breaking downe the fence there, contrary to a paine laid xiii^{s} iiii^{d}.

Also wee present Martha Erindle for the like xiii^{s} iiii^{d}.

8° die april 1689

Wee the Jury doe find that the said Richard Stansfield hath a way over the said Close called Leyes, as is in the Traverse mentioned

by enquiry

[signed] Edmund Deane
Jonathan Kighley
Richard Scarbrough
George Towne

[no endorsement]

R	Nomina Constabulorum	
Halifax	Isaac Wilkinson Gabriel Learoyd sworn	
Sowerby	John Stansfield	sworn
Skircoate	Joseph Robinson	sworn
Ovenden	John Firth	sworn, Jonas Deane deputy
Warley	James Chadwicke	sworn
Wadsworth	William Wilkinson	sworn
Midgley	William Walker	sworn
Rishworth with Norland	Richard Tayler	sworn, James Roper deputy
Stansfield	Richard Stansfield	sworn
Langfield	Thomas Walton	sworn
Heptonstall	William Crabtree	sworn William Greenwood -
Erringdon	Isaac Farrer	sworn

[no endorsement]

membrane 15 continued

View of Frankpledge and Tourn held at Brighouse on 16 October 4 James II [1688]

Panel for Lord King Inquest taken on the oaths of Daniel Walker, Abraham Langley [*Lumme* in draft], Isaac Bates, William Garlicke, Robert Drake, Joseph Crowther, Jonathan Threapland, Anthony Lea, Edward Crosland, Christopher Brooke, William Liversedge, and Geoffrey Ramsden, [also *Gilbert Ramsden* in draft], jurors.

HIPPERHOLME WITH BRIGHOUSE John Brooke, gen, constable, and his fellows presented Joshua Wright as constable.

RASTRICKE Isaac Dawson, constable, and his fellows presented Joseph Thornton as constable.

FIXBY Robert Drake, constable, and his fellows presented Samuel Dyson as constable.

NORTHOWROME John Ambler, constable, and his fellows, presented Samuel Crowther as constable.

Item, they presented John Crowther for not repairing the footpath to Northowrome £3 1s 4d.
SHELFE Jeremy Brookesbanck, constable, and his fellows presented Joshua <Knight> as constable.
QUARMBY George Dyson, constable, and his fellows presented George Dyson (sic) as constable.
DALTON Joshua Eastwood, constable, and his fellows presented Joseph Dyson as constable.
HARTESHEAD cum CLIFTON William Poplewell and Joshua Haworth, constables, and their fellows presented William Child as constable.
STAINLAND James Gleidhill, constable, and his fellows presented Geoffrey Ramsden as constable.
BARKISLAND Joseph Holdroyd, constable, and his fellows presented Joseph Houldroyd as constable.

Sum of court [blank]

[in draft, membrane 80 dorse: election of constables]

Hipperholme with Brighouse John Brooke, gen, constable, Jeremy Robinson, [Robert] Hanson, Michael Jagger and John Smith, sworn men, presented Joshua Wright as constable, who deputed Jeremy Robinson, who was received and sworn.
Rastrick Isaac Dawson, constable, Nicholas Boothroyd, James Batty, Samuel Rigley and John Whitehead, sworn men, presented Joseph Thornton as constable, who deputed John Hirst....
Fixby Robert Drake, constable, Moses Heaton and Thomas Whitehead, sworn men, presented Samuel Dyson.
Northowram John Ambler, constable, John Sharpe, Joseph Wilson, Jeremiah Jagger and Jonathan Bairstowe, sworn men, presented Samuel Crowther.
Shelfe Jeremy Brookesbanck, constable, Samuel Bentley, Samuel Spencer and Samuel Whyteley, sworn men, presented Joshua Knight.
Quarmby George Dyson, constable, Thomas Denton, Isaac Houlroyd, William Dyson and George Dyson, sworn men, presented George Hey.
Dalton Joshua Eastwood, constable, Thomas Kilner, sworn man, presented Joseph Dyson.
Hartishead with Clifton William Poplewell and Joshua Haworth, constables, John Brooke, Samuel Lumme, John Flather and Samuel Lunne, sworn men, presented Joshua Hanson and William Child.

membrane 81

Stainland James Gleidhill, constable, Abraham Crowther and John Sykes, sworn men, presented Geoffrey Ramsden.
Barkisland Joseph Holdroyd, constable, Jonathan Hanson, Henry Crosley, Samuel Rawson and Jeremy Crosley, sworn men, presented Joseph Houlroyd.

[in draft, after membrane 81]
A
Brighouse Curia Let' tenta ibidem
16° die 8bris 1688 Panel for King
Daniel Walker sworn

Abraham Lumme	Joseph Crowther	Christopher Brooke
Isaac Bates	Jonathan Threapland	William Liversedge
William Garlicke	Anthony Lea	Geoffrey Ramsden
Robert Drake	Edward Crosland	Gilbert Ramsden

Thomas Denton was elected grave of Scammonden for two messuages called Crofthouse, and was sworn.

William Garlicke was elected grave of Rastricke for the current year for land called Heys lands.
[no endorsement]

B
October the 16th 1688
Paynes layde at the Court leete houlden at Brigghouse.
Imprimis We lay in payne Samuell Wade to amend his lane betwixt his owne house and the wood falle head, and scowre his ditch on the side of the lane betwixt and Martinmas next, in payne of $13^s 4^d$.
Item We present Mr Clife for not make in a sufficient foote way and not scoweringe his ditch and swithing his hedge over his inge head leadinge towards the wester croft accordeinge to former paynes.
Item We present Mr Clife for not scowereinge his ditche in the lane side leadinge to Sinderhills accordeinge to former paynes.
Item We lay in payne Mr Clife to amend the foot way over his ingehead and scower his ditch and switch hedge leadeing towards Westercroft, in payne of $13^s 4^d$.
Item We lay in payne Mr Clife to scower his ditch in the lane side leadeinge to wards Sinderhills in payne of $13^s 4^d$.
[signed] Daniell Walker marke
Joseph Crowther Samuell B Bentley

Anthony Lea Samuel Spencer
Samuell Whietle presentors
Jeremy Brookesbanke Constable
Hipperholme with Brighouse [*rectius* Shelfe]

[no endorsement]

C

Rastricke Bill at the Court leet holden at Brighouse, October the 16th 1688

It is laid in paine that the [Common] fence adjoyning on the Common of Rastricke shall be made and kept in sufficient and <lawful> repaire at all times hereafter between Houlroyd Yate and the Upperedge Yate, and for every person concerned makeing default therein to forfeite 1^{l} 19^{s} 11^{d}

Other paines or presentments we have none.

Witness our hands

Traverse Onely we present John Bothroyd for makeing an Inmate in his now dwelling house in Rastricke

[signed]
The marke of
Nicholas + Bothroyd
The marke of
James I Batty
John Hirst Constable

The marke of
Samuell S Rigley
The marke of
John T Whitehead
Rastricke

[endorsed] Daniell Walker / Joseph Crowther

D i

Fixby Bill at the Court Leet holden at Brighouse October 16th 1688

Wee say that since the last Court Leet or before wee have not found or knowne any person or persons thing or things presentable. Witnesse our hands

[signed] The marke of
Moses MH Heaton

The marke of
Thomas T Whitehead
Fixby

[endorsed]
Daniell Walker / William Liversedge / Christopher Brooke

D ii

October 16 1688 Fixby

Item We lay in paine any persons or persons that [ride]ath or driveath any horse or horses over the close of land called or knowne by the name of Hie feild, for everie offender $3^s\ 4^d$

[signed] Robert Drake

[no endorsement]

E

Northowram paines for Lord at Court houlden at Brigghouse by us whose names are heare under subscribed.

Item Wee lay in paine that George Stockes doe fence ofe his Scarr that lyeth after Lowether Riden betwixt this and Martelmus next in paine of $10^s\ 4^d$

Item Wee lay in paine that Jo. Nolson doe dike his dikes and scour it that goeth to Smallbrigg over anent Jonathan Threapland betwixt this and Martelmus next in paine of $4^s\ 4^d$

Item Wee lay in paine that James Scoberd and Jo Crowther and Mr Wood <doe> mend the way so farr as theire ground lyeth after ground side betwixt this and Martelmus next in paine for ever one of them $4^s\ 4^d$

Item Wee lay in paine that Willum Snowdin fence of the wayside that lyeth after his ingeside betwixt this Martelmus next in paine of $10^s\ 4^d$

Item Wee present Jo Crowther not for mending of foot way that leadeth up to Northowram $3^{li}\ 1^s\ 4^d$

[signed] Daniell Walker The presenters Jo Sharpe
Joseph Crowther Joseph Willson
Jeremiah Jagger
Jonathan Barstow

Northowrome John Ambler Constable

[no endorsement]

F

October the 16th 1688

Item we lay in pain John Kershaw, Jeremy Batley, and John Frost to amend the way betwixt Hoilehouse and Lightliffe Chappel to make a sufficient foot causway and set stoops to keep horses of, in pain of 30s

Item we lay in pain Nathan Whitley and Nathan Firth to make good the foot bridge called Bottom Hall Bridge, in pain of 20s

Item we lay in pain Widdow Brighouse to amend the way in the deep lane betwixt Finkil Street end and the bottom of her five day work, in pain of 20s

All these to be repaired betwixt and the first of December next, in pain of the summs above written.

Item we lay in pain Thomas Kay to repair the foot bridge going over into Abraham Walker ground toward Nathan Baxters, to be repaired betwixt and the time above mentioned, in pain 10s

[signed] Robert H Hanson his mark / Jeremiah + Robinson his mark / Michael M Jagger mark / John Smith

Item we present Henery Brook, Samuel Smith, Gilbert Sturdy, Mr Edward and Mr Abraham Langley for not mending the high way betwixt Knowltop and Hellewell sike according to the former pains in the summ of 20s.

by enquiry

[endorsed] Daniell Walker / Joseph Crowther / William Liversedge / Christopher Brooke / Jeffery Ramsden

G

Quarmby Bill at the Court Leet holden at Brighouse the 16th day of October 1688

Wee say that since the last Court Leet or before wee we (sic) have not found or knowne any person or persons thing or things presentable within our said Liberty.

Witnesse our hands

Onely we lay in paine that the Common fence betweene John Pillins and the Outlane shall be made and kept in sufficient repaire, and for every person concerned makeing default therein at any time hereafter to forfeite

1^{l} 19^{s} 11^{d}

[signed] William Dyson / Isaac Houroyd / Georg Dyson / Thomas Denton

Quarmby

[no endorsement]

H

Dalton bill

Whee the said Constable of Dalton and Thomas Kilner presentor doe here say that those paines <which> whee did lay the last Court day are performed and done, and that whee have not any paines or presenments (sic) consarening our Hye whayes or any coman anoyance that whee know of, but that omne bene All is well and in good order.

[signed] Daniell Walker / Joshua Eastwood Constable / Abraham Lum / Thomas + Kilner Presenter

October the 16, 1688

Christopher Brook

Dalton

[no endorsement]

I

Hartishead cum Clifton bill

October 16th 1688 Brigghouse Court

As our former paines are all amended wee therefore find nothinge to present

Witnesse our hands

[signed] Daniell Walker
Abraham Lum
William Liversedge
Joshua Haworth
William (Poplewell marke
John + Breare marke
Samuell S L Lumne marke

Hartishead cum Clifton

[no endorsement]

J

October the 16th 1688 Stainland bill

Thes are to Certifie the Jury of this Courte that wee doe not find any thing painable or presentable for the present. Wittnes our hands

[signed] Daniell Walker
Jeffery Ramsden
Abraham Crowther
John I Sikes
John Gledhill Constable

Stainland

[no endorsement]

K

October the 16th 1688

Thes are to Certifie to the Jury of this courte that wee doe not find any thing painable or presentable for the present. Wittnes our hands

[signed] Daniell Walker
Joseph Crowther
Abraham Lum
Jonathan Hanson
Samuell R Rawson
his marke
Joseph Houlroid Constable

Barkisland

[no endorsement]

L

October the 16th 1688

Item I present any person or persons that goeth or rydeth through the Welling and them that belongeth Hall house 4s 4d

The ocorsier Jo Sharpe

[no endorsement]

M

[Names of constables]

Hipperholme with Brighouse	Joshua Wright, sworn, Jeremiah Robinson, deputy
Rastricke	Joseph Thornton, sworn, John Hirst, deputy
Fixby	Samuel Dyson, sworn
Northowrome	Samuel Crowther, sworn
Shelfe	Joshua Knight, sworn
Quarmby	George Hey, sworn
Dalton	Joseph Dyson, sworn
Hartishead with Clifton	Joshua Hanson sworn for Hartishead and William Child for Clifton
Stainland	Geoffrey Ramsden, sworn
Barkisland	Joseph Houlroyd, sworn

membrane 15 continued

View of Frankpledge and Tourn held at Burton on 17 October 4 James II [1688]

Panel for Lord King Inquest taken on the oaths of Godfrey Crosland, James Hinchliffe, John Rhodes, John Battye, John Coldwell of Cumberworth, Richard Cockill, Joshua Rhodes, George Roebucke, Humphrey Wilson, Philip Earnshawe, John Allott, John Hinchliffe and Adam Lindley, jurors.

They presented that Joseph Bilcliffe of Cumberworth made affray and drew blood from William Rich on 5 July past *mercy 10s*

Item, they presented that Thomas Parkin of Shelley made affray and drew blood from William March of Cumberworth on 4 July past *mercy 10s*

KIRKBURTON George Roebucke, constable, and his fellows presented William Moone as constable.

SHELLEY Robert Broadhead and John Hey, constables, and their fellows presented John Peace as constable.

SHEPLEY Joseph Hobson, constable, and his fellows presented Joseph Hobson as constable.

CUMBERWORTH [HALF] Thomas Kirkwood, constable, and his fellows presented William Oxley as constable.

EMLEY Robert Hare, constable, and his fellows presented John Page as constable.
FLOCKTON Richard Carter, constable, and his fellows presented John Walshawe as constable.
THURSTONLAND Thomas Morehouse, constable, and William Boothe presented Abraham Lockwood as constable.
HOLME Richard Morton, constable, and his fellows presented Joshua Roades as constable.
FULSTONE township jurors said that all was well.
SCHOLES township jurors said that all was well.
WOOLDALE township jurors said that all was well.
CARTWORTH township jurors said that all was well.
AUSTONLEY township jurors said that all was well.
HEPWORTH township jurors said that all was well.
THWONGE township jurors said that all was well.

[in draft, membrane 82 dorse: presentation of constables]
Kirkeburton George Roebucke and John Haigh, constables, and John Bell, George Meller, Robert Hirst and John Hardy, sworn men, presented that Samuel Wood and William Moone were elected to the office of constable for the coming year, and they were sworn.
Shelley Robert Broadhead and John Hey, constables, and John Wood, Edward Jessop, Arthur Lee and Thomas Silvester, sworn men, presented that John Peace ...
Shepley Joseph Hobson, constable, and John Bray, William Hirst, Richard Earnshawe and John Longbotham, sworn men, presented that William Greene ... and he deputed Joseph Hobson.
Cumberworth Thomas Lockwood, constable, and Joseph Child and William Marsh, sworn men, presented William Oxley ...
Elmley Robert Hare, constable, and John Lockwood, Thomas Moore, Adam Donkerley and John Lockwood, sworn men, presented John Page ...
Flockton Richard Carter, constable, and Thomas Bedford, John Crowther, Richard Wilcock and James Gouldthorpe, sworn men, presented John Walshaw ...
Thurstonland Thomas Morehouse, constable, William Brooke, Jarret Collier, Henry Jellott and Robert Hall, sworn men, presented Abraham Lockwood ...
Holme Richard Morton, constable, Timothy Eastwood and William Earnshaw, sworn men, presented Joshua Roades ...

membrane 83

Fulston George Roebucke, Edward Langley, Henry Hirst and William Crosland presented -
Scholes Abraham Hamon and Thomas Booth, sworn men -
Wooldale Edward Duckenfield, John Thorpe, Samuel Bramold and Gamaliel Brooke, sworn men -
Cartworth James Littlewoood, Abraham Roberts, Joshua Roberts and Robert Ellis, sworn men -
Austonley Abraham Meller and Thomas Brooke, sworn men -
Hepworth Josias Berry, Robert Beever, John Hall and George Hattersley, sworn men -
Thwonge Michael Midgley and Robert Saunderson, sworn men -

membrane 15 dorse

Holme (118) It was attested by William Morehouse, lords' tenant, that John Morehouse of Lindley on 24 August 1687 surrendered into the lords' hands half a messuage and all houses, barns, structures, closes, tenements and hereditaments thereto appending in Fulstone in the graveship of Holme, now occupied by Joshua Shaw or his assigns at an annual lords' rent of 10¾d, compounded: to the use of Joseph Morehouse, brother of the said John, his heirs and assigns for ever. Agreed: entry fine, 2s 8¼d

Holme (119) It was attested by Josiah Berry, lords' tenant, that John Dokeson of Eden Booth on 6 May 1687 surrendered into the lords' hands a messuage or cottage in Hepworth and a mistall (*armentar'*) appurtenant, a croft, a garden adjoining, a little close called Ashdole, a little close called Paddocke, with all ways, waters, watercourses, liberties, profits, easements, emoluments and hereditaments in Hepworth, now occupied by Robert Bever or his assigns at an annual lords' rent of 3d, compounded: to the absolute use of the said Robert Bever, his executors, administrators and assigns from 2 February last past for 60 years at an annual rent to the said John Dokeson, his heirs and assigns of 18s payable at Whitsun and Martinmas in equal portions, and paying all taxes and assessments due. Should the rent fall into arrears on rent day, John Dokeson, his heirs and assigns might enter and distrain and remove, drive away and impound the distraint until the arrears were paid, returning any surplus. Agreed: entry fine, 4½d.

- (120) It was attested by John Batty, lords' tenant, that Abraham Swallowe on 16 June last surrendered into the lords' hands and quitclaimed to James Beever, his heirs and assigns for himself, his heirs and assigns for ever all state, right, title, reversion and demand in a dole of land with wood and underwood in Scholesbancke and abutting on le Smallclough on the north, on running water from Scholes brigge to the east, on the enclosed wood of John Tincker senior to the south, and le Lee on the west, with appurtenances in

Scholes in the graveship of Holme, now occupied by the said James Bever or his assigns at an annual lords' rent of [blank], compounded: to the absolute use of the said James Beever, his heirs and assigns for ever. Agreed: enrolment fine, 6d.

- (121) It was attested by Thomas Booth, lords' tenant, that David Charlesworth on 27 February past surrendered into the lords' hands that residence near the chapel of Holmefirth, with all parlours and rooms appurtenant, and all ways, passage, liberties, privileges, benefits, commodities, easements and emoluments at Holmefirth in Wooldale in the graveship of Holme, now occupied by the said David Charlesworth or his assigns at an annual lords' rent of 2½d, compounded: to the use of Henry Morrie, his heirs and assigns for ever, provided that if David Charlesworth, his heirs, executors, administrators or assigns or any of them paid or caused to be paid to the said Henry Morrie, his heirs, executors, administrators or assigns or any of them £10.10s on 4 June after the date of the surrender at the residence of the said Henry Morrie at Holmefirth, the surrender would become void, but if there were default in payment in any part the property stood to the use of Henry Morrie, his heirs or assigns for ever. Agreed: entry fine, 7½d.

- (122) It was attested by William Morehouse, lords' tenant, that William Hirst of Fulstone on 17 October instant surrendered into the lords' hands a close called le Moorelands and another close called Crookelands, with all ways, waters, watercourses, etc, appurtenant in Fulstone in the graveship of Holme, now occupied by the said William Hirst or his assigns at an annual lords' rent of 12d, compounded: to the use of Richard Hirst his brother, his heirs and assigns for ever when he reached the age of 24 years. Within the year after entry, Richard, his heirs and assigns would pay Anne Hirst and Mary Hirst, his sisters, £8, to be divided equally between them. Agreed, to hold by due service: entry fine, 3s.

- (123) It was attested by John Battye, lords' tenant, that John Greene of Whickleden on 14 November past surrendered into the lords' hands half a messuage called Nether Whickleden and half of all lands appurtenant, namely a house called Newhouse where Jonathan Breare now lived, also the west end of a barn containing three bays called Upperlath, and le Upper Mistall adjoining (except the undivided half of a half bay in the barn, a yard in breadth and five in length, between a shed (*armentar'*) called Nether mistall, and the last bay (*infime' intercapedium*) in the said barn, half the fold to the south, a whole close called Broomefield, a close called Ryefield and le Ryefield wood, a whole close called Netherbothoms, and le Springewood adjoining to the east, two closes called Horsecloses of arable and pasture, a meadow called Whamynge, a close called Kilne Croft of arable and pasture, and a half garden, with all ways, waters, watercourses, profits and commodities appurtenant in Scholes in the graveship of Holme, now occupied by John Greene and Jonathan Breare or their assigns at an annual lords' rent of 3s 5d, compounded: to the absolute use of Abraham Wood, son of Anne Greene, wife of the said John Greene, his heirs and assigns for ever, with reversion of the other half / **membrane 16** / of the said messuage called Nether-whickleden and all lands appurtenant, now occupied by John Greene at an annual lords' rent of 3s 5d after the death of Anne Greene, wife of John Greene, to the absolute use of the said Abraham Wood, his heirs and assigns for ever, paying the said John Greene and (*seu*) Sarah Greene, children of the said John Greene the sum of £15 in one payment within 20 days after the death of Anne Greene, wife of John Greene. For default of payment within the said time the half part of the messuage and lands appurtenant would be to the use of the said John and Sarah Greene and their assigns for 4 years next following. At the end of this time Abraham Wood, his heirs and assigns must pay to Anne Wood, his sister, £15 in one payment; for default of which the half messuage and land would pass to the use of Anne Wood and her assigns for 4 years. The first half would remain with Abraham Wood, with the reversion of the second half. Agreed, to hold by due service: entry fine for immediate possession, 10s 3d, and for the reversion 5s 1½d.

Sum of court [blank]

[in draft, after membrane 86]
A
Burton Curia Let' tenta ibidem 17° 8bris 1688 Panel' pro domino Regis
Godfrey Crosland sworn
James Hinchcliffe
John Rhoad
John Batty
John Coldwell of Cumberworth
Richard Cockhill
Joshua Roads
George Roebucke
<v.s for non-appearance>
\+ John Coldwell of Thurstonland
Humphrey Wilson
Philip Earnshawe
\+ Joshua <non-appearance> Littlewood
John Allott
John Hinchcliffe
Adam Linley

[no endorsement]

B

Paines laid at the Court Leet and Sheriffe Turne holden at Kirkeburton the 17th day of October 1688 by the Constable and Swornemen of Kirkeburton as followeth:

Imprimis we lay in paine that noe manner of person or persons shall carry away either green wood or drie out of other mens ground without licence of the owners thereof, in paine of every time so seen, known or taken 12d

Item we lay in paine that no manner of person or persons shall goe over other mens groundes where there is no usuall way, in paine of every time so seen, knowne or taken 12d

Item we lay in paine that all the Householders within the said towne shall ring their swine and so keep them, in paine of every default 12d

Item we lay in paine that all the Inhabitants within the said towne shall make their fences sufficient joyneing upon hard corn at or before the 11th day of November next and so kepe them, in paine of every default 10s

Item we lay in paine that all the Inhabitants within the said towne shall switch their hedges and scoure their ditches joyneing upon the highwayes be fore the 11 day of November next and so keep them, in paine of every default 10s

Item we lay in paine that no manner of person or persons shall make any foot way but the usuall way over on close belonging to Robert Dickinson called to upper 10 day worke, in paine of every time so seen or known 1s 1d

[signed]	John Bele	Godfrey Crosland
	George Mellar	John Rhodes
	Robert Hurst	John Battye
	John Hardey	John Hinchliffe
	Samuell Woode Constabell	

Kirkeburton

[no endorsement]

C

Paines laid at the Kings Court called the Sherife turne held at Kirke burton the 17 day of October 1688, the Constable and sworne men of Shelley as followeth:

Imprimis we lay in paine that no manner of person or persons shall carry away either green wood or dry out of other mens ground without the licence of the Owners thereof, in paine of every time so seen, knowne or taken 12d

Item we lay in paine that no manner of person or persons shall goe over other mens ground where there is no usuall way, in paine of every time so seen, known or taken 12^{d}

Item we lay in paine that all the Inhabitants within the said towne shall ring their swine and so keep them, in paine of every default 12^{d}

Item we lay in paine that all the Inhabitants within the said towne shall make their fences sufficient joyneing upon hard corne at or before the 11 day of November next and so keep them, in paine of every default 10^{s}

Item we lay in paine that all the inhabitants within the said towne shall switch their hedges and scoure their ditches joyneing upon the high wayes before the 11th day of November next and so keepe them, in paine of every default 10^{s}

Item we lay in paine that no manner of person or persons make any horse way up the Ings belonging to Robert Dickinson, in paine of every time so seen, knowne or taken 10^{s}

Item we lay in paine that Richard Thorpe the elder and Richard Thorpe the younger <remove> the mainer, wood and stones being in the way to the dwelling house of Joseph Green at or before the 31st of this instant October, in paine of 10^{s}

Item we lay in paine that Richard Thorpe the elder and Richard Thorpe the yonger remove the wall at the back of the yate opening into the folde of Joseph Green at or before the 31st day of this instant October, in paine of every such default 10^{s}

[signed] John Wood / Thomas Selvester
Edward Jessop / Arthur Lee
John Peace Cunstable

We lay in paine that noe manner of person or persons shall goe, ride over one close of Richard Cockhills called Little Ing nor one close of Edward Seniers called Wind Milhill, in paine of every time soe seene, known or taken $iii^{s}\ iiij^{d}$

Shelley

[dorse, signed]
Godfrey Crosland / John Rhodes / John Battye / John Hinchliffe

D

Paines laid at the Kings Majestie court called the Sherriffes Turne holden at Kirkburton the 17th day of October Anno domini 1688 by the Cunstable and sworne men of Shepley as followeth:

Imprimis Wee lay in paine that noe manner of person or persons shall carry away either green wood or dry out of other mens ground without

[licence] of the owners thereof, in paine of every time soe seene, known or taken xij^{d}
Item Wee lay in paine that all the housholders within the said town shall ring theire swine and soe keep them, in paine of every default xij^{d}
Item Wee lay in paine that all the inhabitants within the said town shall make theire fences sufficient joyneing upon hard corne before the xjth of November next and soe keep them, in paine of every default x^{s}
Item Wee lay in paine that all the inhabitants within the said town shall switch their hedges and scour their ditches joyneing upon the high ways at or beefor the xjth of November next, in paine of every default x^{s}
[signed] Godfrey Crosland
Joh Bay and William Hirst John Rhodes
Richard Yearnshawe and John Longbotham, John Battye
sworne men John Hinchliffe
Shepley
[no endorsement]

E

Paines laid at the Kings Majestie court called the Sheriffes Turne held at Kirkburton the 17th day of October Anno domini 1688 by the Cunstable and sworne men of Cumberworth as followeth:
Imprimis Wee lay in paine that noe manner of person or persons shall carry away either green wood or dry out of other mens ground without licence of the owners thereof, in paine of every time soe seen, known or taken xij^{d}
Item Wee lay in paine that all the housholders within the said town shall ring theire swine and soe keep them, in paine of every default xij^{d}
Item Wee lay in paine that all the inhabitants within the said town shall make theire fences sufficient joyneing upon hard corn before the xjth of November next and so keep them, in paine of every default x^{s}
Item Wee lay in paine that all the inhabitants within the said town shall switch their hedges and scoure theire ditches joyneing upon the high wayes at or before the xjth of November next and so keep them, in paine of every default x^{s}
Item Wee lay in paine that Thomas Shaw shall make his fence sufficient in the Pilling bothame beetween George Green and him, the said Thomas Shaw, at or before the xjth of November next and so keep them, in paine of every default v^{s}

Item Wee lay in paine that noe manner of person or persons shall goe over John Couldwell barrows ing where there is noe usuall way, in paine of every time so seen, known or taken xij^{d}

Item Wee lay in paine that Edward Kenyon shall make his fence sufficient <and scour his ditch> between his hinging and John Couldwell hinging at or beefore the xxvth of March next and soe keep it, in paine of every default xij^{d}

Item Wee lay in paine William Morehouse shall switch his hedge and scoure ditch beetwene his heady cloase, James Frith heady cloase, and his owne land, and make it sufficient at or before the xxvth day of March next and so keep it, in paine of every default iij^{s} iiij^{d}

Item Wee present Joseph Biltcliff for a blood and a fray upon <the body of> William Rich the 5th day of July last past x^{s}

Item Wee present Thomas Parkin for a blood and a fray upon <the body of> William Marsh the 4th of June last past x^{s}

[signed] Joseph Child, John Rhodes
William Marsh, John Battye, Godfrey Crosland
John Hinchliffe

Cumberworth

[no endorsement]

F

Paines laid at the Kings Majesties Court called the Shirriffes Turne holden at Kirkburton the 17th October Anno domini 1688 by the Cunstable and sworne men of Emley as followeth

Imprimis Wee lay in paine that noe manner of person or persons shall carry away either green wood or drie out of other mens grownd without licence of the owners thereof, in paine of every time soe seene, known or taken xij^{d}

Item Wee lay in paine that all the housholders within the said town shall ring their swine and soe keep them, in paine of every default xij^{d}

Item Wee lay in paine that all the inhabitants within the said town shall make their fences sufficient joyneing upon hard corne before the xjth day of November next and so keep them, in paine of every default x^{s}

Item Wee lay in paine that all the inhabitants within the said Town shall switch their hedges and scoure their ditch joyning upon the highwayes at or before the xjth of November next and soe keep them, in paine of every default x^{s}

Item Wee lay in paine that John Marsden and John Saunderson shall switch their hedg and scoure their ditch and make their wall sufficient beetwen

Joseph Child yokeley his and their yokeley hill in Emley park at or bee fore the xj[th] of November next and soe keep it, in paine of every default v[s]
Item Wee lay in paine that Joseph Green shall make his fence sufficient beetween Joseph Child and him in Emley parke at or before the xj[th] of November next, in paine of every default x[s]

Elmley

[endorsed]	Robert Hare	Ould constable
	John Lockwood	Thomas Moore
	Adam Donckerley	sworne men

[signed] Godfrey Crosland / John Rhodes/ John Battye / John Hinchliffe

G

Flockton Nethers Bill the 17th of October 1688

Paines laid at the Sheriffe <turne> at Burton by the Constable and Sworne men as followeth

Imprimis Wee lay in pain that no manner of person or persons whatsoever shall cut or carry away either green wood or dry out of other mens ground without consent of the owner thereof, in pain of every such default x[s]
Item Wee lay in pain that no manner of person shall put or drive either horses or sheep or any other goods to the common, not paying any ley or proporcion of pound rent according to the custom of the said towne, upon paine of such default xx[s]
Item *Wee present Richard Morton for breaking down one Steel and hindring the usual foot way over the Lower Quarrell close leading to Nether Flockton [deletion][s]*
Item Wee lay in pain that John Sikes do set and hinge a gate suffitiently between Flockton and Emley commons at or before the 11th day of November next, upon pain of such default iij[s] iiij[d]
Item Wee lay in pain that Joseph Lee set a steel at Kirke Inge Yate for the usuall foot way leading to Flockton Milne at or before the 11th day of November next, upon pain of such default iij[s] iiij[d]

[signed]	Godfrey Crosland	Thomas + Bedford
	John Rhodes	his marke
	John Battye	John x Crowther
	John Hinchliffe	his marke

Flockton

[no endorsement]

H

Paines laid at the Kings Court commonly called the Sherife turne holden at Kirkburton the 17th day of October 1688 by the Constable and sworn men of Thirstyland as followeth:
Imprimis we lay in paine that no manner of person or persons shall carry away either green wood or dry out of other mens ground without the licence of the owners thereof, in paine of every time so seen, known or taken 12d

Item we lay in paine that no manner of person or persons shall goe ever other mens ground where there is no usuall way, in paine of every time so seen, known or taken 12d

Item we lay in paine that all inhabitants within the said towne shall ring their swine and so keep them, in paine of every default 12d

Item we lay in paine that all inhbitants within the said towne shall make their fences sufficient joyneing upon hard corne at or before the 11th day of November next and so keep them, in paine of every default 10s

Item we lay in paine that all the inhabitants within the said towne shall switch their hedges and scoure their ditches joyneing to the high wayes before the 11th day of November next and so keep them, in paine of every default 10s

Item we lay in paine that no manner of person or persons shall cross the landes to goe to the yate in the field above Matthew Lockwoods, in paine of every time so seen or knowne 3s 4d

[signed] Godfrey Crosland
Henery Gillott John Rhodes
Robert Hall John Battye
Abraham Lockwood Cunstable John Hinchliffe
Thurstonland

[no endorsement]

I

Paines laid at Kings Majesties Court called the Sherife turne holden at Kirkeburton the 17th day of October Anno domini 1688 by the sworne men of Holme, namely Timothy Eastwood and William Earnshaw

Imprimis we lay in paine that no maner of person or persons whatsoever shall cutt or carry away either green wood or drye out of other mens grounds without lycence of the right owner thereof, in payne of every default xij

Item we lay in paine that no person or persons go over other mens grounds where there is no accustomed way, in payne of every default xij

Item we lay in paine that all the househoulders within the townshipe aforesaid shall yoke and ring their swine and so keepe them untill the next Court Leet, in payne of every default xij

Item we lay in paine that no person or persons shall put any scabed or infectious beast unto any of the commons belonging to the said towne, in payne of every default xij

Item we lay in payne that all persons who have any fences adjoyning to hard corne that the make the same sufficient before the tenth of next ensuing, in payne of every default xij

[signed] Godfrey Crosland / John Rhodes / John Battye / John Hinchliffe

Holme

[no endorsement]

J

Paines layed thee Kings Majesties Court Houlden at Kirk Burton the 17th day of October 1688 by the Constable and sworne men of Fullston as followeth:

Imprimis we lay in payne that noe maner of person or persons shall cutt or carie away ether greene wood or dry out of other mens ground without lycence of they owner thereof, in paine of everie default 1s

Item wee lay in paine that they that keep any swine shall ringe them and soe keepe them till they next Court day, in payne of everie default 1s

Item wee lay in payne that everie one shall keepe they watters in thier right accastomed courcs by skouringe thiere diches, likewise that everie one shall cutt and swich thiere hedgs where they are anoyance to the hye way, in payne of everie default 1s

Item George Roebucke layes in paine that no maner of person or persons do make any ussuall path or way over one close called the Hinchclife croft, in paine of every default so seen, knowne or taken 1s

Item John Morehouse layes in paine that Edward Langley cutt hys hedge and lopp the trees on one close called the little Ing joyneing <of> one close of hard corne before the first day of January next ensueing, in paine 1s

[signed] William Crosland / Heneri Hurst / Edward Langlley / George Robucke / Godfrey Crosland / John Rhodes / John Battye / John Hinchliffe

Fulstone

[no endorsement]

K

Paines laid at the Kings Majesties Court commonly called Sherriffes Turne houlden at Burton the 17th day of October Anno domini 1688 by the constable and sworne of Scoles as followeth: Abraham Hamor and Thomas Booth

Imprimis Wee lay in paine that noe maner of person or persons whatsoever shall cut or carry away either green wood or dry out of other mens ground without licence of the owner thereof, in paine of every such default xij^{d}

Item Wee lay in paine that noe maner of person or persons whatsoever shall goe over other mens ground where there is noe lawfull way, in paine of everie default xij^{d}

Item Wee lay in paine that all maner of persons whatsoever that hath any swine shall yoke and ringe them and so keep them, in paine for such default xij^{d}

Item Wee lay in paine that all maner of person or persons whatsoever shall scower their ditches joyneing upon the high waies and keep the waters in their antient accustomed coursses, in paine of iij^{s} iiij^{d}

[signed] Godfrey Crosland / John Rhodes / John Battye / John Hinchliffe

Scholes

[no endorsement]

L

Paines laid at the Kings Majesties Court commonly [called] the Sheirrife turne houlden at Burton the 17th day of October Anno Domini 1688 by the Constable and sworne men of Wooldale as followeth:

First Wee lay in paine that noe maner of person or persons whatsoever shall cut or carry away out of other mens ground neither green wood nor dry without lycence of the owner, in paine of every such default xij^{d}

Alsoe Wee lay in paine that all persons whatsoever that hath any swine shall yoke and ring them and soe keep them, in paine for such default iij^{s} iiij^{d}

Alsoe Wee lay in paine that noe maner of person or persons whatsoever shall goe over other mens ground where there is noe lawfull way, in paine of every default xij^{d}

Alsoe Wee lay in paine that all maner of persons whatsoever shall scower their ditches joyneing upon the high waies and keep the waters in their antient accustomed courses, in paine of v^{s}

[signed] Edward Duckinfield Godfrey Crosland
John Tuhorp John Rhodes
Samuell Bramall John Battye
Gamalliell Brooke John Hinchliffe

Wooldale

[no endorsement]

M

Paines laid at the Kings Majesties Court commonly [called] Sheirrifes Turne houlden at Burton the 17th day of October Anno Domini 1688 by the Constable and sworne men of Cartworth as followeth:

Imprimis Wee lay in paine that noe maner of person or persons whatsoever shall cut or carry away either green wood or dry out of other mens ground without licence of the owner thereof, in paine of every default xij^d

Item Wee lay in paine that noe maner of person or persons whatsoever goe over other mens ground where there is noe lawfull way, in paine of every default xij^d

Item Wee lay in paine that all maner of person or persons whatsoever that hath any swine shall yoke and ring them and soe keep them, in paine of every default v^s

Item Wee lay in paine that all maner of persons whatsoever shall scower their ditches joyneing upon the high waies and keep the waters in their antient accustomed coursses, in paine of iij^s iiij^d

[signed] Robert R Ellis marke
James Littlewood
Joshua I Roberts his marke

Item wee lay a paine that Joshua Heape, Richard Hinchliffe, Henry Kaye and John Hinchliffe doe amend one antient way from Lanehead to Hinchliffe Mill and keep the water in the accustomed courses before the 20th of November next in paine of 39^s

Abraham A Roberts his marke
Godfrey Crosland
John Rhodes / John Hinchliffe / John Battye
Cartworth

[no endorsement]

N

Burton At the View of Francpledge and Court Leet of our Soveraigne lord the king with the turne holden there the 17 day of October 1688

Pains layd by the Constable and sworn men of Austonley

Imprimis Wee lay in paine that noe maner of parsons cut down or carry away eather green wood or dry out of other mens grounds without the licence or consent of the owner thereof, in pain of every burden soe known j^s o^d

Item Wee lay in pain that noe parson travell on other mens grounds where there is noe usuall way, in pain of eeavery default soe seen or known j^s o^d

Item Wee lay in pain that all parsons scour and dres there water courses and diches adioineing to the hy ways and soe keep them at all tims, in pain of every default soe known iij iiij

Item Wee lay in pain that all parsons yoke and ring there swine and soe keep them at all tims, in pain of every default soe known j^s o^d

Item Wee lay in pain that noe parsons put or turn forth any scabbed horses or other infectious cattell on any of the Lords Commons, in pain of every default soe seen or known x^s o^d

[signed] Abraham Mellor M
William W Kennion

Item James Hinchlife doth lay in paine that noe maner of parson or parsons whatsoever shall put or drive any sheep or other cattell into a certaine parcell of land of the said James Hinchclife called Goodbentclough, in paine for such default x^s

Item Wee lay in paine that noe parson or parsons shall *turne* <hinder> the watter for runing overthwart Taylor lane, in paine of every time soe seen, known or taken iij^s $iiij^d$

[signed] Godfrey Crosland / John Rhodes / John Battye / John Hinchliffe
Austonley

[no endorsement]

O

Burton At the View of Francpledge and Court Leet of our Soveraigne lord the King with the turne holden ther the 17 day of October 1688

Pains layd by the Constable and sworn men of Hepworth

Imprimis Wee lay in paine that no maner of parsons cut down or carry away either green wood or dry out of other mens grounds without the licence or consent of the owner thereof, in pain of every burden soe known j^s o^d

Item Wee lay in paine that noe parson travell on other mens grounds where there is noe usuall way, in pain of every default soe seen or known j^s o^d

Item Wee lay in pain that all parsons scour and dreas there water courses and diches adioineing to the hy ways and soe keep them at all tims, in pain of every default soe known iij^s $iiij^d$

Item Wee lay in pain that all parsons yoke and ring there swine and soe keep them att all tims, in pain of every default soe known j^s o^d

Item Wee lay in pain that <no> parsons put or turn forth any scabbed horses or other infectious cattell on any of the Lords Commons, in pain of every default soe seen or known x^s o^d

[signed] Robert Bever
Josias Berry
John Hall
George Hattersley

Item Wee lay in pain that noe manner of parson make a way over the West Feild head, in pain of every default j^s o^d

Wee lay in pain that Joseph Addy make the fence <sufficient> betwixt Indrod and West feild *in pain* betwixt this and second of Feberiwary, in pain of 5^s o^d

[signed] Godfrey Crosland / John Rhodes / John Battye / John Hinchliffe
Hepworth

[no endorsement]

P
Paines laid at the Kings Majeties Court commonly called Sherrifes Turne houlden at Burton the 17th day of October Anno Domini 1688 by the Constable and sworne men of Overthongue as followeth
Imprimis Wee lay in paine that noe maner of person or persons whatsoever shall cut or carry away either green wood or dry out of other mens ground without licence of the owner thereof, in paine of every default xij^{d}
Item Wee lay in paine that all persons whatsoever that hath any swine shall yoke and ring them and soe keep them, in paine of every default iij^{s} iiij^{d}
Item Wee lay in paine that noe maner of person or persons whatsoever shall goe over other mens ground where there is noe lawfull way, in paine of every default xij^{d}
Item Wee lay in paine that all maner of persons whatsoever shall scower their ditches joyneing upon the high waies and keep the waters in their antient accustomed coursses, in paine of x^{s}

[signed] Robert Sanderson / Michael + Midgley his mark / Godfrey Crosland / John Rhodes / John Battye / John Hinchliffe
Overthwonge

[no endorsement]

Q Burton At the View of Franke Pledge and Court Leet of our Soveraigne Lord the King with the Turne holden there the 17th day of October in the year of our Lord 1688
Item We the Jury doe present Joseph Bilcliffe <of Cumberworth> for makeing an affray and draweing of blood upon the body of William <Richy> the fifth day of July last by the oath of William Marsh in x^{s}
Item We doe present Thomas Parkin of Shelley for makeing an affay and draweing of blood upon the body of William Marsh of Cumberworth the fourth of June last by the oath of the said William Marsh in x^{s}
[signed] Godfrey Crosland / James Hinchliffe / John Rhodes / John Battye / John Couldwell / Richard Cockell / Joshua Roades / George Robucke / Humfrey Wilson / Phillip Earnshaw / John Allott / John Hinchliffe / Adam Lindley /
by enquiry

[no endorsement]

R

[in Latin]	Names of Constables	
KIRKBURTON	Samuel Wood and William Moone	sworn
SHELLEY	John Peace	sworn
SHEPLEY	Joseph Hobson, deputy	sworn
CUMBERWORTH	William Oxley	sworn
ELMLEY	John Page	sworn
FLOCKTON	John Walshawe	sworn
THURSTONLAND	Abraham Lockwood	sworn
HOLME	Joshua Roades	sworn

membrane 16 continued

Wakefield view of frankpledge and court leet held on 6 April 1 William & Mary [1689]

Panel for the King and Queen Inquest taken on the oaths of William Shutleworth, Richard Yoward, Thomas Harris, Anthony Bland, Samuel Jackson, John Smith, Timothy Hirst, John Leake, Robert Webster, Henry Ellis, John Forrest, William Preston, William Robinson, and Henry Hemingway, jurors.

They presented that Joseph Burrnet of Durtcarr took profit of herbage from a common balk belonging to the pinder (*impensator'*) lying near le Bottom field in Criglestone *amerced 6s 8d*

Item, Thomas Marshall of Wakefield made affray and drew blood from Jonas Shauu of the same *amerced 10s*

Item, William Nantcliffe built and encroached on the common called Outwood *amerced 3s 4d*

NORTHGATE William Warde, constable, and his fellows presented Susan Carter of Ossett for using false weights *amerced 12d*

STANLEY Joseph Smith, constable, and his fellows presented Joseph Sellars for digging stones on the common *amerced 5s*

SANDALL Robert Beckwith, constable, and his fellows presented that all was well.

WALTON with BRETTON Joseph Wright, constable of Walton, and William Brooke, constable of Bretton, and their fellows presented that all was well.

HORBURY Japhet Heald, constable, and his fellows, presented that all was well.

OSSETT John White, constable, and his fellows, presented the inhabitants of Gawthorpe for not hanging (*perpender'*) sufficient gates at Gawthorpe stoops *amerced 12d*
NORMANTON Thomas Broadley, constable, and his fellows presented John Newsome for not making his fence against Houlclough *amerced 12d*
Item, they presented George Wareing for putting contagious goods (*bona*) on the common *amerced 3s 4d*
SOOTHILL Josiah Clapham, constable, and his fellows presented that all was well.
DEWSBURY Michael Ellis, constable, and his fellows presented that all was well.
WESTARDSLEY Timothy Kitson, constable, and his fellows presented that all was well.
CRIGLESTONE John Hirst, constable, and his fellows presented that all was well.
ECCLESHILL James Wilson, constable, and his fellows presented that all was well.

Sum of court [blank]

[in draft, membrane 87]
KIRKEGATE Thomas Bethell, constable
WESTGATE Richard Norfolke, junior, constable
NORTHGATE William Warde, constable
STANLEY Joseph Smith, constable
SANDALL Robert Beckwith, constable
WALTON with BRETTON Joseph Wright, constable for Walton, John Barker, deputy: William Brooke <did not appear>, constable for Bretton

membrane 87 dorse

HORBURY Japhet Heald, constable
OSSETT John White, constable <did not appear>
NORMANTON Thomas Broadley, constable
SOOTHILL Josiah Clapham <for non appearance xs >
DEWSBURY Michael Ellis, constable
WESTARDSLEY Timothy Kitson, constable
CRIGLESTONE John Hirst, constable
ECCLESHILL James Wilson, constable

[in draft, after membrane 87 dorse]
A

Panel of jurors, 6 April 1689
William Shuttleworth, sworn

Francis Mawde		
Richard Yoward	John Smith	Henry Ellis
William Shuttleworth	Timothy Hirst	John Forrest
Thomas Harris	*Thomas Totty*	William Preston
Anthony Bland	John Leake	William Robinson
Samuel Jackson	Robert Webster	Henry Hemingway

John Burton
Timothy Bolton sworn affeerers
Thomas Carter, sworn pinder for Horbury

B

Wakefeild

Att the view of Franck Pledge and Court Leet holden theire the sixth day of Aprill in the first yere of the raigne of our soveraigne lord and lady William and Mary by the Grace of God King and Queen of England etc, Annoque domini 1689

Wee present all inhabitants and raisarts within the jurisdiction of this Court for not appeareing at the said court, every one of them for his default sixpence apece 0^s 06^d

[signed]	William Shuttleworth	John Smith
	Richard Yoward	Timothy Hurst
	Thomas Hariss	John Leake
	Anthony Bland	Robert Webster
	Samuell Jackson	Henry Ellis
		John Forist
		William Priston
		William Robinson
		Henry Hemingway

Timothy Bolton
John Burton
by enquiry

[no endorsement]

C

Wakefeld Att the view of Franck Pledge and Court Leet holden there the sixth day of Aprill Anno Domini 1689

traversed Wee the Jury there sworne for our Soveraigne Lord and Lady the King and Queen doe present Joseph Burnett of Dirtcarr for takeing the profitts and herbage of a common balke belonging to the Pinder lyeing neere unto the Bottom field in Criglestone vj^{s} viij^{d}

[signed] William Shuttleworth fered by us
Richard Yoward Timothy Bolton
William Robinson John Burton
John X Leake
Samewel Jackson

by enquiry

[no endorsement]

D

Wakefeld Att the view of franck pledge and court leet holden there the sixth day of Aprill in the first yeare of the raignes of our soveraigne Lord and Lady William and Mary by the grace of God King and Queen of England etc, Anno Domini 1689

Tr[aversed] Wee the Jury there sworne for our Soveraigne Lord and Lady the King and Queen doe present Isaac Rawling for takeing Twenty sheep from the Pinder of Horbury 3^{s} 4^{d}

Item wee present John Leake for breaking the Lords pinfold att Stanley 3^{s} 4^{d}

Item wee present Thomas Marshall of Wakefield for makeing a fray and drawing blood upon the body of Jonas Shauu of the same 10^{s} 0^{d}

Item wee present Joseph Longley for digging upp the common and getting stones upon the Outwood within the jurisdiction of this court xxxix^{s} xj^{d}

Item wee present Michael Addy of Barnsley for killing a bull and not baiteing him in Wakefield

Item wee present William Nantcliffe for building and encroaching upon the common called Outwood iij^{s} iiij^{d}

[signed] William Shuttleworth
Richard Yoward fered by us Timothy Bolton
Samuell S Jackson his marke John Burton
Anthony Bland

by enquiry

[no endorsement]

E

Westgate Bill

Sworne men

[signed] Thomas Johnson / Joseph Armistage / Francis Allon

Omne Bene
Westgate

[no endorsement]

F

The presentment for Norgate

Mr John Murgitroyd and Jonathan Stocks for a blood and a fray 10^{s} 0^{d}
Robert Barke for not paving his door 1 0
Jane Langstaff for false weights 1 0
Susanna Carter of Osset for the same 1 0
Henry Plaisterer for a common annoyance 1 0

[signed] William Naylor
Thomas Marshall — fered by us
George Walton — Timothy Bolton
Marke Winterburne — John Burton

William Shuttleworth / Richard Yoward / William Robinson / Thomas Harris / Anthony Bland

Northgate

[no endorsement]

G

Stanla presentments Woodside

Joseph Langla for didgin up the coman and getting of stones 00 05^{s} 00
Joseph Selle for diggin up of Cla and selling it out of the parrish 00 03 04
Widdow Robbinson of Wackfeild for unscouered diches at Brodford 00 03 04
Will Mitchel of Allathorp for a turning his scabed horses unto the coman, which <is> a noyance to all the nabers and unscouered ditches 00 03 04

[signed] William Shuttleworth — Thomas T Jayey
John Smith — Gorge Hebdin
Timothe T Horste mark — Will Rodela
William P Prostton — Samuel Borke

fered by us
Timothy Bolton John Barton

Stanley

[no endorsement]

H

Sandall bill

Antney Croschay | Abram Robart
Thomas Kershey | Josaway Ackcoun

Omnia bene
Sandall

[no endorsement]

I

John Barker constable for Walton cum Bretton
Timothy Hirst jurey man

omnia bene
Walton cum Bretton

[no endorsement]

J

Horbury bill

Omane bene

Sworne men: George Isiott / John Wadsworth / John Haigh

Horbury

[no endorsement]

K

April 25th

Ossett Bill for presentments

Imprimis we present Mr Richard Nettleton for not scouringe his ditches toward the kings high street 00 05 00

We present the inhabitance of Gawthrope for not hanginge a sufficient yate at Gawthrope stoups betwixt and the day appointed by us 00 01 00

[signed] John White Constable
Richard Teery / Samuell Copley / John Land / John Sugden
four sworn men

[signed] William Shuttleworth / Richard Yoward / William Robinson / Anthony Bland

fered by us Timothy Bolton John Burton

Ossett

[no endorsement]

L

Normanton Bill of presentments

Inprimis we present John Newsom for his fence being not made against houstelough 0^l 1^s 0^d

Item we present Will Asshall for commoning without right 0 0 6
Item John Bedford for putting to the common without right 0 0 6
Mrs Lovitt for a peice of fence being a noyance to the highwayes betwixt Heu lane end and the field yate 0 1 0
George Warine for putting infectious goods to our common 0 3 4
[signed] his marke
Thomas Broadley + Constable
William Bluett John + Standidge <his marke>
Richard + Jubb <his marke>
Will + Ashall <his mark> By Law men
Normanton
[endorsed]
William Shuttleworth / Richard Yoward / William Robinson / Anthony Bland / John Smith / John + Leeack mark
fered by us Timothy Bolton / John Burton

M

Soothill Bill
Concarning presentments: All is well
[signed] Henry Hemingway Jureman
Richard Wode / Robard Rodes his R mark
Soothill
[no endorsement]

N

Dewsbury Bill Omnea bane
[signed] his marke Michall Ellis
John I Thornes
his marke his marke his marke
Joshua + Toll Isack S Smith John O Day
Dewsbury
[no endorsement]

O

Westardisley bill Timothy Kitson Constable
sworne men
Antony Williamson / Daneille Netlton
Omna bane
[signed] Daniel Nettleton / Antony Williamson
Westardsley

[no endorsement]

P

The Constable of Criglestone Bill

As upon a diligent Inquiery aboute all things touching our office, we whose names are subscribed doe finde noe default but omne bene.

[signed] John Hirst Constable
Robert Cooke
Richard Michiell four men
Mathew Law
Timothy Milner
Criglestone

[no endorsement]

Q

Eccleshill bill the 6 of Aprill 1689

We have no presentments

[signed] James Hobson Constable
John Barraclough last sworne man
Eccleshill

[endorsed] King

membrane 16 continued

Halifax view of frankpledge and court leet, held on 8 April 1 William and Mary [1689].

Panel for King and Queen Inquest taken on the oaths of Richard Scarbrough, Joshua Whitehead, Joshua Dearden, gen, Jonas Boardall, Abraham Brigge, Thomas Oldfield, Edmund Wadsworth, Richard Patchett, Michael Oldfield, Thomas Barker, John Gibson, John Utley, and Richard Thomas, jurors.

Sowerby (124) It was attested by John Hargreaves senior, gen, lords' tenant, that William Thomas of Redicarr in Wadsworth, yeo, on 3 April instant surrendered into the lords' hands all that messuage with appurtenances in Soyland in <Sowerby in the graveship> of Sowerby and all houses, barns, structures, folds, gardens, lands, tenements, meadow, closes, pasture, ways, passages, water, watercourses, liberties, profits, commodities, easements, emoluments and hereditaments appurtenant, now occupied by James Bilsbury or his assigns at an annual lords' rent of 2s 4d, compounded: to the use of Michael Firth of Height in Barkisland, gen, his heirs and assigns for ever. Agreed, to hold by due service: entry fine 7s.

HALIFAX Isaac Wilkinson and Gabriel Learoyd, constables, and their fellows presented that Abraham Scott did not repair the way against his house at the lower end of the town *amerced 5s*

Item, Henry Ramsden did not repair the way against his house at the lower end of the town *amerced 20s*

Item, Joshua Dunn did not repair <the way against> his house in le Back Lane *amerced 24s*

SOWERBY John Stansfield, constable, and his fellows presented that all was well.

SCIRCOATE Joseph Robinson, constable, and his fellows presented that all was well.

OVENDEN John Firth, constable, and his fellows presented that all was well.

WARLEY James Chadwicke, constable, and his fellows presented that all was well.

WADSWORTH William Wilkinson, constable, and his fellows presented that all was well.

MIDGLEY William Walker, constable, and his fellows presented that all was well.

RISHWORTH with NORLAND Richard Tayler, constable, and his fellows presented that all was well.

STAN[S]FIELD Richard Stanfield, constable, and his fellows presented that all was well.

LAN[G]FIELD Thomas Walker (sic), constable, and his fellows presented that all was well.

HEPTONSTALL William Crabtree, constable, and his fellows presented that all was well.

ERRINDEN Isaac Farrer, constable, and his fellows presented that all was well.

membrane 16 dorse

Sowerby (125) It was attested by John Hargreaves senior, gen, lords' tenant, that Joseph Wilson of Wood in Soyland in Sowerby, yeo, and Jane now his wife, she examined separately by the steward, on 15 December last surrendered into the lords' hands that messuage with appurtenances called le Wood in Soyland in Sowerby in the graveship of Sowerby and all houses, edifices, barns, structures, folds, gardens, land, tenements, meadow, closes, pasture, feedings, ways, waters, watercourses, liberties, profits, commodities, easements, emoluments and hereditaments appurtenant, now occupied by the said Joseph Wilson or his assigns, also a cottage now occupied by Dinah Robertshaw or her assigns, at an annual lords' rent of 17d, compounded: to the use of Joshua Whiteley of Holmehouse in Barkisland, yeo, his heirs and assigns for ever. Agreed: to hold by due service, entry fine, 4s 3d.

- (126) It was attested by John Hargreaves senior, gen, lords' tenant, that Joseph Wilson of Wood in Soyland in Sowerby, yeo, on 15 December last surrendered into the lords' hands, remitted and quitclaimed all rights, etc, including power of redemption, in the messuage called le Wood in Soyland in the graveship of Sowerby and four closes of land, meadow and pasture appurtenant thereto known as le Bank above the house, le Inge under the house, le Inge bothome close and le Holme att Waterside, with all houses, edifices, barns, structures, folds, gardens, land, tenements, meadow, closes, ways, waters, watercourses, liberties, profits, commodities, easements, emoluments and hereditaments as occupied by the said Joseph Wilson and a certain Simeon Patchett or their assigns and now by Joseph Wilson or his assigns etc at an annual lords' rent of 12d, compounded: to the use of Joshua Whiteley of Holmehouse in Barkisland, yeo, his heirs and assigns for ever. He gave 6d for enrolment of the quitclaim.

- (127) It was attested by John Heape, lords' tenant, that Abraham Feilden of Soyland in Sowerby, yeo, on 30 December last surrendered into the lords' hands the reversion after his death of all four closes of land, meadow and pasture with appurtenances, and a barn appurtenant near Farra Height in Soyland in Sowerby, and all ways, passages, waters, watercourses, liberties, profits, common of pasture and turbary, easements, emoluments and hereditaments lately occupied by the said Abraham and his assigns at an annual lords' rent of 3s 3d, [compounded] and for 12d not compounded: to the use of Mary Fielden of Soyland, spinster, and her assigns for her lifetime and after her death to the use of Martin Feilden of Halifax, bookbinder, his heirs and assigns for ever. Agreed: Mary Fielden gave the lords 20¼d for the reversion of the compounded land, and a further [blank] for the land not compounded. Martin Fielden also gave 20¼d for the reversion of the compounded land when it happened, and for the non-compounded land [blank].

- (128) It was attested by John Hargreaves junior, lords' tenant that Robert Preistley of Bayteinges in Sowerby, yeo, and Henry Preistley on 19 March last surrendered into the lords' hands a close of land, meadow and pasture with appurtenances in Sowerby in the graveship of Sowerby known as le Kilne Inge or Lanerhill, occupied as appurtenant to a messuage in Sowerby now held by Joshua Stanton or his assigns, with all ways, waters, watercourses, liberties.., common of pasture and turbary, advantage and hereditaments, being customary land, held at an annual lords' rent of [blank], compounded: to the use of Richard Hoyle of Godley in Northowrome, yeo, his heirs and assigns for ever. Agreed, to hold by due service: entry fine [blank].

Hipperholme (129) It was attested by John Richardson, lords' tenant, that Ambrose Noble and George Noble and Thomas Noble of Halifax, sons of George Noble of the same, chapman, by his late wife Grace, daughter of Edward Jackson late of Halifax, yeo, deceased, on 1 February last surrendered into the lords' hands all the two closes of land, meadow and pasture with appurtenances in Northowrome in the graveship of Hipperholme adjacent to Halifax Brooke and near le Norrbrigg there, with all ways, watercourses and easements, now occupied by the said George Noble senior or his assigns at an annual lords' rent of 8d, compounded: to the use of Francis Wilkinson near Norbrigg in Northowrome, tanner, his heirs and assigns for ever. Agreed, to hold by due service; entry fine 2s.

- (130) It was attested by John Hargreaves junior, lords' tenant, that Jeremy Rossendale of Skircoate, gen, on 17 October last surrendered into the lords' hands all that messuage with appurtenances in Hipperholme in the graveship of Hipperholme and all houses, edifices, barns, structures, folds, orchards, gardens, lands, tenements, meadow, closes, pasture, feedings, ways, waters, watercourses, liberties etc, lately occupied by James Phillippes or his assigns and now by Thomas Kitson or his assigns at an annual lords' rent of [blank], compounded: to the use of the said Thomas Kitson of Hipperholme, clothier, his executors, administrators and assigns as from 2 February last for 14 years at such an annual rent, and under such covenant, provisions and conditions as expressed in a pair of indentures of the same date as the surrender made between the same Jeremy and Thomas. Agreed: entry fine [blank].

- (131) It was attested by John Hargreaves junior, lords' tenant, that Jonas Ingham of Blakehill in Northowrome, yeo, on 9 March last surrendered into the lords' hands all the messuage in Northowrome known as le Newhouse near an ancient messuage called Blakehill, and all houses, edifices, structures, yards, gardens and easements appurtenant, the south and east of a fold as now so divided, a smith's shop or smithy, a 'henhouse', and a 'swinestye' lately built thereon, with a garden, a croft on the east side of the house, a close of land and meadow called le Long Inge, now subdivided into two, a barn at the upper end of Le Long Inge, another close of land, meadow and pasture called le Hawroydes, another close of arable and pasture called le Nether Charwell bothom, another called le Little Ryeding, and a similar three closes of land and pasture called Overbancks, now occupied by the said Jonas Ingham or his assigns, a cottage or residence lately built, standing above the east part of a fold, now occupied by John Hardistye and Abraham Firth or their assigns, and all ways, waters, watercourses, liberties .. appurtenant, and freedom for ever to use the ways and passages at all times across the two closes lately of the inheritance of John Bairstowe of Ovenden appurtenant to the messuage called Blakehill and called les Rye Pighell and Churchwell bothome, to carry 'manure' into the close called Rydeings and carry annually 'the cropps thereof' and come and go with milk between the messuage called Newhouse and the last mentioned closes. These were copyhold and owed an annual lords' rent of 2s 9d, compounded (the liberties of passage by John Bairstowe and his heirs, and the right to win (*acquirere*) coal (*carbon'*) in the said close called Overbancks or delve a 'new pitt' being excluded from the surrender): to the use of John Hargreaves senior of Halifax, attorney (*scriptor'*), and John Murgatroyde of Warley, yeo, and their heirs with the intent that John Hargreaves and John Murgatroyde, yeo, their heirs and the surviver of their heirs stood / **membrane 17** / seised of the messuage, etc in trust for such uses as expressed in a tripartite indenture made between Jonas Ingham, of the first, John Hargreaves and John Murgatroyde of the second, and Miles Ingham of Blakehill, clothier, youngest son of Jonas of the third part. Agreed that John Hargreaves and John Murgatroyde hold to the uses mentioned in the indenture. Entry fine, 8s 3d.

- (132) It was attested by John Hargreaves junior, lords' tenant, that Susan Flather of Halifax, widow, lately wife of Thomas Flather junior, late of Northowrome, clothier, deceased, on 12 March last surrendered into the lords' hands an annuity or sum of £5 payable annually from the messuage called Briggroyde with its appurtenances in Northowrome in the graveship of Hipperholme, and all houses, structures, land, closes and grounds now occupied by Thomas Flather senior or his assigns: to the use of Anne Flather, Joseph Flather, Susan Flather and Sarah Flather, children of the late Thomas Flather and Susan, lately his wife, and their assigns, for the natural life of Susan Flather senior, payable at Whitsun and Martinmas in equal parts, payments starting from the date after the death of Thomas Flather senior. Should payment in full or in part be delayed by 20 days, they might enter the messuage and distrain until satisfaction was made. Agreeed: entry fine, 4s 2d.

Sowerby (133) It was attested by John Hargreaves junior, lords' tenant, that Robert Preistley of Bayteings in Sowerby, yeo, and Henry Preistley of the same, son and heir of the said Robert, on 19 March last surrendered into the lords' hands the freedom to dig and win < 'peates, turffes and flaghts' > for their necessary use as occupiers of those three messuages in Soyland now occupied by Nathan Whitley, Josiah Siddall and Joshua Staineton or their assigns, now sold by the said Robert Preistley to Richard Hoyle of Godley in Northowrome, yeo, and his heirs in a piece of 'Mossie ground' (*muscosi fundi*) in Soyland laying by Bayteingsdike and Mansheade, estimated at 10 acres, and stack (*Anglice, to reare*) and dry them to carry away with men, horses and carts, and the use of the usual ways at the usual times, at an annual lords' rent of ½d, compounded: to the use of the said Richard Hoyle, his heirs and assigns for ever. Agreed: entry fine, 1½d.

Sum of court [blank]

[in draft, membrane 88 dorse, list of constables]

Halifax	Isaac Wilkinson and Gabriel Learoyde
Sowerby	John Stansfield
Skircoate	Joseph Robinson
Ovenden	John Firth, constable, Jonas Deane, deputy
Warley	James Chadwicke
Wadsworth	William Wilkinson
Midgley	William Walker
Rishworth with Norland	Richard Tayler, constable, James Roper, deputy
Stansfield	Richard Stansfield
	membrane 89
Langfield	Thomas Walton
Heptonstall	William Crabtree, constable, William Greenwood, deputy
Erringden	Isaac Farrer

[in draft, after membrane 93]

A

Halifax Court Leet held on 8th April 1689

Panel for King and Queen

Richard Scarbrough sworne

Joshua Whitehead	Thomas Oldfield	Thomas Barker
Joshua Deardon, gen	Edmund Wadsworth	John Gibson
Jonas Boardall	Richard Patchett	John Utley
Abraham Brigge	Michael Oldfield	Richard Thomas

[no endorsement]

B

Panel for King and Queen between parties

Richard Scarbrough etc, as above, less Richard Thomas

Abraham Clegg pro 70 year

John Eastwood pro 60 yeares

John Barker

Robert Stansfield

[no endorsement]

C

Aprill the 6 day 89

Gabrill Learoide for forestalling the markett and bying butter and selling it the same day, contrary to law.

Elizabeth Coultris for the licke.

Dorothe Roberts for the licke and bying egs and selling the same day.

[signed] Joshua Willson / Robert Dyson

by enquiry

[endorsed] These we leave to Mr Steward to be considered of according to the contents of the statute.

[signed] Richard Scarbrough / Joshuah Dearden / Thomas Oldfield / Richard Patchett

D

Halifax [Court Leet held on 6 April 1689]

<I John Blagburne> *Wee the Jury there sworne for our Soveraigne Lord and Lady the King and Queen* doe lay in paine that Henry Feilden doe turne the water into its antient course out of one close of the said Henry Feilden <lyeing> *scituate* att Lighthasles within the jurisdiction of this court unto our messuage scituate att Lighthasles aforesaid, now in the occupation of Thomas Blagburne, before the eighteenth day of May next, in paine of xxxix^{s} xj^{d}.

[signed] Richard Scarbrough
Joshuah Dearden   John Blagburne
Thomas Oldfield
Abraham Brigge   by enquiry

[no endorsement]

E i

Presentment

Abrham Scott for not mending the gate against howseing in botam in town 00. 5^{s}. 0

Henry Ramsden for not mending the way against his howseing in the botam town 1. 0. 0

Josua Dunn for not mending the way against his howsing in the baklaine 1. 4. 0

Mr Lister for not mending the way against his howsing in new gate end 0. 6. 0

Mr Robert Alinson for not mending the way against his housing 1. 00. 0

Mr Ramsden of Crowstone for not mending the way against his howsing 0. 13. 4

Samuell Newton for not mending the way against his howsing in Swin market 0. 8. 0

Mr Thomas Harton of London for not mending the highway against his housing 0. 16. 0

paines of the last Court Light

Robert Gledill for not mending the Hieway Cabidglane end 0. 2. 0

Mr Antribus for not mending about his houseing 0. 13. 4

Daniell Jackson for not mending against Old Hall 0. 6. 0

Mr Jermih Bently for not mending cawse Bak Hall 0. 2. 0

Natheniell Holdstead for not mending befor Henry Lakes houseing 0. 6. 0

Mr Harton for not mending before his howsing top town 0. 2. 6

William Scot for not mending befor his howsing 0. 1. 0

John Windl for not mending his way about his house 0. 2. 0

Benjmen Bateis for not mending the way about his howsing 0. 5. 0

Johnthan Windl for not mending his way about his housing and for not taking up his maner 0. 1. 0

Richard Scarbrough for not mending about his housing 0. 3. 0

John Dixson for not mending befor his housing 0. 0. 6

Widow Jackson for not mending befor her housing 0. 3. 0

Mr Corer for not mending befor his howsing and lathing 0. 3. 0

Jonthan Glover and John Wilson for not mending befor James Dickinson house 0. 1. 0

George Bently for not mending thy way befor and about his howsing 0. 5. 0

Wiliam Walker for <not> mending the way befor his howsing on green 0. 2. 0

John Ellam for not mending befor his lathing on green 0. 1. 0

Timothy Wadsworth for not mending the way about his howsing 0. 5. 0

Thomas Edwards for coman anoyence in the hie way 0. 2. 0

old John Brigg for turning the water out of course 0. 5. 0

Richard Baraclugh for not mending the way at Southgat end 0. 5. 0

Halifax

[no endorsement]

E ii

Josua Dunn for not mending the way befor his houseing botam town 2s. 0
Mr Pour for not mending the way against his house in Corn market 10. 0
Mr Henry Ramsden for not mending hie way at Starr 0. 5. 0
Mr Thomas Thornell for not mending about his houseing at Hart Horn 0. 5. 0
Mr John Richardson for not mending befor his housing botam town 0. 1. 0
Mr William Burkby for not mending befor his housing botam town 0. 5. 0
Mr Lunn for not mending before the Kiln 0. 1. 0
Mr Jermiah Bently for not mending his walls as goes to the brig 10. 0

Constables of Hallifax

[signed] Gaberill Learoyd / Isaac Wilkinson / Michaell Waugh

presenters Aaron Horner / John Hilous / James I Soutill / John Wilson / William Wamoit / Francis F Dixson his marke

[signed] Richard Scarbrough / Joshuah Dearden / Thomas Oldfeild / Richard Patchett / Joshua Whithead / Abraham Brigge / Michaell Oldfield

[no endorsement]

F

Sowerby Bill Aprill the 8th 1689

Wee the Constable and sworne men for Sowerby doe not find anythinge painable or presentable within our townshippe: Witnesse our hands

[signed] John Stansfeld constable
John Crossby / Samuell Holden / Josia Siddale / John Siddale
Sowerby

[endorsed] Richard Scarbrough / Joshuah Dearden / Thomas Oldfield

G

The Constable of Skirttcoatt Bill Aprill 8th 1689

who saith that their high ways are in good repair, stockes, buts, cucking stoole and pindfold also, and we have no presentments.

Overseers Joseph Mellin / Anthony Milner
Constable Joseph Robinson

[signed] Richard Scarbrough / Joshua Whithead / Joshuah Dearden / Thomas Oldfeild

[no endorsement]

H

John Firth the Constable of Ovenden *October the 26 day 1688* the hie way leading betwen Jonas Deanes and Mixden Milne are amended October the 26 day 1688: the way leading north betwen Jonas Deanes and Cockill are amended all in due time. The buttes and pinfold and cookstole is all in good repaire. The hie wayes in good repaire. The way leading to 2 colpits lying betwen Thomas Prestley ground north west and Jacob Battes ground north east we pe[in]d it in 1 pound 19 shillings and a 11 pence, giving 60 dayes time to amend it in

[signed] John IF Firth / Daniel Garfoorth / Jonathan Akroyd
Richard Scarbrough / Joshua Whithead / Abraham Brigge/ Michaell Oldfield

Ovenden

[no endorsement]

I

Warley Bill Aprell the 8 89

This is to all those whome itt may concarne that all ouer hie wayes are in good repayre. Ouer buttes and stockes and cockstole and pinfould is all in good repayre, and for frays and bludwipes wee doe not know of aney, and all thinges given in charge wee doe not know of aney.

[signed]	Richard Scarbrough	John Murgatroyd	Constable
	Joshua Whithead	Cristopher Wadsworth	
	Joshuah Deardene	Thomas Adkinson	
	Richard Patchett	Presenters	

Warley

[no endorsement]

J

The Bill for Wadsworth the 8th of Apirell 1689

The High way all in good Repare.

The Cuck Stoole the same.

The Stockes the same and all things else in charge is performed to the best of our Knowledge.

The buts the same.

[signed]	William Willkin	constable
	Richard Scarbrough	Jonas Shackllton
	Joshua Whithead	Paull Greenwood

Michaell Oldfield Isack Dowerst
Richard Thomas Joseph Smallwood [written over erasure]
presenters
Wadsworth

[no endorsement]

K

Midgley Bill

This may certifie whom it may concern that our butts, stocks and pinfold are all in good repair, our highways likewise. [And] for affrayes and bloodwipes, rogues and vagabonds, or any other matter belonging our office, we know of none within our Liberty of Midgley.

[signed] Jos: Sunderland Constable James Shaw
Dan + Brear <mark> John + Beamond <mark>
Thomas + Blackbrough new presenters
Midgley

[endorsed] Richard Scarbrough / Joshuah Dearden / Thomas Oldfeild / Thomas Barker

L

Aprell 8th 1689

The constable of Rusworth come Norland, who saith their Highways are good Repaire, stocks, butts and pindfold also. And wee have noe presentments.

[signed]
Isack I Botumley <his mark> George W Whittley <his mark>
Overseers
Michael Sootell
John Crowther
James Roper Constable

[signed] Richard Scarbrough / Joshua Whithead / Thomas Oldfeild / Richard Patchett

Rishworth cum Norland

[no endorsement]

M

Stansfield Bill Aprill the 8th 1689

These are to informe the good men of the Jury that scab'd horses and ston'd horses of our Comon wee have none. Ouer butts, stocks and cuckingstoole

are in good repaire, and all the hy wayes that was painde the last court are amended.
Now wee lay a paine of one hy way in Stansfield leading betweene Stansfield Kilne and the Crostone in thirteene and foure pence if it be not amended between and the next court.
Also wee lay a paine of one hy <way> in Stansfield leading betweene Ridge yeate and Hawkkstones in fifteene shillings if it be not amended betweene and the next court.
Wittness ouer hands
[signed] Richard Stansfield Constable | Amory Eastworth
James Stansfeild
Richard Scarbrough | his
Joshua Whithead | John I Horsfell
Thomas Oldfeild | mark
Richard Patchett | his
James I Greenwood
Stansfield [mark]
[no endorsement]

N i

Langfield Bill Aprell the 8th 1689
These are to informe the good men of the Jury of scab'd horses and stoned horses of ouer Common wee have none.
Ouer butts and stocks are in good repaire.
All the hy wayes that was pained the last court are amended within the time.
Now wee lay a paine of one hy <way> in Langfield leadeing betweene Jack-lee yeate and Salterrake in twenty shillings, if it be not amended betweene and the next court.
Also wee lay a paine of one hy way in Langfield leading betweene Nicholas Ogdens and Langfield Common in twenty shillings, if it be not amended between and Midsummer next.
Also wee lay a paine of one hy way in Langfield leading betweene Stootly yeate and Load yeate in five shillings, if it be not amended between and the next court.
Wittnesse ouer hands
[signed] Thomas Walton Constable | John Ingham
Abraham Clegge
Daniel x Greenwood <his mark>
Abraham A Heape <his mark>
[signed] Richard Scarbrough / Joshua Whithead / Abraham Brigge /

Michael Oldfield

Langfield

[no endorsement]

N ii

Langfield

Also wee lay apaine of one hy <way> in Langfield leading betweene Stansfield bridge and the bridge stone betweene an roomfield in tenne shilling, if it be not amended betweene and Midsommer next.
Also wee lay apaine of one hy way in Langfield leading betweene roomefield and Todmorden water in tenne shillings, if it be not amended betweene and Midsommer next.
Wittness ouer hands

[signed]	Thomas Walton Constable	John Ingham
		Abraham Clegge
	Richard Scarbrough	Daniell x Greenwod his mark
	Joshuah Dearden	Abraham A Heape his mark
	Thomas Oldfeild	
	Richard Thomas	

[no endorsement]

O

April the 8th 89

Heptonstall Bill

Wee foure together with the Constable do inform the Court as followeth: Our hye wayes in Heptonstall togather <with> our buts, stocks, pinfould, cookestole are in good repair.
We lay apaine of 20^{s} shillings upon the way leading betwixt Whitreaps Clogh and Greenhill end in Stansfield to be amended betwixt and the 24th of June by the inhabitants thear unto ajoyning or whon it doth concern. What was pained the last court leet is amended. Other misdemenors we know none.

[signed]	Richard Scarbrough	[1]John Horsfull
	Joshua Whithead	[1]Jonathan Crabtre
	Joshuah Dearden	[1]Timothy Horsfull
		John Fyswycke
		[1]William Greenwood Constable

Abraham Brigge / Michael Oldfield / Thomas Oldfield / Richard Scarbrough (sic)

[1] In same hand

Heptonstall

[no endorsement]

P

Aprill the 8th day 1689

Erringden Bill for the Constable

Butts and Stoks and Ways are in Good Repeair: and as for all other things we know none.

[signed] John Thomas Isaack Farrar Constable
John Farrar
Henry Sunderland
Henry Ridehough Presenters
Erringden

[endorsed] Richard Scarbrough / Joshua Whithead / Abaraham Brigge / Michaell Oldfield

membrane 17 continued

Brighouse view of frankpledge and court leet held on 9 April 1 William and Mary [1689]

Panel for the King and Queen Inquest taken on the oaths of Joseph Lister, Francis Prestley, William Garlicke, Thomas Lacy, Thomas Johnson, Jonathan Threapland, Joseph Wood, Samuel Apleyeard, William Hanson, Thomas Dyson, Henry Hanson, Michael Bentley and John Ramsden, jurors.

HIPPERHOLME Joshua Wright, constable, and his fellows presented that all was well.

RASTRICKE Joseph Thornton, constable, and his fellows presented that all was well.

FIXBY Samuel Dyson, constable, and his fellows presented that all was well.

NORTHOWROME Samuel Crowther, constable, and his fellows presented that all was well.

SHELFE Joshua Knight, constable, and his fellows presented that William Cliffe, clerk, did not scour his ditch adjoining the vennel leading to Sinderhills as previously pained *amerced 13s 4d*

Item, William Cliffe did not make <sufficient> the footpath, nor scour his ditch, nor switch his hedge across le Ingehead leading to Wester Croft as previously pained *amerced 13s 4d.*

QUARMBY George Hey, constable, and his fellows presented that all was well.

DALTON Joseph Dyson, constable, and his fellows presented that all was well
HARTISHEAD <with CLIFTON> Joshua Hanson and William Child, constables, and their fellows presented that all was well.
STAINLAND Geoffrey Ramsden, constable, and his fellows presented that all was well.
BARKISLAND Joseph Houlroid, constable, and his fellows presented that all was well.

Rastrick (134) It was attested by Robert Ramsden, lords' tenant, that John Hoyle of Rastricke, clothier, and Anne Hoyle of the same, spinster, on 2 January last surrendered into the lords' hands and quitclaimed for ever all rights, title, interest, remainder, reversion, hereditament, possible claim or demand in the messuage called Brigroyde with its appurtenances in Rastricke with all houses, structures, folds, gardens and two closes of land, meadow and pasture called le Great Inge and le Little Inge and all ways, waters, watercourses, liberties and hereditaments whatsoever appurtenant, now occupied by the said John Hoyle or his assigns at an annual lords' rent of [blank], compounded: to the use of Lady Everid' Thornhill, her heirs and assigns for ever. Fine for enrolment, 6d.

Sum of court [blank]

[in draft, membrane 94 dorse]

Hipperholme cum Brighouse	Joshua Wright constable, Jeremy Robinson deputy
Rastricke	Joseph Thornton constable, John Hirst deputy
Fixby	Samuel Dyson constable
Northowrome	Samuel Crowther constable
Shelfe	Joshua Knight constable
Quarmby	George Hey constable
Dalton	Joseph Dyson constable
Hartishead cum Clifton	Joshua Hanson constable: William Child constable
Stainland	Geoffrey Ramsden constable
	membrane 95
Barkisland	Joseph Houlroyd constable

[in draft, after membrane 95 dorse]

A

Brighouse Court Leet, 9° April 1689

Joseph Lister, gen, sworn

Francis Preistley	Jonathan Threapland	Thomas Dyson
William Garlicke	Joseph Wood	Henry Hanson
Thomas Lacy	Samuel Appleyeard	Michael Bentley
Thomas Johnson	William Hanson	John Ramsden

William Ramsden sworn constable of Clifton
Edward Ibberson sworn pinder of Lindley
William Ramsden sworn pinder of Rastricke

[no endorsement]

B

Hipperholme cum Brighouse Bill

Imprimis Wee lay in paine Joseph Wright, John Hanson and Abraham Mallinson for not mending the lane leading from John Thorps to Spoutehous in each of them v^s

Item We lay in paine Stephen Hird, John Houldroyd for not makeing a sufficient foote causee betwixt Hipperholme towne to the stile leading towards Coley Chappell in each of them v^s

Item We lay in paine Joshua Wright for not switching his hedges against his grounds in the lane leading from Hipperholme towards Priestly Greene and to make a sufficient horse causie as hath beene formerly betwixt and Midsumer next, in paine of each of them v^s

Item We lay in paine Jonathan Priestly junior, Widow Empsall, Joseph Firth, Joseph Halliday for not mending their way leading fro Empsall Pond to Priestley Greene, in each of them v^s

Item We lay in paine Francis Priestley, Joseph Halliday and Joseph Firth for not mending the Greene against their grounds of Priestley Greene, in each of them vj^s 8^d

Item We lay in paine Joseph Sucksmith, Mrs Langley and John Roberts to mend the lane against their grounds betwixt Helliwell Sicke and Broad Lane end betwixt and Midsumer next, in each of them v^s

Item We laine in paine Jonathan Priestley and John Roberts to amend the lane against their grounds leading from Sowood house to John Rishworths and to make a sufficient foote causie betwixt and Midsumer next, in paine of each of them v^s

Item We lay in paine John Whiteaker that he amend the foote causie and switch the hedge leading from Henry Gills to Lightclif Chappell betwixt and Midsumer next, in paine of v^s

Item We lay in paine Henry Gill to pull downe the wale of James Shackleton hous end and to make a stile for the footeway as formerly <betwixt and Midsumer next>, in paine of x^s

Item We lay in paine that Henry Brooke scower the ditch leading from Gilbett Sturdeys to his house *in paine of* betwixt and Midsumer next, in paine of v^s

Item We lay in paine that Samuel Smith switch the hedge and scower the ditch and mend the foote causie leading from his house to John Moses betwixt and Midsumer next, in paine of v^s

Item We lay in paine Richard Hudson for turneing the water out of its antient course to the annoyance of the foote way leading betwixt Hipperholme Wells and the laine ends betwixt and Midsumer next, in paine of v^s

Item We lay in paine George Stockes to mend his way against his court wall betwixt and Midsumer next, in paine of v^s

Item We lay in paine James Tettlow to lay open the stile that leads from the top of Tom Royd to Lightcliff Chappll betwixt and Midsumer next, in paine x^s

Hipperholme cum Brighouse

[dorse]

Item We lay in paine James Tettlow that he mend the <foote> way betwixt his house and the woodhead betwixt and Midsumer next, in paine x^s

Item We lay in paine Jeremy Battley, John Gill, and John Frost and Nathan Firth that they mend the way leading betwixt Lightcliffe Chappell and Bothome Hall Brig betwixt and Midsumer next, in paine of xx^s

Item We lay in paine John Crooke that he amend his way that leads from James Litle to *the* his water course betwixt and Midsummer next, in paine of v^s

Item We lay in paine the owner of the lands that adjoynes upon the way leading betwixt Thomas Woodhous hous and Brighous lane head betwixt and Midsumer next, in paine v^s

Item We lay in paine Judah Hoyle that he keepe open the water course that the water may have its antient course thro the towne of Brighous from spoyling the street of Brighous from time to time, in paine of x^s

Item We lay in paine Joseph Rayner that he remove his miden of donge which adjoyns upon Brighous causie betwixt and the 10th May next, in paine of x^s

Item We present Abraham Lum, Paulle Hoyle, Henry Flather, Judah Hoyle and John Nickolls for turning out their swine unyoaked and ronge, on every of them 4^d

[signed] the marke of
Jer: + Robinson constable
the marke of
Jer IZK Hempsall

Jos: Lister
Francis Preistley
Jo: Wood
Samuell Appleyeard

John Smith
Stephen Hird
Abraham A Millner <the marke of>

C

Rastricke Bill at the Court Leet holden at Brighouse the 9th of Aprill 1689
Wee the presentours together with the Constable say that since the last Courte Leet or before we have not seen or knowne any person or persons, thing or things, presentable within our said Townshippe: Witnesse our hands.
Onely we lay in paine that if Isaac Bates of Rastricke doe not before the First day of May next make and hang of his owne proper charge one yate at Bradley lane end, commonly called High Lane Yate, and hang the same yate there in the accustomed place on this side or before the said First day of May next comeing, for such default to forfeit 10s

[signed] Samuell Rigley — John Bothroyd
S his marke — his I marke
John Whitehead — Joshua Hall
his I marke — his I marke
John Hirst Deputy Constable
Jos: Lister / Francis Preistley / Jo: Wood
Rastricke

[no endorsement]

D

Fixby Bill at the Court Leet at Brighouse the 9th of Aprill 1689
We the presenters and Constable say that since the last Courte Leet or before we have not seen or knowne any person or persons, thing or things, presentable within our said Townshippe: Witnesse our hands.

[signed] Thomas Whitehead — Jos: Lister
his T marke — Francis Preistley
Joshua Brooke — John Wood
his I marke
The marke of — Thomas Johnson
Z
Samuell Dison Constable
Fixby

[no endorsement]

E

Northowram paines laid at the Court Leet houlden at Brighouse by us whose names are hear under subscribed, Aprill the 9th 1689.

Inprimes Wee lay in paine Joshua Sonyer, John Horldsworth and George Odey to dyke thear dikes that the water may have free passige away, and to mend the lane sufitiantly betwixt and Midsumer next, in every one of them 00^{li} 06^{s} 08^{d}

Ittem Wee lay in paine Michall Ramsden and William Gill to open thear dikes and to take in the watter at the accostomed places in the lane from Michall Ramsdens to the north lane end betwixt and Midsumer next, in either of them 00 03 04

Ittem Wee lay in paine William Gill and Jeremy Swift to take in the watter at the accustomed places and to mend the way sufitiantly from William Gill lane up the way that goeth to north lane soe farr as thear ground lieth betwixt and Midsumer next, in ether of them 00 03 04

Ittem We lay in paine George Bothamly and Joshua Hopkin to mend the cause and to turne of the water frome the said cause and make the way more passable betwixt and Midsumer next, in ether of them 00 06 08

Ittem Wee lay in paine Joshua *Hopkin* Hodshon and William Snowden, William Shepard to mend the cause sufitiantly from William Greens up to the top of Pule lane betwixt and Midsumer next, in every <one> of them 00 06 08

Ittem Wee lay in paine William Gill and John Wells to mend the Barms-Hill lane sufitiantly betwixt and Midsumer next, in ether of them six shillinges eight pence 00 06 08

Ittem Wee lay in paine George Oddey to mend the cause betwixt the yate that leadeth to his owne house and the lower end of his croft and to mend the Brigg stone at the Croft Botam betwixt and Midsumer next in three shillinges four pence 00 03 04

[signed]	Joseph Lister	Samauall Crouther Constable
	Francis Preistley	Jeremy Jaggar
	Jonathan <marke> Threapland	Jonathan Bairstow
		John Knowles
		James Greaves presentors

Northowrome

[no endorsement]

F i [pinned to F ii]

Shelfe Appriell 9th 1689

Samuell Wardman doth laye in payne any parson that shall make a waye over his Greate Inge, treadinge his corne (except it be from the steel at the Mountaine Ingeside to the steell in the Great Inge over against the Mountaine steelle), in paine of Twentie shillings 20^{s}

[signed] Joseph Lister
Francis Preistley per Samuell Wardman
Joseph Wood

[no endorsement]

F ii

Apriell the 9th

Shelfe Paines layed at the Court leet houlden at Brigghouse

Imprimis Wee laye in payne Benjaman Jagger that he amend the lane suffitientley over against his grownds from the smithie greene to Widdow Sunderlands Intake, in payne of $13^{s}\ 04^{d}$

Item Wee laye in payne Samuell Wade to amend the lane from against his owne house to Samuel Whiteley intack-end sufficiently and scower his ditch on the uper side of the lane betwixt and Midsomer next, in payne of $13^{s}\ 04^{d}$

Item Wee laye in payne Joshua Benn that he amend the way rownd about his Hadhill Intake betwixt and Midsomer next, in payne of $06^{s}\ 08^{d}$

Item We lay in payne Samuell Bentley and Joshua Benn that they amend the way suffitientley over against their grounds betwixt and Midsomer next, in payne of either of them $06^{s}\ 08^{d}$

Item Wee laye in payne Widdow Brewor that shee amend the way against her intacke to the Brigstone, in payne of $06^{s}\ 08^{d}$

Item Wee laye Mr Ellison and Widdow Brewor to amend the waye in the back lane over against their grownds betwixt and Midsomer next, in payne of either of them $03^{s}\ 04^{d}$

Item Wee laye in payne John Burneley, Joseph Sunderland, John Ayckroyd, Abraham Woodhead that they amend the way over against their grounds betwixt and Midsomer next, in payne of every one of them $05^{s}\ 00^{d}$

Item Wee laye in payne Peter Ambler and Abraham Woodhead to amend the waye leadeing up to Giles hill betwixt and Midsomer next, in payne of either of them $03^{s}\ 04^{d}$

Item Wee laye in payne John Brige, Peter Ambler, Daniell Bateman, John Woodhead, John Ayckroyd, Benjamain Jaggor and Mr Ellison that they amen (sic) the waye over against their grownds in Newbrigg lane and laye the Briggstone betwixt and Middsomer next, in payne of everyone of them $03^{s}\ 04^{d}$

Item Wee laye in payne John Brooke and Widdow Waddsworth <and Timothy Smith> that they amend the waye in Hopper lane betwixt and Middsomer next, in payne of everyone of them $03^{s}\ 04^{d}$

Item Wee present Mr Cliff for not scowereing his ditch in the lane side leadeing to Sinderhills accordinge to severall other former paynes 13^{s} 4

Item Wee present Mr Cliff for not makeinge a suffitient foote way and not scoweringe his ditch and swichinge his hedge over his Inge head leadeing to wards Wester croft accordeing to severall other former paynes 13^{s} 4

Item Wee laye in payne Mr Cliff and Samuell Bentley to amend the waye suffitient from the lane side at the back of Mr Cliffe lathe and over his Inge heade and <over> Samuell Bentleys holme leadeinge towards Hallefax, in payne of either of them 01^{li} 19^{s} 00^{d}

Item Wee lay in payne Joshua Knight and James Scoalefield to amend the horse cause from Abraham Tempest house to the head of Cockhill clough head either of them against their owne grownds, in payne of either of them 03^{s} 04^{d}

[signed] Joseph Lister / Francis Preistley / Joseph Wood / Samuell Appleyeard

Samuell Wardman / Samuell Whietley / William Sharpe / John J mark Burneley presentors / Joshua Knight Constable

Shelfe

[no endorsement]

G i

At the Court Leet at Brighouse April 9th Anno domini 1689

Item William Waterhouse of Linley doe lay a paine every person or persons that shall drive or fetch any beasts or horses or make any horse way over or through one croft in Linley called Suncrofte, for every person every time soe offending to forfeite 1^{s}

[signed] Joseph Lister / Francis Preistley / Samuell Appleyeard

William Waterhouse

Quarmby

[no endorsement]

G ii

Quarmby Bill at the Court Leet holden at Brighouse the 9th of Aprill 1689

Wee the Constable and Presentours of Quarmby doe lay in paine that if Anne Clay and James Ryley of Linley doe not before the Tenth day of May next repaire and make passable for horses with packs and loads the way betweene the Salter lane bottome and the Birchincliffe, for such default 6^{s} 8^{d}

Item wee lay in paine that if James Haigh or John Haigh or any other of the inhabitants of Linley doe leave the yate open called Lidyate Lane yate, or the yate called Townend yate, and not shut the same immediately after they have occasion to passe that way, for every such default xij^{d}

Other paines or presentments we have none.

Witnesse our hands

[signed] Thomas Denton / William Morehouse / Thomas Haigh
John Sykes / George Hey
William H Hanson his marke Constable
Joseph Lister / Francis Preistley / Joseph Wood
Quarmby

[no endorsement]

H

Dalton Bill

The Court Leett holden at Brighouse Aprill the 9 day 1689

Wee the Ould Presentor together with the Constabell today since the last Court Leett do find no thing presentabel withein our toune, as witnes our handes.

[signed] Joseph Lister Thomas T <his marke> Killner
Francis Preistley Joseph Dyson Constabel
Joseph Wood Thomas Dison
Dalton

[no endorsement]

I

Hartshead cum Clifton Bill at the Court Leet at Brighouse the 9th of Aprill 1689

Wee the Presentours and Constable doe lay in paine that the Hardsoyle yate and Lidyate yate in Clifton be well fenced and sufficiently hung before the tenth day of May next, those that are concerned therein every one to forfeit for their neglect 1^{s}

Item we lay in paine that John Ransley and John Scott doe switch the hedges and scoure the ditches in Thornhill lane and for default thereof either of them to forfeit 6^{s} 8^{d}

Item we lay in paine every person and persons that shall keep any swine without yokes and rings, for every such person so offending to forfeit 3^{s} 4^{d}

Other paines or presentments we have none.

Witnesse our hands:

[signed] John Flather + his marke The Mark of William ┌ Child

Constable
Samuell SL Lumme his marke
Hartishead cum Clifton
[endorsed] Joseph Lister / Francis Preistley / Joseph Wood / Henery his H mark Hansen

J

Stainland Bill Apprill the 9th 1689
These are to scartifie to the Jury of this Court that wee doe not find anything painable or presentable at this present.
Wittnes our hands:
[signed] Abraham Crowther Jeffery Ramsden Constable
John I Sickes marke
Joseph Lister / Francis Preistley / Joseph Wood / Michael Bentley
Stainland
[no endorsement]

K

Apprill the 9th 1689
Barkisland Bill
Item wee lay in pain that no parson or parsons shall pull downe any fence or make any way over one close of land called the Great Lightlyroyd belonging to George Houlroid of Barkisland, in paine for every default 3s 4d
[signed] Henery H marke Crosley / Jeremiah Crosley / Joseph Houlroid
Constable
[signed] Joseph Lister / Francis Preistley / Joseph Wood / John Ramsden
Barkisland
[no endorsement]

membrane 17 continued

Burton view of frankpledge and court leet held on 10 April 1 William and Mary [1689]

Panel for King and Queen Inquest taken on the oaths of Richard Morton, Luke Wilson, James Fraunce, John Tinker, John Battye, Joshua Tinker, John Fitton, Thomas Firth, Thomas Dey, Thomas Morehouse, George Kay, Thomas Peace and Robert Hare, jurors.
KIRKEBURTON Samuel Wood and William Moone, constables, and their fellows presented that all was well.

SHELLEY John Peace, constable, and his fellows presented that all was well.
SHEPLEY Joseph Hobson, constable, and his fellows presented that all was well.
CUMBERWORTH William Oxley, constable, and his fellows presented that all was well.
ELMLEY John Page, constable, and his fellows presented that all was well.
FLOCKTON John Walshawe, constable, and his fellows presented that all was well.
THURSTONLAND Abraham Lockwood, constable, and his fellows presented that all was well.
HOLME Joshua Roades, constable, and his fellows presented that all was well.
FULSTONE township presented that all was well.
SCHOLES township presented that all was well.
WOOLDALE township presented that all was well.
CARTWORTH township presented that all was well.
AUSTONLEY township presented that all was well.
HEPWORTH township presented that all was well.
THWONGE township presented that all was well.

membrane 17 dorse

Holme (135) Hester Wilson, wife of Luke Wilson, and Anne Genn, daughters and next heirs of Henry Genn, late of Totties, deceased, came before the steward and paid 15s 2¼d for leave to inherit all the compounded land and [blank] for uncompounded land at Totties with other land in Scholes late of the inheritance of the said Henry Genn and held in copyhold, with all ways, waters, watercourses, easements, profits and commodities appurtenant in Wooldale and Scholes in the graveship of Holme, all now occupied by Elizabeth Genn and Daniel Cartwright or their assigns at an annual lords' rent of 5s 2¾d, compounded, except for a close called Greenhillbanck, being parcel of the same, held at an annual lords' rent of 2d, non-compounded, following the death of Henry Genn. Agreed.

- (136) It was attested by Luke Wilson, lords' tenant, that Humphrey Wilson of Wooldale Towne End on 8 April instant surrendered into the lords' hands the reversion after the death of the said Humphrey of a messuage at Wooldale Towne End with all houses, barns, structures, stables, folds, orchards, gardens and yards appurtenant, and all closes of arable, meadow or pasture commonly called le Croft adjoyneing to the house, another called Wardcroft adjoining le Croft, another called Wellynge adjoining the barn, another called Bentonyhill adjoining Wellynge, another called Longynge or Weetynge also adjoining Wellynge, another called Everoyde, also all several doles called Byerdole land lying in the several fields of Wooldale, namely a dole to the north side of le West field, another on the upper side of le Middle field, another lying in le Wheat Croft, two doles in a field called Oldhouse, another lying in le Kirkeroyds, and two doles in le Morecroft, with all other land, etc, and all ways, waters, watercourses, profits, liberties, privileges, benefices, easements, emoluments and hereditaments appurtenant in Wooldale in the graveship of Holme, now occupied by the said Humphrey Wilson or his assigns at an annual lords' rent of 1s 10d, compounded: to the absolute use of John Wilson of Netherthwonge, son and heir of the said Humphrey, and Mary, now wife of the said John Wilson, their heirs and assigns for ever. Reversion agreed: entry fine, 2s 9d.

- (137) It was attested by James France, lords' tenant, that Joshua Charlesworth of Mossedge on 4 April instant surrendered into the lords' hands a messuage or residence at le Overhill house with all barns, structures, folds, gardens and appurtenances, and all land, closes, meadow, pasture, wood, underwood and appurtenances, also a close at le Netherhill house called Great Brearley and a close called Brearlee head, and another called Broadynge, now in two closes, with all edifices built threon, with all ways etc, in Cartworth in the graveship of Holme, now occupied by Thomas Winpenie or his assigns at an annual lords' rent of 5s, compounded: to the use of Thomas Winpenie, his executors, administrators and assigns from 2 February last for 19 years at an annual rent of £14, payable to the said Joshua Charlesworth, his heirs and assigns, at Whitsun and Martinmas in equal parts, with leave to distrain if late by 14 days. Agreed: entry fine, 7s 6d.

- (138) It was attested by John Tincker, lords' tenant, that Elizabeth Genn, widow, on 20 June last surrendered into the lords' hands a messuage called Greenhillbanck, a barn, a garden, a fold, and all houses and structures appurtenant, and all those closes of arable, meadow and pasture known as le Bryanroyd, le Banck, le Croft, le Flat, le Greenshill field (now in two closes), le Browe and le Inge, with all ways, etc in Wooldale in the graveship of Holme, now occupied by Daniel Cartwright or his assigns at an annual lords' rent of 3s 8d, compounded (except for the close called Banck, non-compounded): to the use of the said Daniel Cartright, his executors, administrators and assigns from 2 February last for 22 years at an annual rent to Elizabeth Genn, her heirs and assigns of £8 3s 4d, payable at Whitsun and Martinmas in equal parts within 20 days of falling due, and paying all taxes and rates levied during the term (except on assessments for maintenance of 'footarms' and service as officers, ministers and constables), with repairs to the buildings, known, *Anglice,* as *Mosse and Morter*, during the term, and leave to distrain if there were default of payment within 20 days, returning any surplus. Agreed: entry fine 5s 6d for compounded land and [blank] for the non-compounded.

- (139) It was attested by John Batty, lords' tenant, that Josiah Berry of Hepworth and Dinah Berry his mother on 21 November 1687 surrendered into the lords' hands a house in which the same Josiah Berry now lived, with all structures appurtenant at the west end of a fold lying to the south of the same house, a garden at the west end of the house, another house lately built on the south of the said fold, and a parcel of ground at the lower end of the house, now with 'a draw well', with all folds, profits and commodities appurtenant in Hepworth in the graveship of Holme, now occupied by the said Josiah Berry or his assigns at an annual lords' rent of 3¼d, compounded: to the use of George Morehouse, his heirs and assigns for ever, on condition that if Josiah Berry, Dinah Berry, or either, their heirs, executors, administrators or assigns, or any one paid or cause to be paid to the above George Morehouse, his executors, administrators or assigns the sum of £31 10s on 28 September next after the surrender at the residence of George Morehouse at Stonybanck the present surrender would become void. Agreed that subject to such conditions George Morehouse, his heirs and assigns hold the property for ever. Entry fine, 9¾d.

Sum of court [blank]

[in draft, membrane 96 dorse]
List of constables, namely
Kirkburton Samuel Wood and William Moone
Shelley John Peace
Shepley Joseph Hobson
Cumberworth William Oxley
Elmley John Page
Flockton John Walshawe
Thurstonland Abraham Lockwood
Holme Joshua Roades
Fulston [blank]
Scholes [blank]
Wooldale [blank]

membrane 97

Cartworth [blank]
Austonley [blank]
Hepworth [blank]
Thwong [blank]

[in draft, after membrane 99]

A

Burton Court Leet panel, 10 April 1689

Richard Morton, sworn

Luke Wilson	Joshua Tincker	Thomas Morehouse
James France	John Fitton	George Kay
John Tincker	Thomas Firth	Thomas Peace
John Batty	Thomas Day	Robert Hare

John Pogson sworn constable of Shepley

Richard Firth sworn pinder of Kirkeburton

[no endorsement]

B

Item I present Henry Copley <of Skelmonthorpe> for not keepeing the usuall way to the coale pit in Hoyton broome belonging to Robert Hare, for every default 00^{li} 01^{s} 00d

Item I present Thomas Shaw of Emley parke for not keepeing the usuall high way to the coale pit in Hoyton broome belonging to Robert Hare, for every such default 00 01 00

[signed]	Richard Morton	Luke Wilson
	John Tincker	James France
	John Battye	Joshua Tinker
	John Fitton	Thomas Firth
	Thomas Peace	Thomas Morehous
	Gorge Kaye	Thomas Daye
	Robert Hare	

by enquiry

[no endorsement]

C

Paines laid at the Kings majesties court called the Shirrifs turne holden att Kirkeburton the 10th day of Aprill 1689

By the Constable and sworne men of Kirkeburton as followeth

Imprimis wee lay in paine that noe manner of person or persons shall cut or carry away either greene wood or drie out of other mens ground without licence of the owners thereof, in paine of every time soe seene, knowne or taken xij^{d}

Ittem wee lay in paine that all manner of person or persons whatsoever shall yoke and ringe theire swine and soe keepe them untill the next court day, in paine of every default xij^{d}

Ittem wee lay in paine that noe manner of person or persons whatsoever shall put any scab'd or infectious horses upon any of the Commons belongeinge to Kirkeburton, in paine of every default x^{s}

[signed] John Chapel Richard Morton
John Hardey John Battye
Robert Hurst Thomas Firth
Michel Pites Thomas Peace
Kirkeburton

[no endorsement]

D

Paines laid by the Constable and sworne men of Shelley at the Kinges Court called the Sherrifes turne holden at Kirkeburton the 10th day of Aprill 1689

Inprimis We lay in paine that no manner of person or persons shall carry away either green wood or dry out of other mens ground without the licence of the owners thereof, in paine of every time so seene, knowne or taken 12^{d}

Item We lay in paine that no manner of person or persons shall goe or ride over other mens ground where there is no usuall way, in paine of every time so seen, known or taken 1^{s} [written over 3^{s} 4^{d}]

Item we lay in paine that all the householders within the said towne shall yoke and ring their swine and so keepe them, in paine of default 12^{d}

Item We lay in paine that no manner of person or persons within the said towne shall put any scabbed horse or other infected beast unto any of the Commons belonging to the said towne, in paine of every time so seen, known or taken 10^{s}

[signed] Arthur Lee Richard Morton
Thomas Silvester Luke Wilson
Edward Tinker James France
John Denton John Tincker
Shelley

[no endorsement]

E

Paines laid by the Constable and sworne men of Shepley at the Kinges Court called the Sherrifes turne holden at Kirkeburton 10th Aprill 1689

Imprimis We lay in paine that no manner of person or persons shall carry away either dry wood or green out of other mens ground without the licence of the owners thereof, in paine of every time so seen, known or taken 12^{d}
Item We lay in paine that no manner of person or persons shall goe or ride over other mens ground where there is no usuall way, in paine of every time so seen, known or taken $1^{s}\ 0^{d}$ [written over $3^{s}\ 4^{d}$]
Item We lay in paine that all the householders within the said towne shall yoke and ringe their swine and so keepe them, in paine of every default 12^{d}
Item We lay in paine that no manner of person or persons shall put any scabbed horse or other infected beast unto any of the Commons belonging to the said towne, in paine of every time so seen, known or taken 10^{s}
Item We lay in paine that Joseph Garside shall not turne the water out of the usuall course in the Hall sike, in paine of every such default 10^{s}
[signed] John Hobson
Joseph Swallow

Item We lay in paine that no one turn the water out of the usuall water course in the March lane contrary to custom, in pain of every such default 10^{s}

Richard Morton / Luke Wilson / John Tincker / James France
Shepley

[no endorsement]

F

Paines laid by the Constable and sworne men of Cumberworth halfe at the Kinges Court called the Sherrifes turne holden at Kirkeburton 10th Aprill 1689
Imprimis We lay in paine that no manner of person or persons shall carry away either green wood or dry out of other mens ground without the licence of the owners thereof, in paine of every time so seen, known or taken 12^{d}
Item We lay in paine that no manner of person or persons shall goe or ride over other mens ground where there is no way, in paine of every time so seen, knowne or taken $1^{s}\ 0^{d}$ [written over $3^{s}\ 4^{d}$]
Item We lay in paine that all the householders within the said towne shall <yoke and> ringe their swine and so keepe them, in paine of every default 12^{d}
Item We lay in paine that no manner of person or persons within the said towne shall put any scabbed horses or other infectious beast unto any of the Commons belonging the said towne, in paine of every time so seen, known or taken 10^{s}

Item We lay in paine that Richard Goodale of Cumberworth do make sufficient fence betwixt one close in his possession called Parcar and the Common at or before the 10th day of May next, in paine of such default 5^{s}

[signed] Joseph Childe Richard Morton
George Priest Thomas Peace
Thomas Firth
John Battye
Cumberworth

[no endorsement]

G

Paines laid by the Constable and sworne men of Emley at the Kinges Court called the Sherrifes turne holden at Kirkeburton the 10th of Aprill 1689

Imprimis We lay in paine that no manner of person or persons shall carry away either dry wood or green out of other mens ground without the licence of the owners thereof, in pain of every time so seen, known or taken 12^{d}

Item We lay in paine that no person or persons shall goe or ride over other mens ground where there is no usuall way, in paine of every time so seen, known or taken $1^{s}\ 0^{d}$ [written over $3^{s}\ 4^{d}$]

Item We lay in paine that all the householders within the said towne shall yoke and ringe their swine and so keepe them, in paine of every default 12^{d}

Item We lay in paine that no manner of person or persons within the said towne shall put any scabbed horse or other infected beast unto any of the Commons belonging the said towne, in paine of every time so seen, known or taken 10^{s}

Item We lay in paine John Blaker do make his fence sufficient betwixt Richard Woofenden *Nether* Nettlebeddes and his, in paine of such defaulte $0^{li}\ 3^{s}\ 4^{d}$ [written over illegible sum]

Item We lay in paine that no manner of persons do make any way with horse or teame over two closes belonging to Richard Woofenden, the one called the Great Close, the other called *Nether* <Nettlebedes>, in paine of every time so seen, known or taken $13^{s}\ 4^{d}$ [written over $01^{li}\ 00^{s}\ 00^{d}$]

Item We lay in paine that Widow Hepworth and John Hepworth do make their fence sufficient betwixt Matthew Taylor field piece and their tom thorne betwixt this day and the 1st of <June> *May* next, in paine of such default $13^{s}\ 4^{d}$ [written over $00^{li}\ 10^{s}\ 00^{d}$]

Item We lay in paine that no manner of persons shall make any foot way over Mr Richardson Banke closes, in paine of every time so seen, known or taken $00^{li}\ 01^{s}\ 00^{d}$

Item We lay in paine that the occupiers of Christopher Bingley land adjoyneing to Emley moore do make their fence sufficient before the first day of *May* <June> next, in paine of such default
0^{li} 6^{s} 8^{d} [written over illegible sum]
**Item* We lay in paine that Widow Hepworth and John Hepworth do sett their hedge in the right place betwixt [ ] [blank]*
Item We lay in paine that Joseph Marshall do make all his fences sufficient betwixt him and Peter Warbleton before the first day of May next, in paine of such default 0^{li} 03^{s} 4^{d} [written over 01^{li} 0^{s} 0^{d}]
Item We lay in paine that no manner of person or persons doe make any foot way over the old roide belonging to William Field, in paine of every time so seen, known or taken 00^{li} 01^{s} 00^{d}
Item We lay in paine that Matthew Marshall doe make his fence sufficient betwixt him and Dame Allot before the 1st of <June> *May* next, in paine of each default 00^{li} 03^{s} 04^{d}
Item We lay in paine that every one occupieing any land joyneing to the high way in Emley parke doe make the wayes sufficient before the first day of *May* June, in paine of such default 00 06 08

[signed] Adam Donkersley — Richard Morton
John Lockwood — Luke Wilson
John Gleadhill — Joshua Tinker
John Childe sworne men — Thomas Morehouse
Elmley

[no endorsement]

H

Paines laid at the Kings Majesties Court called the Shiriffes turne holden at Kikeburton the 10th day of Aprill 1689

by the Constable and sworne men of Flockton Nether ass followeth:

Inprimis Wee lay in paine that no maner off person or persons whatsoever shall cut or cary away either greene wood or dry out off other mens ground without licence of the owner thereof, in paine of every time soe seene, knowne or taken xij^{d}
Wee lay in paine that all maner of person or persons whatsoever shall ringe and yoke their swine and soe keepe them, in paine of every default xij^{d}
Wee lay in paine that no maner of person or persons whatsoever shall put any scabed or infectious horses or meares unto the said Comon belonging the said towne, in paine of everie time so seene or knowne or taken x^{s}

Wee lay in paine that all maner of persons belonging the townshipe switch their hedges, scearse theire diches, wich is a common anoyance <to> the high way, for every fault xij^d
Wee lay in paine that George Robouthur of Hee Burton doe hinge a yate a tope of John Sickes closes above Thomas Walshawes beffor the sixth day of May in 3^s 4^d *xij^d*
[signed] James T Goulthorp sworn man John Walshaw Constable
Flockton
[signed] Richard Morton / Thomas Peace / Thomas Firth / John Battye
[no endorsement]

I

Peanes laid by the Constable and sworne men of Thurstoland at the Kings Court called the Shirife turne houlden at Kirkeburton the 10 day of Aperill 1689
Item we lay in paine that no maner of parson or parsons shal cut and cari away greene wood or drye out of other mens grounds, in peane of every time so seen, knowne or taken 5^s
Item We lay in paine that no maner of parson or parsons shal [goe] over other mens grounds where there is no way, for everi default
1^s 0 [written over 3^s 4^d]
Item We lay in peane that no maner of parson or parsons goe over the Elys Clife where there is no way, in peane of every time so seene, knowne or taken 1^s 0 [written over 3^s 4^d]
[signed] Joshua Tinker Richard Morton
William Lockwood John Battye
sworne men John Tincker
Robert Hare
Thurstonland
[no endorsement]

J

Burton At the View of Francpledge and Court Leet of our Soveraigne Lord and Lady the King and Queen, with the Turne, hold there the tenth day of April in the first year of their reigne, Anno domini 1689

Paines layd by the Constable and sworn men of Holme
Imprimis Wee lay in pain that no persons carry away green wood or dry out of any mans grounds without the owners leave, in pain of every default 1^s
Item That all persons yoake and ring their swine and soe keep them at all times, in pain of every default soe known 1^s

Item That all persons scour their water courses adjoineing to the hyways and soe keep them, in pain of every default iij^{s} iiijd
Item That no persons travel over other mens grounds where there is noe usuall way, in pain of every default 1^{s}
Item That noe persons put any scabbed horses or other infectious cattell to the Commons, in pain of every default x^{s}
[signed] George Heptonstall Richard Morton
his H marke John Battye
William W Earnshaw Thomas Firth
his marke Thomas Peace
Holme
[no endorsement]

K Paines laid att his Majesties Court Leet commonly called the Scheiriffs Turne houlden att Kirkeburton on the 10th day of Aprill Anno domini 1689 by the Cunstable and sworn <men> of Foulstone as followeth
Imprimis We lye in pane that no manner of person or persons shall cut or carrie away out of other mens ground either green wood or dry without the licence or consent of the owner thereof, in paine of every default 01^{s}
Item We lay in pane that no manner of person or persons do put or let att libertie any scabed or infectious <beast> on to any of the Commons belonging to the towne, in paine of every defaut 10^{s}
Item We lye in paine that every one keep the water in its right accustomed courses by scouring of their ditches, in paine of every default 01^{s}
Item We lye in pane that every one that keep swine do yoke them and ring them and so keep them till the next court day, in paine of every default 01^{s}
Item We lye in paine that all manner of person or persons do fence their hedges and scoure their ditches joyning unto any ones hard corne, in <pane> of every default 01^{s}
[signed] Richard Morton Daniell O Bray his marke
Thomas Firth Thomas Morehous
Thomas Peace George Robuck
Richard Sonyor
John Battye
Fulstone
[no endorsement]

L

Paines laid at the King and Queen Court commonly call'd the sheirrif turne holden at Burton the 10th day of Aprell Anno Domini 1689 by the Constable and sworn men of Scoles as followeth:

Imprimis Wee lay in paine that noe maner of person or persons whatsoever shall cut or carry away either green wood or dry out of other mens ground without licence of the owner, in paine of every default xij^{d}

Item Wee lay in paine that all persons whatsoever that hath any swine shall yoke and ring them and soe keep them, in paine of every such default xij^{d}

Item Wee lay in paine that all maner of persons whatsoever shall scower their ditches joyneing upon the high waies and keep the waters in their antient courses, in paine for such default iij^{s} iiij^{d}

Item Wee lay in paine that noe maner of person or persons whatsoever shall put any scabbed or infectious beast to any of our commons, in paine for every such default x^{s}

Item Wee lay in paine that noe maner of person or persons whatsoever shall goe over other mens ground where there is noe lawful way, in paine of every default xij^{d}

Item Wee lay in paine that those of the inhabitants of Foulstone which did formerly repaire one bridge commonly called Mearehouse Bridgge, lately decayed and broken downe, that the said inhabitants doe before the 24th day of June next ensueing set up and make a suffitient bridge there, according as formerly hath been, in paine for such default [blank]

[signed] Abraham Woodhead
Thomas B Booth
his marke

Item Wee lay in paine that noe maner of person shall goe over or through one wood called Milne hirst wood where there is noe way, in paine of every such default xij^{d}

Item Wee lay in paine that all persons make their fences suffitient joyneing to the afforesaid wood before the 24th of July next and soe keep them, in paine of iij^{s} iiij^{d}

[signed] Richard Morton / Robert Hare / Luke Wilson / James France Scholes

[no endorsement]

M

Burton At the View of Francpledge and Court Leet of our Soveraigne Lord and Lady the King and Queen with the Tourne holden there the Tenth day of April in the first year of their Raigne, Anno dominique 1689

Paines laid by the Constable and the sworne men of Wooldall

Imprimis Wee lay in pain that no manner of persons (sic) or persons cutt down or carry away either green wood or dry out of any other mens grounds without the owners lycence, in pain of every default soe known 0^{li} 1^{s} 0^{d}
Item Wee lay in pain that all persons scour and drentche their ditches and watercourses adjoineing to the hy ways and soe keep them at all times, in pain of every default soe known 0 iij. $iiij^{d}$
Item Wee lay in pain that no person or persons goe or travell over any other mens grounds where there is noe usuall way or footpath, in pain of every default soe known 0 1^{s} 0
Item Wee lay in pain that all persons yoake and ring their swin and soe keep them at all times, in pain of every default so known 0 1^{s} 0
Item Wee lay in pain that noe person or persons set any cur or other dog at any mans sheep or other cattell or sleat any mans sheep upon the Commons, in pain of every default soe known 0 3^{s} $iiij^{d}$ [written over vj^{s} $viij^{d}$]
Item Wee lay in pain that noe persons put or turne forth any scabbed horses or other infectious cattell to any of the Commons, in paine of every default soe known 0 x^{s} 0
Item Wee lay in pain that noe person or persons passe or travell in over or through one parcell of ground in the occupacion of John Thorp called Croft or Brow lyeing betwixt his house and Spout, in pain of every default soe seen or known 0 1^{s} 0
**Item* Wee lay in pain that the severall occupiers of the grounds lyeing above John Castle house at Inghead doe keep the water in their grounds in the right courses there, that the same may descend and run down John Castle ynge over the way into the Sow Close, as of right it ought, and keep the same from cuming down the lane into the town of Holmefirth, in pain of every default soe known 0 x^{s} 0*

[signed] Thomas Hudson — Richard Morton
John + Tayler — Luke Wilson
Joshua I Ellis — James France
Joshua H Heeley — John Battye
Wooldale

[no endorsement]

N

Paines laid at the King and Queens court commonly called Sheiriffs Turne houlden at Burton the Tenth day of Aprell anno domini 1689 by the Constable and sworne men of Cartworth as followeth:

Imprimis Wee lay in paine that noe maner of person or persons whatsoever shall cut or carry away either green wood or dry out of other mens ground without licence of the owner thereof, in paine of every default xij^{d}

Item Wee lay in paine that all persons that hath any swine shall yoke and ring them and soe keep them, in paine of such default xij^{d}

Item Wee lay in paine that all maner of persons whatsoever shall scower their ditches joyneing upon the high waies and keep the waters in their antient accustomed coursses, in paine of every such default iij^{s} iiij^{d}

Item Wee lay in paine that noe maner of person or persons whatsoever shall put any scabed or infectious beast to any of our Commons, in paine for every such default x^{s}

Item Wee lay in paine that noe maner of person or persons whatsoever shall goe over other mens ground where there is noe lawfull way, in paine of every default xij^{d}

[signed] Robert $^{\text{his mark}}$ Hinchcliffe
R
Joseph I Hinchcliffe
his mark
John Hinchcliffe
Henry Morton

Item wee lay in pain that no persons travell over or through the grounds of Richard Hoyland called the Inge and the Over Modwoodleys, in pain of every default xij^{d}

Richard Morton / Luke Wilson / James France / Robert Hare

Cartworth

[no endorsement]

O

Burton At the View of Francpledge and Court Leet of our Soveraigne Lord and Lady the King and Queen in the Tourne holden there the Tenth day of Aprill in the first year of their raigne, anno domini 1689

Paines laid by the Constable and the sworne men of Austonley

Imprimis Wee lay in pain that no manner of person or persons cutt down or carry away either green wood or dry out of any other mens grounds without the owners lycence, in pain of every default soe known 0^{li} 1^{s} 0^{d}

Item Wee lay in pain that all persons scour and drentch their ditches and water courses adjoineing on the hywayes and soe keep them at all times, in pain of every default soe known 0 iij^{s} iiij^{d}

Item Wee lay in pain that no persons goe or travell over any other mens grounds where there is noe usuall way or foot path, in pain of every default soe known 0 j^{s} 0

Item Wee lay in pain that all persons yoake and ring their swine and soe keep them at all times, in pain of every default soe known 0 j^{s} 0

Item Wee lay in pain that noe person or persons set any cur or other dog at any mans sheep or other cattell or sleat any mans sheep upon the Commons, in pain of every default soe known 0 3^{s} iiij^{d} [written over 0 vj^{s} viij^{d}]
Item Wee lay in pain that noe persons put or turne forth any scabbed horses or other infectious beasts or cattell to any of the Commons, in pain of every default soe known 0 x^{s} 0
Item Wee lay in pain that no persons travell over one close of Richard Croslands called the Hanging royd betwixt Bothoms and Hinchliffe Mill, in pain of every default soe knowne 0 j^{s} 0 [written over iij^{s} iiij^{d}]
Item Wee lay in pain that noe persons travell in over or through one close at Boothhouse called Boothhousebank in the occupacion of John Brooke out of the usuall way there and likewise one other close called Netherbanke, in pain of every default 0 j^{s} 0 [written over iij^{s} iiij^{d}]
Item Wee lay in pain that all persons keep the right foot path in one bothom called Round bothom in the occupacion of Joshua Eastwood, in pain of every default soe known 0 j^{s} 0 [written over iij^{s} iiij^{d}]
[signed] John B Brooke
Richard K Kay

Item that no persons travell out of the way in one close of Joshua Eastwood called Shroggs, in pain of every default 0 j^{s} 0

Richard Morton / Luke Wilson / James France / John Tincker
Austonley

[no endorsement]

P

Burton Att the View of Francpledge and Court Leet of our Sovereaigne Lord and Lady the King and Queen with the Turnne holden there the Tenth day of April in the First year of their Raigne, Annoque domini 1689

Paines layd by the Constable and the Sworne men of Hepworth

Imprimis Wee lay in pain that no manner of persons whatsoever cutt down or carry away either green wood or dry out of any other mens grounds without the owners lycence, in pain of every default so known 0^{li} 1^{s} 0^{d}
Item Wee lay in pain that all persons scour and drentch their ditches and water courses adjoineing upon the hy wayes and soe keep them at all times, in pain of every default soe known 0 iij^{s} iiij^{d}
Item Wee lay in pain that no person or persons goe or travel over any other mens grounds where there is no usuall way or footh path, in pain of every default soe known 0 j^{s} 0
Item Wee lay in pain that all persons yoake and ring their swine and soe keep them at all times, in pain of every default soe known 0 j^{s} 0

Item Wee lay in pain that no person or persons sett any curr or other dog at any mans sheep or other cattell or sleat any mans sheep upon the Commons, in pain of every default soe known 0 3^{s} iiij^{d} [written over vj^{s} viij^{d}]
Item Wee lay in pain that no persons put or turne forth any scabbed horses or other infectious beasts or cattell to any of the Commons, in pain of every default soe known 0 x^{s} 0
Item Wee lay in pain that noe persons travell out of the footpath in one close in the occupacion of Robert Beever called Hobcroft or fetch or drive any cattell over or through the same at any time or times thereafter, in pain of every default 0 j^{s} 0 [written over 0 iij^{s} iiij^{d}]
Item Wee lay in pain that Christopher Kaye younger make up his ditch and fence betwixt his grounds called Dein royds and the grounds of John Brown called Deinroyds (sic) and soe keep the same, in pain of every default
0 10^{s} 0 [written over 1^{li} .. illegible]

[signed] John I Brown his marke
Godfrey + Beever his marke
Richard Morton / Luke Wilson / James France / Robert Hare
Richard Z Healiwell his marke
William W Shaw his marke
Hepworth

[no endorsement]

Q

Burton At the View of Francpledge and Court Leet of our Soveraigne Lord and Lady King and Queen with the Tourn holden there the Tenth day of April in the First year of their Raigne Annoque domini 1689

Paines layd by the Constable and the Sworne men of Thonge

Imprimis Wee lay in pain that no person or persons cutt down or carry away either green wood or dry out of any other mens grounds without the owners lycence, in pain of every default soe known 0^{li} j^{s} 0^{d}
Item Wee lay in pain that all persons scour and drentch their ditches and watercourses adjoineing on the hy wayes and soe keep them at all times, in pain of every default soe known 0 iij^{s} iiij^{d}
Item Wee lay in pain that no person or persons goe or travell over any other mens grounds where there is noe usuall way or foot path, in pain of every default soe known 0 j^{s} 0
Item Wee lay in pain that all persons yoake and ring their swine and soe keep them at all times, in pain of every default soe known 0 j^{s} 0

Item Wee lay in pain that no person or persons set any cur or other dogg at any mans sheep or other cattel or sleat any mans sheep upon the Commons, in pain of every default soe known 3^s 4^d [written over vj^s $viij^d$]
Item Wee lay in pain that no persons put or turn forth any scabbed horses or other infectious beasts or cattel to any of the Commons, in pain of every default soe known 0 x^s 0
Item Wee lay in pain that no persons put down the fence or carry away either green wood or dry from the fence or grounds in one close of Richard Hoyland called Padock, in pain of every default soe known 0 j^s 0
[signed] Richard H Hoyland Richard Morton / Thomas Peace / Robert Hare/
Michael M Midgeley / Luke Wilson
Thwonge

[There is writing on the right margin, but it is too tattered to read.]
[no endorsement]

INDEX OF PERSONS

Persons have been listed alphabetically, but entries may not all refer to the same person. Where the number is printed in bold lettering this normally indicates that the person is a panellist. Where, however, such a person is styled 'sworn man' without any indication of a township, he has signed a bill presented at the Court Baron.

Ackcoun, Jos., sworn man for Sandal 132
Addy, Joseph 125: Michael, of Barnsley 130
Adear, Jonas 99
Ainley, Edward 86
Akroyd, John 153*: Jonathan, sworn man for Ovenden 143
Alinson, Mr Robert 141
Allanson, Robert 93: jr, of Ovenden, yeo 94
Allen, Francis, of Wakefield 83, 87: sworn man for Westgate 130
Allot(t), Dame 164: John **111, 115, 126**
Ambler, John, constable for Northowram 104, 105, 108: Peter 153*
Antrobus, Mr 97, 141
Appleyard/ Apleyeard, Richard 28: Samuel xii, **147, 149, 150, 154***
Archer, Thomas 1, 39
Armitage, Henry, sworn man for Kirkgate 84, 86: John 5, 28: Joseph, gen, of Outwoodside, Wakefield xi note, 30-31: dep grave of Stanley 5, 19: sworn man for Westgate 84, 86, 130: Thomas, bart x, 1, 39
Arthington, Cyril, esq 1, 39
Ash(all), William, sworn man for Normanton 85, 133
Ashley, John, of Dewsbury 9, 12
Asshall, Will 133
Atkinson, Mr Robert, sr 97: Thomas, presenter for Warley 143

Bairstowe, John, of Ovenden 138: Jonathan, presenter/ sworn man for Northowram 105, 108, 152
Barber, John 26: Thomas, of Wintersett, yeo 8, 12, 13, 23
Bargh, Joseph 9, 34*: Thomas, of Wakefield, grocer 9-10, 34: William, of Wakefield, grocer, son of 9-10, 34
Barke, Robert 131
Barker, John 139: (dep) constable for Walton 90, 128, 132: Thomas **134, 139, 144**
Barraclough, John, sworn man for Eccleshill 85, 90, 134: Richard 141

Bat(t)ley, Jeremy 108, 150
Bate(i)s, Benjamin 141: Isaac, of Rastrick 151
Bateman, Daniel 153: William xii, **83, 85**
Bates, Christopher **104, 106**: Isaac viii, 8, **104, 106**: James **90, 96, 98, 99, 100**
Batley, John xii, 4
Batte, Jacob 143
Batty(e), James, sworn man for Rastrick 105, 107: John xiii, **111, 115, 116, 117, 119, 120*, 121, 122*, 123*, 124, 125, 126*, 156, 160*, 161, 163, 165*, 166*, 168**: lords' ten 113, 114, 159
Baxter, Nathan 109
Baynes, William 36
Be(e)ver, Godfrey, sworn man **59**: sworn man for Hepworth 171: James 113-4: Robert 113, 170: sworn man for Hepworth 113, 125: William, sworn man **59**
Beale, George 22, 24: Henry, gen 22, 24
Beamond, John, presenter for Midgley 144
Beardshaw, Abraham, constable for Dewsbury 84, 85
Beatson, Daniel, of Humley Mooreside, clothier 37
Beckitt, Edward, sworn man for Sandal 84, 87: constable for Sandal 90
Beckwith, Robert, constable for Sandal 83, 84, 127, 128
Bedford, John 133: Thomas, sworn man for Flockton 112, 120: sworn man for Horbury 85
Bell, John, sworn man for Kirkburton 112, 116
Belton, Anne, of Mount Sorrill, widow 32
Benn, Joshua 153*
Benson, Robert, esq, heirs of 1, 39
Bentley, George 141: Jeremy 97: Mr Jeremiah 141, 142: Michael **147, 149, 156**: sworn man for Stansfield 92, 101: Samuel 153, 154: sworn man for Shelf 105
Berry, Edward 8: Josiah, lords' ten 113: of Hepworth 159: Dinah mother of 159: sworn man for Hepworth 113, 125
Bethell, Thomas, constable for Kirkgate 83, 84, 90, 128
Bilcliffe, Joseph, of Cumberworth xiii, 111, 119, 126
Bilsbury, James 31, 134
Bingley, Christopher 164: Matthew, of Norwich, whitesmith 35, 38: Mary wife of 35, 38
Birkhead, Henry, lords' ten 35: of Lightcliffe, yeo 38
Bla(c)ker, John 26, 163
Blagbrough, Thomas, sworn man for Midgley 92, 100

Blagburne, John 140: Thomas, presenter for Midgley 140, 144
Bland, Anthony x, 86, **127, 129*, 130, 131, 132, 133**: of Wakefield, clothworker, 5: Anne wife of 5
Blaymires, Jonas, co-constable of Halifax 90, 92, 98
Bluitt, William, sworn man for Normanton 85, 133
Boardall, Jonas 94, **134, 139**
Bolton, Timthy, affearer for Wakefield 129*, 130*, 131*, 132, 133
Booth(e), Thomas, lords' ten 114: sworn man **28**: sworn man for Scholes 113, 122, 167: William, constable for Thurstonland 112
Boothroyd, John 107: sworn man for Rastrick 151: Michael, sworn man for Rastrick 105, 107
Bothomley, Elizabeth 96: George 152: Isaac, overseer/ sworn man for Rishworth 92, 100, 144: Jeremy 96: sworn man for Rishworth 92: John, of Croftehouse, clothier 96: Richard, of Croftehouse, clothier 96
Boyes, Benjamin, lords' ten 95: sworn man 27: Richard, of Halifax, clerk 15-16, 22: Elizabeth wife of 22
Bradford, Robert ix*,**18, 25, 27, 33, 37**: grave of Ossett 5, 27
Bradley, John, of Gawthorpe, cardboard-maker 19
Braithwaite, James, sworn man for Westgate 84, 86
Bramold, Samuel, sworn man for Wooldale 113, 123
Bray, Daniel, sworn man for Fulstone 166: John, sworn man for Shepley 112, 118
Brearcliffe, John, grave of Hipperholme x: sworn man **28**
Breare, Daniel, presenter/ sworn man for Midgley 92, 100, 144: John 110: Jonathan 114-5: Joseph **1, 6, 7**
Brewor, Widow 153*
Brigge, Abraham xii, **134, 139, 140, 142, 143, 145, 146, 147**: John 141, 153: Judith 94-5: of Warley, spinster 95: Robert 1, 39
Briggs, John, dep grave of Wakefield 5
Brighouse, Widow 108
Bro(a)dhead, Edmund 5, 28: Josiah 5, 28: Richard 5, 28: Robert, co-constable for Shelley 111, 112
Broadley, John 97: Thomas, constable for Normanton 83, 85, 90, 128*, 133
Bromley, John, gen, of Wakefield xi note, 30
Brook(e), - 27: Christopher **106, 107, 109***: Gamaliel, sworn man for Wooldale 113, 123: Henry 109, 150: John xiv, 153, 170: gen, constable of Hipperholme 104, 105: sworn man for Austonley 170: sworn man for Hartshead 105: Joshua, sworn man for Fixby 151: Mary 35-36: Mercy 35-36: Richard, of Lepton 28: grave of Holme 5: Sarah 83, 86: spinster 1, 39: Thomas 35-36: sworn man for Austonley 113 : William,

co-constable for Walton with Bretton 83, 84, 90: constable for Bretton 127, 128: sworn man for Thurstonland 112
Brookesbanck, Jeremy, constable for Shelf 105*, 107: Mary ix
Brown(e), John 171: sworn man for Heworth 171: William, co-constable for Walton with Bretton 83, 84, 88
Burgh (Burck), Samuel, sworn man for Stanley 84, 87, 131
Burkby, Mr William 142
Burneley, John 153: presenter for Shelf 154
Burnett, Jonas viii-ix: Joseph viii-ix: of Dirtcar 127, 129
Burrow, Thomas, constable for Westgate 83, 84: sworn man **29**
Burton, John, affearer for Wakefield 129*, 130*, 131*, 132, 1313
Butterfield, Henry, sworn man for Ovenden 92, 99

Carter, Richard, constable for Flockton 112*: Susan, of Ossett 127, 131: Thomas, pinder for Horbury 129
Cartwright, Daniel 157, 158
Casson, Robert **83, 85, 86*, 87, 88, 89***
Castle, John 168
Castlehouse, William 22, 24: constable for Horbury 83, 85
Cawbert, James, of Elland Hall, yeo 9
Cawthorne, John **22, 24***
Chadwicke, James 1, 39: constable for Warley 91, 92, 104, 135, 139
Chaister, Widow 84, 89
Chappell, James, sworn man for Walton 84, 88: John, sworn man for Kirkburton 161
Charlesworth, David 114: Joshua, of Mossedge 158
Chesman, John, of Leeds, flax-dresser 15, 22, 26: Elizabeth wife of 26
Child, John, sworn man for Emley 164: Joseph 120: sworn man for Cumberworth 112, 119, 163: William, constable for Clifton 105*: co-constable for Hartshead 148*, 155
Chipchase, George, of Wakefield, pewterer 4-5: Elizabeth wife of 4: John, cloth-worker 4-5
Chirrieholme, Thomas, gen, gov of Wakefield Grammar School 3
Clapham, Elizabeth, widow 1: Josiah, constable for Soothill 84, 85, 90, 128*
Clarke, Benjamin, gen 1, 4, 7: of Stanley, gen 15: s of 7, 15
Clarkson, John ix, **14, 16, 33, 37**: grave of Alverthorpe 5: of Newton 29
Clay, Anne viii, 154: John 94
Clegg, Abraham 139: sworn man for Kirkgate 84, 86: sworn man for Longfield 92, 101, 145, 146: George, of Sowerby, yeo 94

Cliffe, John, of Carleton, yeo 31: Elizabeth wife of 31: Mr 106, 154*: William, clerk 147
Cockcroft, Gregory 93: John son of 93: Agnes wife of 93
Cockill, Richard **111, 115,** 117, **126**
Collier, Jarret, sworn man for Thurstonland 112
Cooke, Robert, sworn man for Crigglestone 85, 89, 134
Copley, Henry, of Skelmonthorpe 160: Samuel, sworn man for Ossett 85, 88, 132
Co(u)ldwell, John 119: of Cumberworth **111, 115, 126**: of Thurstonland 115
Coultris, Elizabeth 140
Cowlen, John, searcher for hides at Halifax 93
Cowpe, Benjamin **1, 6, 7**
Crabtree, Jonathan, sworn man for Heptonstall 92, 102: William, constable for Heptonstall 91, 92, 104, 135, 139, 146: sworn man for Erringden 93, 102
Craven, William, knt 1
Crawshawe (Croshey), Anthony, sworn man for Sandal 84, 87, 132
Croft, John **83, 85**
Cromacke, John, of Morley, rope-maker 29, 32, 33: Dorothy wife of 29, 32, 33
Crooke, John 150
Crosby, John, sworn man for Sowerby 142
Crosland, Dorothy, widow 37: Edward **104**: Godfrey xiii, 5, 28, **111, 115, 116, 117, 118, 119, 120*, 121, 122*, 123*, 124, 125, 126***: Richard 170: Thomas 1*, 39: William, sworn man for Fulstone 113, 122
Crosley, Henry, presenter/ sworn man for Barkisland 106, 156: Jeremy, presenter/ sworn man for Barkisland 106, 156: John, sworn man for Sowerby 92, 98
Crowther, Abraham, presenter/ sworn man for Stainland 106, 110, 156: John 105: sworn man for Flockton 112, 120: sworn man for Rishworth 92, 100, 144: Joseph **104, 106*, 107, 109, 110**: of Northowram 2: yeo 95, 108: Samuel, constable for Northowram 104, 105, 111, 147, 148, 152: William, sworn man for Ovenden 92, 99
Currer, John 93: sworn man for Sowerby 92, 98: Mr 141
Cusworth, Robert ix, **8, 11, 14, 16, 17, 24, 27, 29, 32, 33, 37**
Cuttell, Thomas 5, 28

Dalston, John, of Heathhall, kt and bart 31
Dawson, Isaac, constable for Rastrick 104: Joshua, constable for Stansfield 91, 92, 101: William, of Horbury **1, 6, 7**: of Rastrick **1, 6, 7**

Deane, Edmund, gen xii, **90, 96, 97, 98, 99*, 100*, 101*, 102*, 103*, 104**: Jonah/Jonas 143: dep constable for Ovenden 92, 104, 139
Dearden, Joshua xii, **134, 139, 140*, 142*, 143, 144, 146***
Dearnelie, John 5, 28
Denton, Edward, lords' ten 25*: John, of Hey Croft 96: sworn man for Shelley 161: Thomas, grave of Scammonden 6, 106: sworn man for Quarmby 105, 109, 155: William, of Hey Croft, yeo 96
Dewhirst, Isaac, presenter for Wadsworth 144: John, sworn man for Wadsworth 92, 100
Dey, John, sworn man for Dewsbury 85, 89, 133: Thomas **156, 160***
Dickinson, James 141: Robert 116, 117: constable for Sandal 83, 84, 87
Dixon, - , daughters of 97: David, of Burnlee, salter 3: Edward 1*, 39: Francis, sworn man for Halifax 92, 98: George 2-3, 7: John, sr, of Sowerby, yeo 34: of Bentleyroid, yeo 25: jr 25, 34: William 1, 39
Dixson, Francis 142: John 141
Dobson, James 6, 27: Samuel, sworn man for Soothill 85
Dodgson, John 91, 98: Thomas **14, 16, 17**
Dodsworth, Thomas **24, 27**
Dokeson, John, of Eden Booth 113
Donkerley, Adam, sworn man for Emley 112, 120, 164
Drake, Joseph, co-constable of Halifax 90, 92, 98: Robert **104**: constable for Fixby 104, 105, 108
Draper, John, sworn man for Kirkgate 84, 86
Duckenfield, Edward, sworn man for Wooldale 113, 123
Dunn, Joshua 97, 135, 140, 142
Dyson, George, constable for Quarmby 105*: sworn man for Quarmby 105, 109: Joseph, constable for Dalton 105*, 111, 148*, 155: Robert 140: Samuel, constable for Fixby 104, 105, 111, 147, 148, 151: Thomas **147, 149, 155**: William, sworn man for Quarmby 105, 109

Ealroyd, Jonathan, sworn man for Ovenden 99
Earnshawe, John xiii: Philip **111, 115, 126**: Richard, sworn man for Shepley 112, 118: William, sworn man for Holme 112, 121, 166
Eastwood, John 139: Joshua 170*: constable for Dalton 105*, 109: Timothy, sworn man for Holme 112, 121
Eastworth, Amory, sworn man for Stansfield 145
Edwards, Thomas 141
Ellam, John 141
Ellis, Henry **127, 129***: James 35, 39: Joshua, sworn man for Wooldale 16 8: Michael, constable for Dewsbury 84, 85, 89, 90, 128*, 133: Richard 8,

13, 16, 18, 22: gen, gov of Wakefield Grammar School 3: Robert, sworn man for Cartworth 113, 124
Ellison, Mr 153*
Empsall, Jeremy, sworn man for Hipperholme 150: Widow 149
Erindle, Martha 103

Fairbancke, George, of Mouldson Place, yeo 96
Fairbarne, George 9, 13, 17, 19, 22, 23
Farrer, Charles 8: Isaac, constable for Erringden 91, 93, 104, 135, 139, 147: James, constable of Sowerby 91, 92, 98: John xii, 6, 27: sworn man for Erringden 147: Robert, sworn man for Longfield 92, 101 William, esq 1, 39
Fearnley, Isabel, of Gawthorpe, widow 19
Fearnside, John, of Northowram, yeo 95: Mary wife of 95
Feilden, Abraham, of Soyland, yeo 136: Henry 140: Martin, of Halifax, bookbinder 136: Mary, of Soyland, spinster 136
Fell, Joshua, sworn man for Dewsbury 85, 89
Field, William 164
Firth, Abraham 137: John, constable for Ovenden 91, 92, 99, 104: of Watergreene, yeo 94: 135, 139, 143: Joseph 149*: Luke 5, 28: Michael, gen, of Height 94, 134: Nathan 108, 150: Richard, pinder of Kirkburton 160: Thomas xiii, 2, **156, 160*, 161, 163, 165, 166***
Fitton, John **156, 160***
Flather, Anne 138: Henry 150: John, presenter/ sworn man for Hartshead 105, 155 Joseph 138: Sarah 138: Susan, of Halifax, widow 138: jr 138: Thomas, jr, of Northowram, clothier 138: sr 138
Fletcher, John, sworn man for Erringden 93, 102
Forrest, John **127, 129***: sworn man for Ossett 85, 88
Foster, John, sworn man for Normanton 88: Thomas 33
Fournes, Samuel, gen, heirs of 1, 39
Fraunce, James xiii, 5, **156, 160*, 161, 162, 167, 168, 169, 170, 171**: lords' ten 158: sworn man **27, 28***
Frith, James 119
Frost, John 108, 150
Fyswycke, John, sworn man for Heptonstall 146

Garforth, Daniel, sworn man for Ovenden 99, 143
Garlicke, William ix, 8, **104, 106, 147, 149**: grave of Rastrick 6, 106
Garside, Joseph 162
Genn, Anne 157: Elizabeth 157: widow 158: Henry, of Totties 157

George, marquis of Halifax 1, 39
Gibson, John **134, 139**
Gill, Henry 149*: John, gen x, 1, 39, 150: William 152*: constable for Soothill 84, 85
Gillott, Elkanah, sworn man for Halifax 92, 98 see also Jellott
Gle(a)dill, John, sworn man for Emley 164: Robert 141
Gledis, Robert 97
Gleidhill, James, constable for Stainland 105, 106, 110: Jeremy, infant 93: John 10: Martha, widow 93: Mary, infant 93: William 2-3
Glover, Caleb 83, 87: Daniel 83, 87: Jonathan 141 Robert 83, 87: Thomas 83, 87
Godson, John, sworn man for Normanton 88
Goodale, Richard, of Cumberworth 163
Goodall, Jeremy, of Gawthorpe, farmer 19
Goodwin, Edward, gen 1*, 39
Gouldthorpe, James, sworn man for Flockton 112, 165
Greaves, James, presenter for Northowram 152
Greene, George 118: Henry 3: John 3: of Whickleden 114-5: Anne wife 115: Joseph 117, 120: Sarah 115: spinster 30: William 152: constable for Shelley 112
Greenwood, Ambrose, sworn man for Heptonstall 92, 102: Daniel, sworn man for Longfield 145, 146: James, sworn man for Stansfield 145: John, sworn man **38**: Paul, sworn man for Wadsworth 143: Thomas, of Mytham 91, 103: William, dep constable for Heptonstall 92, 104, 139, 146
Grice, Richard, gen 4: gen, lords' ten 26*
Gunson, Robert, affearer at Wakefield 86*, 87, 88*, 89*
Gupwell, John xii, **22, 24, 83, 85**

Hadfield, John, jr 10: sr 10: Elizabeth wife of 10
Haigh, James 5, 28, 155: John ix, 5, **8, 11, 12*, 13, 14, 15, 18, 19, 20, 21***, 22, **25**, 26, **27**, 155: of Horbury, yeo 8, 11, 23: grave of Alverthorpe 38: grave of Sandal 14: dep grave of Horbury and Thornes 5, 17, 27: co-constable for Kirkburton 112: sworn man for Horbury 85, 132: Oliver 14: Thomas, sworn man for Quarmby 155
Haineworth, Robert 93: Mercy wife of 93
Haldsworth, Samuel 6, 27
Hall, John, of Wakefield, tanner 31: sworn man for Hepworth 113, 125: Jonathan 2, 7: gen 22: Judith dau of 22: Joseph, of Sandal Magna, yeo 8-9, 12, 23, 29, 32: lords' ten 31: sworn man 14, 17: Joshua, sworn man

for Rastrick 151: Robert, sworn man for Thurstonland 112, 121: Sarah, of Thornes, widow 31: William **1*, 6, 7,** 39: of Wakefield, barber 15: Margaret, wife of 15: of Woodhouse Lane, shoemaker 30-31: Elizabeth wife of 30-31

Halleley, John, of Earlsheaton 4

Halliday, Joseph 6, 28, 149*: Richard 30, 31

Halstead, Nathaniel 97, 141: Robert **90, 96, 100**

Hamer, James, constable for Rishworth 91, 92

Hamon, Abraham, sworn man for Scholes 113, 122

Hanson, Abraham 95: Henry 147, 149, 156: John 149: Jonathan, sworn man for Barkisland 106, 110: Joshua, constable for Hartshead 105, 111, 148*: Robert, sworn man for Hipperholme 105, 109: William **147, 149, 155**: jr 1, 6, 7

Hardistye, Abraham 95; John 137

Hardy, John, sworn man for Kirkburton 112, 116, 161

Hare, Robert xiii, **156, 160*,** 160*, **165, 167, 169, 171, 172**: constable for Emley x, 112*, 120

Hargreaves, Daniel, sworn man for Soothill 85: jr, lords' ten 95, 96: John x: of Halifax, attorney xi: dep grave of Hipperholme 6: (dep) grave of Sowerby 6, 38: sr, gen, lords' ten 2, 9, 14, 20, 21, 94, 95, 134, 135, 136: jr 20, 21: jr, lords' ten 136, 137*, 138*: sr, of Halifax, attorney 138: sworn man **27**: Susanna 20, 21

Harris, Thomas xii, **83, 85, 86*, 87, 88*, 89, 127, 129*, 131**

Harrison, Gervase **16, 17*, 19, 33, 37**: John **1, 6, 7, 83, 85, 87**: sworn man for Walton x, 84, 88: Richard xi, 33*: Thomas, sworn man x**, 29, 38**: lords' ten 3

Harrupp, William, lords' ten 3

Hartley, Edith 11

Harton, Mr 141: Mr Thomas, of London 141

Hatfield, Francis **14, 16, 17**: gen, of Stanley 22-3: Anne dau of 23

Hattersley, George, sworn man for Hepworth 113, 125

Haward, William, gen, gov of Wakefield Grammar School 3

Haworth, Joshua, co-constable for Hartshead with Clifton 105*, 110

Haye, Jonas, sworn man **28**

Heald, Japhet, constable for Horbury 83, 85, 90, 127, 128

Healiwell, Richard, sworn man for Hepworth 171

Heape, Abraham, sworn man for Longfield 145, 146: John, lords' ten 136: Joshua 124

Heaton, Moses, sworn man for Fixby 105, 107

Hebden, George 24, 27: sworn man for Stanley x, 84, 87, 131

Heeley, Joshua, sworn man for Wooldale 168
He(m)mingway, Henry **127, 129***: searcher for hides at Halifax 93: John 9, 13: Richard **18, 19, 20, 21***
Heptonstall, George, sworn man for Holme 166
Hepworth, John 163, 164: Thomas 83: Widow 163, 164
Hey, George, constable for Quarmby 105, 111, 147, 148, 155: John, co-constable for Shelley 111, 112
Heyworth, Thomas 88
Hide, Samuel 36: sworn man **29**
Higins, Mrs 88
Hileley, Henry, of Sowerby, yeo 18, 19-21: John, of Earlsheaton, yeo 9: Elizabeth wife of 9
Hilous, John 142
Hinchliffe, James xiv, **111, 115**, 125, **126**: John xiii, **24, 27, 28, 111, 115, 116, 117, 118, 119, 120*, 121, 122*, 123*, 124,** 124, **125, 126***: grave of Holme ix-x, 21: 27: sworn man for Cartworth 169: Joseph, sworn man for Cartworth 169: Richard 124: Robert, sworn man for Cartworth 169
Hird, Stephen 149: sworn man for Hipperholme 151
Hirst, Anne 114: Henry, sworn man for Fulstone 113, 122: John 7, 8, 10: constable for Crigglestone 84, 85, 89, 90, 128*, 134: deputy constable for Rastrick 111, 148, 151: sworn man for Rastrick 105, 107: Mary 114: Richard 114: Robert, sworn man for Kirkburton 112, 116, 161: Simeon 5, 28: Timothy **127, 129*, 131**, 132: William, of Fulstone 114: sworn man for Shepley 112, 118
Hitchon, Abraham, coheirs of 27: of - Brooke 6
Hobson, James, constable for Eccleshill 134: John, sworn man for Shepley 162: Joseph, (dep) constable for Shepley 111, 112, 127, 157, 159
Hodgson, Abraham, searcher for hides at Halifax 93: John 99
Hodshon, Joshua 152
Hol(d)royd, Benjamin, of Halifax, mason 91: Joseph, constable of Barkisland 105, 106, 110, 111, 148*, 156
Holden, Daniel, sworn man for Sowerby 92, 98: Samuel, sworn man for Sowerby 142
Holgate, George 27: grave of Sowerby 5
Hollings, Isaac, of Horton 95
Hollingworth, John 83, 86: William sworn man **27**
Holmes, Henry, sworn man for Halifax 92, 98
Holroyd, Martha 14: Sarah 14
Hopkin, Joshua 152
Hopkinson, John, gen 4

Horldsworth, John 152
Horne, Cotton, gen 19: William, gen 1, 39: of Wakefield, gen 16, 19: sworn man **29**
Horner, Aaron 142
Horsfall, John, jr/ sr, sworn man for Heptonstall 92*, 102*, 146: sworn man for Stansfield 92, 101, 145: Jonas, of Heptonstall 103: Timothy, sworn man for Heptonstall 146
Horton, Mr, of Sowerby 97
Houl(d)roid, George, of Barkisland 156: John 149: Isaac, sworn man for Quarmby 105, 109
Howitt, Martha, widow 10
Hoyland, Richard 169, 172: sworn man for Thong 172
Hoyle, Anne, of Rastrick, spinster 148: James, servant ix, 52, 53: John 8: of Rastrick, clothier 148: of Shawe 25: Judah 150*: Paul 150: Richard, of Godley, yeo 138-9: William, sworn man for Halifax 92, 98
Hudson, Richard 100, 150: Thomas, sworn man for Wooldale 168
Hunt, Thomas **29, 32**: sworn man for Horbury 85
Hutton, William, constable for Eccleshill 84, 85, 90

Ibberson, Edward, pinder of Lindley 149
Ibbettson, Thomas 6, 27
Illingworth, Richard 94
Illott, Edward, sworn man **14, 17**
Ingham, John, sworn man for Longfield 92, 101, 145, 146: Jonas, of Blakehill, yeo 137: Miles, of Blakehill, clothier 138
Ingland, Matthew 88
Issott, George, sworn man for Horbury 85, 132: William, sworn man **24**

Jackson, Daniel 97, 141: Edward, of Halifax, yeo 137: Mary, of Alverthorpe, widow 35, 39: Samuel **127, 129*, 130***: Widow 141
Jagger, Benjamin 153*: Jeremiah, presenter/ sworn man for Northowram 105, 108, 152: Michael, sworn man for Hipperholme 105, 109
Jaques (Jacks), Thomas, sworn man for Stanley 84, 87, 131
Jellott, Henry, sworn man for Thurstonland 112, 121 see also Gillott
Jessop, Edward, sworn man for Shelley 112, 117
Johnson, Robert, heirs of 1, 39: Thomas 12, 13, **147, 149, 151**: clerk 1, 39: of Painthorpe 14: grave of Sandal 5, 16: sworn man for Westgate 84, 86, 130
Jubb, Richard, sworn man for Normanton 85, 133

Kay(e), Christopher, jr 171: George **156, 160***: Gervase, co-constable for Walton with Bretton 83, 84: Henry 124: Jeremy, of Copthurst, yeo 18, 20, 36: Joshua **33, 37**: Thomas 109
Kent, Elizabeth xi note, 30, 33: John xi note, 30, 33: Mary 30: Richard 27: Thomas, of Stanley, yeo xi note, 30-31: wife of xi note, 33
Kenyon, Edward 119: William 125
Kershawe, John 108: Thomas, sworn man for Sandal 84, 87, 132
Kighley, John 83, 86: Jonathan xii, **90, 96, 97, 98, 99*, 100*, 101*, 102*, 103*, 104**: Widow 3
Kilner, Thomas, sworn man for Dalton 105, 109, 155
Kirkman, Robert 33
Kirkwood, Thomas, constable for Cumberworth 111, 112
Kirsell, John, sworn man **17**
Kirshaw, Joseph, of Soyland, yeo 14: Nathan, of Soyland, yeo 14
Kitching, Isaac, sworn man for Warley 92, 99
Kitson, John 1*, 39: Thomas 137: of Hipperholme, clothier 137: Timothy, constable for West Ardsley 84, 85, 90, 128*, 133
Knight, Joshua 154: constable for Shelf 105*, 111, 147, 148, 154
Knowles, John, presenter for Northowram 152: Jonas, constable for Longfield 91, 92, 101
Knutton, John, sworn man for Walton 84, 88

Lacy, Thomas **147, 149**
Lake, Henry 141
Lancaster, Edward 83, 86
Land, John, sworn man for Ossett 132
Langley, Abraham **104**: Mr 109: of Preistley 21: Edward 122: Mr 109: sworn man for Fulstone 113, 122: John, of Northowram 2: Mrs 149
Langstaff, Jane 131
Law, Benjamin, gen 1, 39: John, sworn man for Longfield 92, 101: Matthew, sworn man for Crigglestone 85, 89, 134: Richard, gen, heirs of 1, 39
Lea, Anthony **104, 106, 107**
Leake, John ix, xi-ii, xiii, **1, 6, 7, 14*, 16, 83, 85,** 87, **127, 129*, 130,** 130, **133**
Learoyd, Gabriel 140: co-constable for Halifax 90, 92, 104, 135, 139, 142
Lee, Arthur, sworn man for Shelley 112, 117, 161: Joseph 120: Obediah, clerk, vicar of Wakefield, gov of Grammar School 3
Leeke, Robert, gen 4
Levet, Mrs 88
Lindley, Adam **111, 115, 126**

Lister, John, of Horton, gen 90, 97: Joseph xii, **147, 148, 150, 151*, 152, 153, 154*, 155*, 156***: Mr 140: Thomas **90, 96, 98**
Litle, James 150
Littlewood, James, sworn man for Cartworth 113, 124: Joshua 115
Liversedge, Oliver 5: Richard 1, 39: of Boothroyd (Dewsbury) 31: yeo 15: William **104, 106, 107, 109, 110**
Lockwood, Abraham, constable for Thurstanland 112*, 121, 127, 157, 159: John xii, **90, 96, 97, 98, 100*, 101*, 102*, 103**: sworn man for Emley 112, 120, 164: Matthew 121: Thomas, constable for Cumberworth 112*: William, sworn man for Thurstonland 165
Longbotham, John, sworn man for Shepley 112, 117
Longley, Joseph 130, 131: Mr 97
Lovitt, Mrs 133
Lum(me), Abraham **106, 109, 110***, 150: Joshua 8: Mr 97: Samuel, presenter/sworn man for Hartshead 105, 110, 156
Lunn(e), Mr 142: Samuel, sworn man for Hartshead 105

Mallinson, Abraham 149
Mamond, William, sworn man for Halifax 92, 98
Mann, John, of Liversedge Lodge (Birstall), clothier 15
Mansfield, Robert **14, 16, 29, 32***
Marsden, Francis, sworn man for Ossett 85, 88: John 119
Marsh, William, of Cumberworth 111, 119, 126: sworn man for Cumberworth xiii, 112, 119
Marshall, Joseph 164: Major **90, 96**: Matthew 164: Thomas, of Wakefield 127, 130: sworn man for Northgate 84, 131
Mason, Peter 83: Mr 86
Mathewman, Richard xiii: gen, lords' ten 70
Mawde, Daniel 38: gen **8, 11, 12*, 13, 14, 16, 17, 22, 24*, 29*, 32***: gov of Wakefield Grammar School 3: lords' ten 10, 22: sworn man **38**: Francis 129: Gideon, gen ix, xii, **1, 6, 7, 14, 16, 17*, 19, 20, 21*, 29, 32*, 83, 85, 86*, 87, 88*, 89**: John, of Halifax ix, 50-3: gen, of Wakefield 8, 11, 13, 23: Jonathan ix, 50-3: Mary, of Halifax ix, 49-53: jr 53: Sarah ix, 51: Thomas, gen, of Doncaster 8, 11, 12, 13, 23
Mawdsley, John **1, 6, 7, 33, 37**
Meller, Abraham, sworn man for Austonley 113, 125: George, sworn man for Kirkburton 112, 116
Mellin, Joseph, overseer/ sworn man for Skircoat 92, 98, 142
Midgley, Abraham, sworn man for Erringden 93, 102: Josiah 93: Michael 5, 28: sworn man for Thong 113, 126, 172: Richard 6, 27: sworn man **38**:

Samuel, constable for Midgley 91, 92, 100: Susan 94-5: W, sworn man **38**: William, gen, lords' ten 93*: of Halifax, gen 18, 20-1
Midlebrooke, William, lords' ten 4*
Milner, Abraham, sworn man for Hipperholme 151: Anthony, overseer for Ovenden 142: sworn man for Skircoat 92, 98: Elizabeth 26: of Cawthorne, widow 26: Jeremy xii, **17, 19, 83, 85**: Thomas, of Kirkburton, yeo 26: Timothy, sworn man for Crigglestone 85, 89, 134
Milnes, Alvery **83, 85**
Mitchell, Elizabeth, widow 93: John, gen, of Scoute 94: Mary wife of 94: lords' ten 4: Mr 97: Richard, sworn man for Crigglestone 85, 89, 134: Robert 1, 39: Will, of Alverthorpe 131
Moone, William, co-constable for Kirkburton 111, 112, 127, 156, 159
Moore, Thomas, sworn man for Emley 112, 120
Morehouse, Elizabeth 37: George 159: John 122: of Lindley 113: Joseph 113: Matthew, sworn man **27**: Thomas 25, 29, 34, **156, 160*, 163, 166**: constable for Thurstonland 112: of Ebsonhouse, yeo 18, 21, 36-37: William xiii, 37, 119: lords' ten 113, 114: sworn man for Quarmby 155
Morkill, Thomas, of Newbigginhill, yeo 37
Morrie, Henry 114
Morton, Henry, sworn man for Cartworth 169: Richard xiii, xiv, 120, **156, 160*, 161, 162, 163, 164, 165*, 166*, 167, 168, 169, 170, 171, 172**: constable for Holme 112*
Moses, John 150
Mosley, Joseph 10
Moxon, William xi, **29, 32, 33**
Murgatroyde, James, lords' ten 94
Murgitroyd, Mr John 131: of Warley, yeo 138: constable for Warley 143

Nantcliffe, William 127, 130
Naylor, Anne 29-30: Charles, gen, gov of Wakefield Grammar School 3: George 29-30: gen, of London 24: grave of Horbury 5: Henry, lords' ten 31, 91: Isaac, lords' ten 34: Joseph 29-30: Mary, of Wakefield, widow 35: Richard 29-30: of Wakefield, clothier 19: Mary wife of 19: Thomas, of Clifton 1, 39: William, sworn man for Northgate 84, 131
Neale, Elizabeth, of Barkisland, spinster 25
Nettleton, Daniel, sworn man for West Ardsley 85, 133: Mr Richard 88, 132
Nevile, Francis, esq, of Chevett, gov of Wakefield Grammar School 3
Newsom(e), John 128, 132
Newton, Samuel 97, 141
Nicholson, Benjamin, constable for Warley 91, 92, 99

Nickolls, John 150
Noble, Ambrose 137: George, jr, 137: sr, of Halifax, chapman 137: Grace (née Jackson), wife of 137: Thomas, of Halifax 137
Nolson, Jo. 108
Norfolke, Richard, jr, constable for Westgate 83, 84, 90, 128
North, John 2, 7, 014: of Horbury, yeo 14: Mary, widow 14
Norton, Samuel 1, 39: gen, of Kettlethorpe 9, 13, 17, 19, 23: sworn man **14**
Nowell, Roger, esq, grave of Stanley x, 5, 17
Nunnes, John, gen 35-6

Oates, Anne, of Dodworth, spinster 4: James, gen, of Murgatroyd 94: Josiah, of Chickingley, yeo 4
Odey, George 152*
Ogden, Nicholas 145
Oldfield, George, lords' ten 94: Michael xii, **134, 139, 142, 143, 144, 146*, 147**: Thomas **134, 139, 140*, 142*, 144*, 145, 146***
Oldroyd, James, constable for Kirkgate 83, 84, 86: John, sworn man **38**: of Alverthorpe, clothier 3 see also Holdroid
Oley, Anne 11: Elizabeth 11: Frances 11: Joseph sr, of Heath (Warmfield) 10-11: Rebecca 26*
Ormeroyd, Peter, sworn man for Stansfield 92, 101
Oxley, William, constable for Cumberworth 111, 112, 127, 157, 159

Page, John, constable for Emley 112*, 127, 157, 159
Parker, Michael **8, 11, 17-8, 19, 33, 37**: of Cawsey 84, 89
Parkin, Thomas xiii, 119: of Shelley 111, 126
Paslay, Thomas xii, **1, 6, 7, 83, 85, 86*, 88*, 89**
Patchett, Richard xii, **134, 139, 140, 142, 143, 144, 145**: Simeon 136
Peace, Elizabeth, of Ossett, spinster 3-4: John, of Ossett 4: constable for Shelley 111, 112, 117, 127, 157, 159: farmer 15: Thomas xiii, **156, 160*, 161, 163, 165, 166*, 172**
Peaker, Samuel xii, **33, 37, 83, 85**: sworn man **29**
Pearson, James 1, 39
Penny (alias Oley) Anne 11
Phillippes, James 137
Pickles, Thomas 93: Mary wife of 93
Pilkington, Lyon, bart 1, 5, 17, 39
Pillin, John 109
Pillington, Daniel 9: Nathaniel 9
Pites, Michael, sworn man for Kirkburton 161

Pitt, Thomas, affearer at Wakefield 86*, 87, 88*, 89*
Plaisterer, Henry 131
Pogson, John, constable for Shepley 160
Pollard, Tempest ix, **8, 11, 12, 13, 14, 16, 22, 24*, 27, 39, 43, 53, 56, 58, 67, 70-2, 75-8, 81**
Poplewell, William, co-constable for Hartshead with Clifton 105*, 110
Potham, William, gen 1*, 39
Potter, William 86
Pour, Mr 142
Powell, Matthew 83, 87
Pre(i)stley, Francis xii, 28, **147, 149,** 149, **150, 151*, 152, 153, 154*, 155*, 156***: co-grave of Hipperholme 6: Henry 136: of Bayteinges 138: Jonathan 28, 149: jr 149: co-grave of Hipperholme 6: Joseph **1, 6, 7**: sworn man **28**: Robert, of Bayteinges, yeo 136, 138: Thomas 28, 143: co-grave of Hipperholme 6: sworn man **27**
Preston, Jonas 8: William **127, 129*, 131**
Priest, George, sworn man for Cumberworth 163
Pymont, John 1, 39

Ramsden, Geoffrey xii, **104, 106, 109, 110**: constable for Stainland 105, 106, 111, 148*, 156: Gilbert 104, **106**: Henry 90, 97, 135, 140, 142: John **147, 149, 156**: Joseph **90, 96**: Michael 152: Mr, of Crowstone 97, 141: Robert, lords' ten 148: Thomas, constable for Skircoat 91, 92, 98: William, constable for Clifton 149: pinder of Rastrick 149
Ransley, John 155
Ratcliffe, James, sworn man for Erringden 93, 102
Rawling, Isaac 130
Rawson, Samuel, sworn man for Barkisland 106, 110
Rayner, Joseph 150: Joshua, constable for Stanley 87
Redman, William xii
Redshawe, George, gen, gov of Wakefield Grammar School 3
Rhodes (Roades), John xiii, 19, **111, 115, 116, 117, 118, 119, 120*, 121, 122*, 123*, 124, 125, 126***: gen 4: Joshua **111, 115, 126**
Rich(y), William xiii, 111, 119, 126
Richardson, Henry 84, 89: Mr John 142: lords' ten 137: Mr 163: Robert 84, 89
Riddlesden, Martha, servant ix, 53
Ridehough, Henry, presenter for Erringden 147
Rigg(e), John 94: Robert 83, 87: Thomas 93, 94: Mary wife of 93
Rigley, Samuel, sworn man for Rastrick 105, 107, 151

Rishworth, John 149
Roades, Francis **22, 24***: Joshua, constable for Holme 112*, 126, 127, 157, 159: Robert, sworn man for Soothill 85, 133
Roberts, Abraham, sworn man for Cartworth 113, 124: sworn man for Sandal 84, 87, 132: Dorothy 140: John 149*: late of Staleywood (Ches), wheelwright 10: Joshua, sworn man for Cartworth 113, 124: William, of Stepney 2-3: Mary wife of 2
Robertshaw, Dinah 135
Robinson, Jeremy, dep constable for Hipperholme 105, 109, 111, 148, 150: sworn man for Hipperholme 105: John 16, 19: Joseph, constable for Skircoat 91, 92, 104, 135, 139, 142: Widow, of Wakefield 131: William xii, **127, 129*, 130, 131, 132, 133**
Robouthur, George, of High Burton 165
Rodes, John, sworn man **24**
Rodley, William, sworn man for Stanley 84, 87, 131
Roebucke, George xiv, **111, 115**, 122, **122, 126**: co-constable for Kirkburton 111, 112, 122: sworn man for Fulstone 113, 166: Humphrey **1, 6, 7**: sworn man 27: John, sworn man **27**
Roper, James, dep constable for Rishworth 92, 104, 139, 144
Ros(s)endale, Jeremy, of Skircoat, yeo 95: gen, son of 95: gen, of Skircoat 137: sworn man **28**
Rose, John, sworn man **29**
Rouse, Deborah 11
Rowley, John **1, 6, 7**
Ryley, James, of Barkisland, yeo 95: of Lindley viii, 154

Sagar, John, gen, of Allerton 95
Saunderson, John 119: Robert, sworn man for Thong 113, 126
Savile, John, clerk 2: gen 30, 31: Thomas, esq, heirs of 1, 39; William, esq, heirs of 1, 8, 13, 17, 18, 39
Scarborough, Richard xii, **90, 96, 98*, 99*, 100*, 102, 103*, 104, 134, 139, 140*, 141, 142*, 143*, 144*, 145*, 146*, 147**
Scatchard, Thomas 30*
Scholey, Richard, deputy grave of Sandal 17
Scoalefield, James 154
Scoberd, James 108
Scoley, Thomas 88
Scott, Abraham 90, 97, 135, 140: John xi,10, 12*, 13, 21, 32, 33, 155: gen, deputy steward xi, 9, 15*, 17*, 19*, 22, 26, 27, 30*, 31, 32, 33*, 34, 37, 38*: Alice dau of 26: Elizabeth wife of 26: gen, of Wakefield 38: gen,

gov of Wakefield Grammar School 3: Robert 12*, 13*, 21, 32, 39: Widow 3: William 141
Scrivener, James **8, 11, 18, 19**: John **18, 19, 20, 21*, 22, 24, 25, 27**
Sedgwicke, Gervase **1, 6, 7**
Sell(ars), Joseph 127, 131
Senier, Edward 117
Senyor, Richard, sworn man for Fulstone 166
Shackleton, James 149: Jonas, sworn man for Wadsworth 143
Sharpe, John 111: sworn man for Northowram 105: William, presenter for Shelf 154
Shauu, Jonas, of Wakefield 127, 130
Shaw, James, sworn man for Midgley 144: Joshua 113: Mr 97: Thomas 118: of Emley park 160: William, sworn man for Hepworth 171
Sheard, Thomas 91, 98
Shep(he)ard, Samuel 25: William 152
Shillitoe, Thomas x, **8, 11, 24, 27, 29, 32**: constable for Crigglestone 84, 85
Shut(t)leworth, William **127*, 129, 130*, 131*, 132, 133**
Siddall, John, sworn man for Sowerby 142: Josiah, sworn man for Sowerby 138, 142
Sikes, John 120 see also Sykes
Silvester, Thomas, sworn man for Shelley 112, 117, 161
Smallwood, Joseph, presenter for Wadsworth 144
Smith, Isaac, sworn man for Dewsbury 85, 89, 133: John **127, 129*, 131, 133**: sworn man for Hipperholme 105, 151: Joseph, constable for Stanley 83, 84, 90, 127, 128: Samuel 109, 150: Timothy 153
Snowden, William 108, 152
Sonyer, Joshua 152
Soothill, James 142: John, sworn man for Rishworth 144: Michael, sworn man for Rishworth 92, 100
Speight, John ix, **24, 27, 33, 37**: William, constable for Ossett 83, 85
Spencer, Samuel, sworn man for Shelf 105, 107
Spin(c)ke, Jeremy, sworn man **17**: Robert, constable for Normanton 83, 85, 88
Stables, John, sworn man for Westgate 84, 86
Stainton, Joshua **90, 96**, 136, 138
Standidge, John, sworn man for Normanton 85, 88, 133
Stanhope, John, esq 1*, 39
Stansfeld, James, sworn man for Stansfield 92, 101, 145: John, constable for Sowerby 91, 92, 104, 135, 139, 142: Richard, constable for Stansfield 91, 92, 104, 135, 139, 145: of Stansfield xiii, 91, 103-4: Robert 139

Stead, Mary, widow 35-36
Stell, Judith, of Halifax, widow 91
Stephenson, Matthew 4: Richard, of Horbury, card-maker 4
Stock(e)s, George 108, 150: John, sworn man **29**: Jonathan 131: Joseph 25
Sturd(e)y, Gilbert 109, 150
Sucksmith, Joseph 149
Sugden, John 90, 96, 101: sworn man for Ossett 132
Sunderland, Abraham viii, 101: Henry, presenter for Erringden 147: John **8, 11, 12**: Jos, constable for Midgley 144: Joseph 153: Widow 153: William **22, 24**
Sutcliffe, Edward 93: constable for Erringden 91, 93: Job 6, 27: Joseph, constable for Heptonstall 91, 92, 102: Samuel 18, 20-1, 34, 38: William, of Hoohoyle, yeo 18, 19-21
Swallow(e), Abraham 113: Andrew 5*, 28*: Anthony 5, 28: Joseph, sworn man for Shepley 162: Richard 1, 39: Robert 5, 28
Swift, Jeremy 152
Sykes, John 165: presenter/ sworn man for Stainland 106, 110, 156: sworn man for Quarmby 154

Taylor, John **29, 32**: sworn man for Wooldale 168: Matthew 163: Richard, constable for Rishworth 91, 92, 104, 135, 139
Tempest, Abraham 154
Terry, Percival **8, 11, 17, 19, 22, 24**: Richard **25, 27**: sworn man for Ossett 85, 88, 132
Tettlow, James 150*
Thewles, Sarah 5, 28
Thomas, Edward, of Waukcliffe, tanner 8, 12, 13, 23: Elizabeth, of Kirk Fenton, widow 8, 12, 13, 23: John, sworn man for Erringden 147: Richard **134, 139, 144, 146**: constable for Wadsworth 91, 92: of Reddicarr, yeo 31: of Stockes, yeo 91-2: William 100: of Reddicarr 31: yeo 134
Thompson, John 30*: Widow 86
Thornell, Mr Thomas 142
Thornes, John, sworn man for Dewsbury 85, 89, 133: Samuel ix, **14, 16, 22, 24*, 29, 32, 33, 37**: lords' ten 4: William, sworn man for Wadsworth 92
Thornhill, Brian 10, 11: Mary, widow of 11: Frances, of Fenay, spinster 25: George, esq 1: of Fixby 10: heirs of 7, 39: Japhet 86: Joseph, constable for Rastrick 104, 105, 111, 147, 148: Lady Everid' 148: Madam, the elder 8
Thornton, Richard, esq, of Wakefield, gov of Grammar School 3

Thorpe, John 93, 149, 168: Susan wife of 93: sworn man for Wooldale 113, 123: Richard, jr 117: sr 117
Thorrold, William, constable for Northgate 83, 84
Threapland, Jonathan xii, **104, 106**, 108, **147, 149, 152**
Tilson, John 36
Tin(c)ker, Edward, sworn man for Shelley 161: John xiii, 10, **156, 160*, 161, 162, 165, 170**: lords' ten 158: sr 113-4: Joshua **156, 160*, 164, 165**
Toll, Joshua, sworn man for Dewsbury 133
Tolson, Richard, esq, of Wath 2: Anne dau of 2: Elizabeth dau of 2: Katherine dau of 2: Edward son of 2: Wilfrid son of 2
Totty, Thomas ix, xii, **8, 11, 14, 16, 17, 29, 83, 85**, 129*: William 8, 13, 16, 18, 22
Towne, George xii, **90, 96, 97, 99, 101, 102, 103*, 104**
Turner, John, sworn man for Walton 84, 88: Nathan 98: William, gen, lords' ten 2: gov of Wakefield Grammar School 3
Turton, John 18, 20, 25, 29, 34, 37: Elizabeth wife of 37

Utley, John **90, 96, 134, 139**

Varley, John, jr, of Ogden 91, 103: sr 91, 103

Wadd, Charles, presenter for Warley 99
Wade, Joshua, of Warley, yeo 94: Samuel 106, 153
Wadsworth, Christopher, presenter for Warley 143: Edmund **134, 139**: John 4: constable of Ovenden 91, 92, 99: sworn man for Horbury 132: Joseph, constable for Stanley 83, 84: Richard, sworn man for Sowerby 92, 98: Timothy 141: Widow 153
Wagstaffe, Robert 2; William 2
Wainwright, John, dep constable for Westgate 84, 86: sworn man for Westgate 84
Walker, Abraham 109: Daniel xii, **104, 106*, 107*, 108, 109*, 110***: John **1, 6, 7, 8, 11, 12, 13**, 37: of Horbury, yeo 8, 12, 13, 23: sealer for hides at Wakefield 85, 86: heirs of 5: Thomas, constable for Longfield 135, 139: of Wakefield, tailor 31: William ix, x, **22, 24-5, 27, 29, 32**, 141: constable for Midgley 91, 92, 104, 135, 139
Walshawe, John, constable for Flockton 112*, 127, 157, 159, 165: Thomas 165
Walton, George, sworn man for Northgate 84, 131: Thomas, constable for Longfield 91, 92, 104, 145, 146
Wamoit, William 142

Warbleton, Peter 154
Warde, John 16, 19: William, constable for Northgate 83, 84, 90, 127, 128
Wardman, Samuel 152-3: presenter for Shelf 154
Waring, George xii, **83, 85, 88***, 128, 133
Waterhouse, John, sr, gen, gov of Wakefield Grammar School 3: Robert, gen, of Whitley 26*: William, of Lindley 154*
Watkinson, Joseph, gen, of Flanshawe, gov of Wakefield Grammar School 3
Waugh, Michael 142
Webster, John, sworn man for Wadsworth 92, 100: Robert 127, 129*
Wells, John 152
White, John, constable for Ossett 83, 85, 88, 90, 128*, 132: Joseph **8, 11, 12, 17, 19, 22, 24, 29, 32, 33, 37**: lords' ten 9; Richard son of 9
Whiteaker, John 149
Whiteakers, Abraham, constable for West Ardsley 84, 85
Whit(e)head, John, sworn man for Rastrick 105, 107, 151: Joshua xii, **134, 139, 142*, 143*, 144, 145*,146, 147**: Thomas, sworn man for Fixby 105, 107, 151
Whiteley, Joshua, of Holmehouse, yeo 136*: Samuel 153: presenter for Shelf 154
Whitley, Anthony 83, 88: Edward, pinder for Ossett 85: George, overseer/ sworn man for Rishworth 92, 100, 144: Nathan 108, 138
Whitwham, Paul, sworn man for Wadsworth 92, 100
Whyte, Francis, esq, gov of Wakefield Grammar School 3: esq, high steward of Manor x, 1, 16, 17, 23*, 27, 35, 36, 38-39, 93
Whyteley, George, sworn man for Kirkgate 84, 86: Samuel, sworn man for Shelf 105, 107
Wiat (*rectius* Wyatt), Edwin, esq, serjeant at law 1
Wilcock, Richard, sworn man for Flockton 112
Wilkin, William, constable for Wadsworth 143
Wilkinson, Francis, gen 1, 39: near Norbrigg, tanner 137: Isaac, co-constable for Halifax 90, 92, 104, 135, 139, 142: John 6, 27, 93: Matthew, gen, of Greenhead 93: Thomas 93: William, constable for Wadsworth 91, 92, 104, 135, 139
Willans, Thomas 83, 87
Williamson, Anthony, sworn man for West Ardsley 85, 133
Wilson, Henry, sr, of Kirkecliffe, yeo 95: Humphrey **111, 115, 126**: of Wooldale Towne End 157-8: Isaac 99: James **1, 6, 7,** 15, **33, 37**: constable for Eccleshill 84, 85, 90, 128*: John 141, 142: of Netherthong 158: Mary wife of 158: sworn man for Halifax 92, 98: Jonathan, dep grave of Holme 5, 27: Joseph, of Wood 135, 136: Jane wife of 135:

sworn man for Northowram 105, 108: Joshua 140: searcher for hides at Halifax 93: Leonard 29: dep grave of Alverthorpe 5: Luke **156**, 157*, **160*, 161, 162, 164, 167, 168, 169, 170, 171, 172**: Hester, wife of 157: Thomas 36: lords' ten 35
Wilton, William, gen xii
Windl, John 141: Jonathan 141
Winpenie, Thomas 158
Winterburne, Mark, sworn man for Northgate 84, 131
Wood, Abraham 115: Charles, sworn man for Warley 92: Edmund 14, 16: John 94: constable for Shelley 112, 117: of Pighell street, blacksmith 94: Joseph xii, **147, 149, 150, 151*, 153, 154, 155*, 156***: sr, of Fould (Northowram) 9: jr, son of 9: sworn man **17**: Mr 108: Richard, sworn man for Soothill 85, 133: Samuel, co-constable for Kirkburton 112, 116, 127, 156, 159: of Pighellstreet, blacksmith 94
Woodhead, Abraham 153*: sworn man for Scholes 167
Woodhous, Thomas 150
Woofenden, Richard 163*
Wormall, William, sworn man **24**
Wright, Joseph 149: co-constable for Walton with Bretton 83, 84, 90, 128: Joshua 149: constable for Hipperholme 104, 111, 147, 148
Wrightson, Robert, gen 1, 39

Yoward, Richard **127, 129*, 130*, 131, 132, 133**

INDEX OF PLACES

Place-names are entered in their modern form, except where this is doubtful. The graveship or township, where given in the text, is added in round brackets. Where the modern name is materially different from the form in the roll the original spelling is given in square brackets.

Adwalton 71
Allerton (Bradford-dale) 95
Almondbury, parish of 3: township of 45
Alverthorpe 3, 35, 39, 42, 49, 56, 58, 76, 79*, 131: bridge at 16: graveship of 3, 5, 8, 13, 14, 16, 17, 18, 19, 22, 23, 29*, 32, 33, 38, 40, 42, 45, 48, 49, 60, 75, 76, 78, 79*
Adders Gate [Adderishgate] (Northowram) 67
Ardsley (East), parish of 30
Armitt Crofts (Sandal) 26*
Austonley (Holme) 5, 28, 74: commons of 170: constablery of 112, 113, 124-5, 157, 169-70

Baitings (Sowerby) 61, 66, 67, 136, 138: dike 139
Ball Green (Sowerby) 62
Barkisland (Sowerby) 25, 61, 62, 65, 66*, 94, 95, 134, 136*, 156: constablery of 105, 106, 110, 148, 156
Barms hill lane 152
Barneside (Hepworth) 44, 54-5, 57, 59, 67, 69
Barnsley 130
Barraclough Lanehead (Southowram) 50
Bailey Hall (Southowram) 48
Bentley Royd 25: Upper/Lower 25, 34
Bingley, parish of 48, 50, 52
Birchencliffe 154
Birstall 15
Blackerhouse (Northowram) 48, 49, 52
Blackhillend (Northowram) 68
Blackstone edge 61, 66
Blackwood (Sowerby) 5-6, 27*
Blake Hill (Northowram) 137, 138
Booth Stead (Warley) 94
Booth House (Austonley 170

Boothroyd (Dewsbury) 15, 31: (Ossett) 46*, 57, 79
Bottom Field (Dirtcar) 40: House (Hipperholme) 47: (Stanley) 22, 24, 60
Bottom Hall Bridge 108, 150
Boy Mill (Sowerby) 6, 27, 68
Bradford 75, 76, 77: parish of 41, 46
Bradford-dale 95
Bradley Lane end 151
Brearley Bridge (Sowerby) 6, 27
Breares, chapel at (Southowram) 50
Bretton, constablery of 127
Brey (Gomersall) 41
Brian Scholes (Northowram) 47
Brighouse 150: causey 150: Lane head 150: street 150: constablery of 104, 105: township of 38
Brigg Royd (Northowram) 138: (Rastrick) 148
Broadford (Alverthorpe) 8, 13, 16, 18: beck 60
Broadroyds (Ossett) 46
Brockholes (Halifax) 99
Brodford (Stanley) 131
Brook Bank (Wakefield) 64
Burnlee (Holme) 2-3
Burton/Kirkburton, court at 37

Cadeby (Sprotbrough) 80
Calder river 68
Carleton (Rothwell) 31
Cartworth 158: commons of 169: constablery of 112, 113, 124, 157, 168-9
Cawsey (Dewsbury) 84, 89
Cawthorpe 26
Cheshire 10
Chevett (Alverthorpe) 3
Chickenley (Dewsbury) 4, 73*, 80: Bank 73
Cinder Hill [Sinderhills] 106, 147, 154
Clay Clough (Sowerby) 61, 67
Cliffe House (Lightcliffe) 76
Clifton 1, 39, 155: constablery of 105*, 148
Closes: see Subject Index for closes, entered under township/ graveship
Clough (Warley) 99
Cockhel (Halifax) 99
Cockhill clough 154

Coley chapel 149
Commons: see Subject Index
Copthurst (Kirkburton) 18, 20, 36
Crigglestone 9, 14, 19, 23, 26*, 40*: Cliffe 40: constablery of 84, 85, 89, 128*, 134: field in 127, 130
Croft: Tailer (Dewsbury) 84, 89: Parrocke (Hipperholme) 47: Walker (Horbury) 68: Suncrofte (Lindley) 154
Croft House (Scammonden) 96, 106: (Sowerby) 6
Cromwell Bottom 50, 53, 62
Crow Hill Shaw (Sowerby) 62
Crowstone 141
Cumberworth 111, 126: commons of 162, 163: constablery of 111, 112, 118-9, 157, 162-3
Cuttyeard (Stanley) 30*

Dalton, constablery of 105*, 109, 148, 155
Dawdike (Sandal) 26
Daw Green (Crigglestone) 26*
Deadman Stone [Dudmanstone] (Almondbury) 45
Deinroyds (Hepworth) 171
Dewsbury 9, 12-13, 15, 54, 73, 79: constablery of 83, 85, 89, 128*, 133: parish of 3, 31, 46, 57, 73
Dick Edge (Holme) 5, 28
Dirtcar (Sandal Magna) 40, 127, 129
Dobroid Steel (Ossett) 46
Dodworth (Silkston) 4
Doncaster 8, 11, 22

Earlsheaton 4, 9, 73, 80
Earnshaw water (Stansfield) 102
Ebson House (Fulstone) 18, 20, 25, 27, 29, 33, 36, 80
Eccleshill, constablery of 84, 85, 90, 128*, 134
Eden Booth 113
Edge End (Warley) 75, 76*
Elland Hall 9
Elys clife (Thurstonland) 165
Emley, commons of 120, 163: constablery of 112*, 119-20, 157, 163: Moor 164: Park 120, 160, 164
Empsall Pond 149
Erringden 18, 19, 21, 48, 92, 101: constablery of 91, 93, 102, 135, 147

Farrar Height (Soyland) 136
Field End Bank (Austonley) 73, 74
Field House (Sowerby) 62
Fenay 25
Fields: See Subject Index
Finkle Street (Hipperholme) 108
Fixby 7*, 10, 11, 63: constablery of 104, 105, 107-8, 147, 151: demesne of 10: Hall 63: wood in 10
Flanshaw (Wakefield) 3, 75: Hall (Alverthorpe) 75
Flockton, common at 120, 164: constablery of 112*, 120, 157, 164-5: Mill 120: Nether 120
Foot (Warley) 68
Fould (Northowram) 9
Fulstone (Kirkburton) 18, 20, 25, 27, 29, 33, 36, 80, 113, 114: commons of 166: constablery of 112, 113, 122, 157, 166

Gawthorpe (Ossett) 19, 73, 79*, 128, 132
Giles Hill (Shelf) 153
Gledallrood (Stanley) 60
Godley (Northowram) 136, 138
Goodbentclough (Austonley) 125
Granhamhey lower yate (Sowerby) 95
Great Gomersal 41
Greenhead (Huddersfield) 93
Greenhill Bank (Holme) 158

Hadhill intake (Shelf) 1530
Halifax 15, 18, 20, 21, 22, 48*, 49, 50, 52, 62, 71, 91, 99, 136, 137, 138*, 154: constablery of 90, 92, 102, 135, 140-2: locations in: Back Lane 97, 135, 140: Bridge 142: Brook 137: Cabidglane 141: Cabidg Lainend 97: Church Lane 97: Cloth Hall 97: Corn market 142: Gate end 97: Gibit Laine end 97: Hart Horn 142: Kiln 142: Lort end 97: Northgate in 53: Norgate end 90: Old Hall 97, 141: Starr 142: Swinemarket 97, 141
Hall sike (Shepley) 162
Hand Green (Warley) 99
Hand Carr (Sowerby) 6, 27
Hardacres (Gawthorpe) 73
Harrison Farm (Warley) 94
Hartley Clough (Stansfield) 101, 102
Hartshead, constablery of 105*, 110, 148, 155-6

Harrod Field (Stanley) 45*, 56*, 87: Lane 87
Hawkstones (Stansfield) 145
Heath (Warmfield) 10, 60, 64
Heath Hall 31
Height (Barkisland) 94, 134
Helliwell Sike (Hipperholme) 109, 149
Heptonstall 102, 103: constablery of 91, 93, 102, 135, 146
Hepworth (Kirkburton) 44, 54-5, 57, 69, 70, 113, 159: commons of 125, 171: constablery of 112, 113, 125-6, 157, 170-1: field in 70, 125
Heys lands (Rastrick) 106
High Hoyland 40
High Lee [Hileley/ Hileleigh] (Sowerby) 18, 20, 21, 33, 38, 40, 45, 48
Hinchcliffe Mill (Austonley) 170: (Cartworth) 124
Hipperholme 6, 38, 47*, 95, 137, 149*: constablery of 104, 105, 108-9, 147, 149: graveship of 2*, 6, 7, 9, 10, 11, 22, 28, 47*, 48, 49, 67, 68, 71, 76, 95*, 137*, 138: Wells 150
Hollingbanke (Sowerby) 93
Holme 21: commons of 166: constablery of 112*, 121-2, 157, 165-6: graveship of 2-3, 5, 10, 18, 20, 21, 25, 27, 28, 29, 33, 36, 44, 55, 56, 57, 60, 67, 69, 70, 73, 76, 80, 113*, 114*, 157, 158, 159
Holme House (Barkisland) 136*
Holmfirth (Wooldale) 114, 168: chapel of 114
Hoo Hole (Erringden) 18, 19, 21, 48
Hopper lane (Shelf) 153
Horbury 1, 4, 6, 14, 23*, 44, 45, 54, 63*, 68, 69, 71, 78, 80-1, 82, 129: constablery of 83, 85, 88, 128, 132: field of 68: graveship of 2, 4, 5, 7, 8*, 11, 12, 13, 14, 24, 27, 29-30, 45, 63, 68, 71, 80
Horton 90, 93
Houlclough (Normanton) 128, 132
Houlroyd yate (Rastrick) 107
Hounley hedge (Ossett) 46
Howden 41, 71, 72
Howroyd (Barkisland) 65, 66
Hoyle Field 96: House (Hipperholme) 108
Hoyton broome 160*
Huddersfield 93
Humleyroyd (Sandal) 9, 12, 13, 14, 17, 19, 22, 23: Mooreside 37:
Hushehill (Sowerby) 91

Inge: Andrew (Dewsbury) 84, 89: Simcarr (Northowram) 2

Ing Head (Shelf) 147: (Sowerby) 6, 27

Jack Bridge (Heptonstall) 102: Lane (Erringden) 102
Jagger Smithy (Hipperholme) 95

Kebroyd ford (Sowerby) 65
Kettlethorpe (Sandal Magna) 9, 17, 19, 23, 40
Kirk Fenton 8, 12, 13, 23
Kirkburton 26: commons of 161: constablery of 111, 112, 116, 156, 160: parish of 18, 20, 36, 44, 54, 69, 80
Kirk Cliff (Soyland) 95
Kirk Field (Stanley) 60
Kirk Ing gate (Flockton) 120
Kirkgate (Wakefield), constablery of 83, 84, 86, 128: streets of 83, 86: Wrengate 86: Moot Hall 86
Kirkheaton, parish of 57
Knoltop (Hipperholme) 109
Knowles 10

Land at le Greene 2: Milnehill (Sowerby) 6
Lane ends (Hipperholme) 47
Lanehead (Cartworth) 124
Leeds 15, 22, 26, 60
Leeds Road (Stanley) 83, 87
Leicestershire 32
Lepton (Kirkheaton) 5, 28, 57
Lightcliffe (Hipperholme) 38, 76: Chapel 108, 149, 150
Lighthazles (Sowerby) 94, 140
Lindley 113, 154*, 155
Little Haworth (Lancs) 62
Littlefieldhouse (Sowerby) 93
Liversedge Lodge (Birstall) 15
London 24, 141: city of 5, 75
Long Edge (Sowerby) 44, 54, 56, 58, 67, 69
Longfield 145: common at 145: constablery of 91, 92, 101, 135, 145-6: Jacklee yeate 145: Salterrake 145
Lower Strangstry 10

Manshead (Soyland) 61, 66, 67, 139
Mapplewelltree (Ossett) 46

March lane (Shepley) 162
Meadow: (Holme) le Broad Lane Close 3: Greatbothome 3: Knacker 3: Whamynge 115
Mear House bridge (Scholes) 167
Midgley 77: constablery of 91, 92, 100, 135, 144
Milne Hill (Sowerby) 27
Milne hirst wood (Scholes) 167
Milne next the House (Sowerby) 68
Mixenden Mill 143
Mooreyate (Sowerby) 95
Morley 29, 32-3, 48
Moss Edge 158
Moulson Place (Stainland) 96
Mountsorrel, Leics 32
Murgatroyd (Warley) 94
Mytham (Stansfield) 91, 103

Nabb (Holme) 5, 28*
Netherthong 158
Nettlebeddes (Emley) 163
New Biggin Hill (Sandal) 37
New Park (Ossett) 4
Newbrigg lane (Shelf) 153
Newhouse (Northowram) 137, 138: (Wickleden) 114
Newton (Alverthorpe) 5, 29
Norland 68: constablery of 91, 92, 135
Normanton, constablery of 83, 85, 88-9, 128*, 132-3
North Bierley (Bradford) 41
North Elmsall 81
Northgate (Wakefield) 9: constablery of 83, 84, 87, 127, 128, 131
Northowram (Hipperholme) 2*, 9, 47*-8*, 49-50, 52, 67, 68*, 71, 76, 94, 95, 105, 108, 136, 137*, 138: constablery of 104, 105, 108, 147, 152: Norbrigg 137
Norwich 35, 38

Ogden 91, 103
Osburnes 10
Ossett 3, 4, 5, 15, 24, 40, 41, 43, 46-7, 57, 73, 79, 127, 131: constablery of 83, 85*, 88, 128*, 132: fields of 4, 41, 46*-7, 57: graveship of 3-5, 9,

15, 19, 27, 29-30, 31, 41, 46*-7, 57, 73*, 79, 80: King's high-street 88, 132
Ossett Lights (Ossett) 41, 57
Otley 67
Outwood (Wakefield) 127, 130
Outwoodside (Wakefield) 30, 31: (Stanley) 73
Ovenden 81, 94, 99, 138: constablery of 91, 92, 135, 143
Over/Lower Paddocke (Northowram) 52
Overhill house (Holme) 158
Overlongbothom (Sowerby) 15, 22, 26
Overmodwoodleys (Cartworth) 169
Overthong (Holme) 5, 28*, 76

Painthorpe (Sandal) 5, 14
Parke yate (Longfield) 101
Parkwall Pale (Ossett) 46, 60, 79
Parrocke (Hipperhome) 47
Pighellstreet (Sowerby) 94
Pilling bothame (Cumberworth) 118
Pitt (Turvin) 80
Priestley 21: Green (Sowerby) 6: (Hipperholme) 28, 149*
Pule lane 152

Quarlers (Northowram) 47-8
Quarmby, constablery of 105*, 109, 147, 154-5: Outlane in 109

Rastrick 1, 6, 62, 107, 148, 151: common at 107: constablery of 104, 105, 107, 147, 151: graveship of 6, 10, 11, 62, 148
Raven Royd (Ossett) 88
Reddicarr (Wadsworth) 31, 134
Reedyshaw (Soyland) 14
Rippling Syke (Ossett) 15, 46, 57
Rishworth with Norland, constablery of 91, 92, 100, 135, 144
Rothwell, parish of 31
Rowtonstall wood 101
Runtingebutts (Ossett) 47

Salter lane bottom 154
Sandal Magna 1, 12, 23, 29, 32, 40, 49: parish of 23, 37, 40

Sandal 9, 14, 16, 17, 23, 58: constablery of 83, 84, 87, 127, 128, 131-2: graveship of 5, 8-9, 10, 14*, 17, 19, 22, 23, 26*, 31, 37, 40*
Scammonden 96*: graveship of 6, 96*
Scholes (Holme) 2, 3, 10, 114, 115, 157: bridge 113: commons of 167: constablery of 112, 113, 122-3, 157, 167
Scholesbancke (Holme) 113
Scout (Northowram) 94
Shacking House (Halifax) 99
Shaley (Wooldale) 2
Shaw (Soyland) 25
Shelf, constablery of 105*, 106-7, 147, 153-4
Shelley 111, 126: commons of 161: constablery of 111, 112, 116-7, 157, 161
Shepley, commons of 152: constablery of 111, 112, 117-8, 157, 161-2
Shotts: see Subject Index
Siddal Hall 47-8
Skelmanthorpe 160
Skircoat 95, 99, 137: constablery of 91, 92, 98, 135, 142
Smallbrigg (Northowram) 108
Smallclough (Holme) 113
Smalley (Stanley) 45*, 56*, 87
Smithie green (Shelf) 153
Soothill, constablery of 84, 85, 89, 128*, 133
Southowram 47-48, 49, 52. 62
Sowdell (Ossett) 46
Sowerby 18, 19, 20, 21, 25, 33, 34, 38, 40, 44, 45, 48, 51, 54, 56, 59, 61, 62*, 65*, 66, 67*, 69-70, 80, 91, 93*, 94*, 95, 134, 135, 136*, 138: constablery of 91, 92, 98, 135, 142: Finkell Street 81: graveship of 5, 14, 15, 18, 20, 21, 22, 25*, 26, 27, 31, 33, 34, 38, 40, 44, 45, 48, 54, 56, 59, 60, 61*, 62*, 65-6, 67*, 68, 69-70, 75, 76, 77*, 80, 81, 91, 93*, 94*, 134, 135, 136*, 138
Sowood House 149
Soyland (Sowerby) 14, 25, 31, 61, 67, 95, 134, 135, 136*, 138-9
Spencer Farm (Hipperholme) 68
Spout (Wooldale) 168
Spouthouse (Hipperholme) 149
Sprotbrough, parish of 80
Stainland 96: constablery of 105, 106, 110, 148, 156
Staleywood, Ches 10
Stammersyke (Stanley) 60

Stanley 5, 15, 19, 23, 30*, 41, 42, 45*, 56*, 60, 73: constablery of 83, 84, 87, 127, 128, 131: fields of 41, 60: graveship of 1, 4, 5, 7, 22-3, 24, 30-1, 41, 60*: pinfold at 130
Stanningden (Sowerby) 61, 65-6
Stansfield 91*, 102, 103*, 145, 146: bridge 146: constablery of 91, 92, 101, 135, 144-5: Cross stone 145: Kiln at 145
Stepney (Middlesex) 2
Stiperden (Stansfield) 102
Stock Lane (Warley) 99
Stockes (Erringden) 92
Stockforthbrooke 61, 66-7
Stony Bank 159
Stubbing (Sowerby) 65, 91: (Scammonden) 96
Swiftplace (Stanningden) 61, 65

Tail Small [Tealsmall] (Ossett) 46
Thong, commons of 172: constablery of 112, 113, 157, 171-2: Over 126
Thornes 29, 31, 83, 87: fields of 35, 39, 42: graveship of 5, 8, 13, 17, 27, 29, 35, 39, 60, 71, 78: Moor 71
Thornhill lane 155: parish of 47
Thorntree (Hipperholme) 95
Thurstonland, constablery of 112*, 121, 157, 165
Todmorden water 146
Tom Royd 150
Topcliffe 63
Totties 157
Tuel Lane (Warley) 99
Turvin (Sowerby) 80

Upper/Netherbinns 50
Upperfieldhouse (Sowerby) 93

Vicaridge (Bingley) 48, 50, 52
Vicars Farm (Warley) 94

Wadsworth (Sowerby) 31, 134: constablery of 91, 92, 99-100, 135, 143
Wainstalls (Warley) 75, 77*
Wakefield 3, 4-5, 8, 9, 11-13, 15, 16, 19, 23, 30, 31, 34*, 35*, 38, 40, 42, 45, 48, 50, 52, 60, 65, 68, 71*, 72, 75, 78*, 79*, 82, 83, 85, 87, 127, 130, 131: court at 17: Free Grammar School at 3; graveship of 4, 5, 9, 15, 34,

35, 41, 45, 64, 71-2, 78: locations in: Bitchhill 9, 34*, 41, 71, 72: Golden Cock 45: Kirkgate 35-6: Northgate 5, 9, 34*, 41, 65, 71, 72, 78, 79, 82: Pinfold House 35-6: Rattonrow/Breadboothes 15: Westgate 78: parish of 30*, 31*, 39, 42, 76
Walton with Bretton, constablery of 83, 84, 88, 127, 128, 132
Warley (Sowerby) 15, 22, 26, 68, 75, 76, 77*, 94*, 95, 138: constablery of 91, 92, 99, 135, 143
Water Green (Sowerby) 94
Wath 2
Waukcliffe 8, 12, 13, 23
West Ardsley, constablery of 84, 85, 89, 128*, 133
Wester Croft (Northowram) 58
Westgate (Wakefield), constablery of 83, 84, 86, 128, 130-1
Westgate Moor (Alverthorpe) 75: (Wakefield) 19
Wheatley (Ossett) 46
Wheatley royd (Sowerby) 5, 27
Wheels Brook (Holme) 5, 28
Whinny Moores (Dirtcar) 40
Whitley 26*: (Thornhill) 47
Wibsey (Bradford) 46
Wickleden (Holme) 3, 10, 114, 115
Will Royd House (Northowram) 9
Wind Hill [Windywell] (Alverthorpe) 8, 13, 17, 18
Winter Edge (Sowerby) 6, 28
Wintersett 8, 12, 13, 23
Wood (Soyland) 135, 136
Wood: Ryefield (Holme) 114
Woodhouse Lane (Ardsley) 30
Wooldale (Holme) 44, 55, 60, 114, 157*, 158*: commons of 168: constablery of 112, 113, 123, 157, 167-8: fields of 158

York, city of 71

INDEX OF SUBJECTS

Affray 91, 98, 111, 119, 126, 127, 130, 131
Annuity 138

Becks: (Alverthorpe) 16, (Broadfore) 60, (Humble Jumble) 78, 79, (Shibden) 2
Bridges: (Bottom Hall) 108, 150, (Brearley) 6, 27, (Halifax) 142, (Humble Jumble) 16, (Jack) 102, (Mear House) 167, (Norbrigg) 137, (Scholes) 113, (Stansfield) 146
Bull-baiting 130

Chancery, decree in 93
Closes:
Alverthorpe: Broad/Lower Inge 75: Broomroyd 75: Doggcroft 56, 58: Dunston 75: Mean/Little/Farr Earley 75: Farwill Lane 76: Fourlands head 75: Gt/Little Gelder Inge 75: Kay 79: Rose Katherine Leys 79: Long 79: Lymegarth 75: Taylors 79: Thistle 75: Througstile 75: Tofts 75: Wowan 75
Austonley: Boothhousebank, Hangingroyd, Netherbanke, Shroggs 170
Barkisland: Gt Lightlyroyd 156
Boothroyd: Upper/Netherhealds, Hill, Upper/Nether Inge, Kittroyde, Wheat 46, 57
Cartworth: Gt Brearley, Brearleehead, Broadynge, Everoyde 158
Cumberworth: Parcar 163
Flockton: Lower Quarrell 120
Fulstone: Hinchclife croft 122
Gawthorpe: High 79: New/Coalpitt 19
Hepworth: Hobcroft 171
Hipperholme: Churchwellbothome 138: New 68: Pighells 71: Rydeings 138: Ryepighell 138: Scale Inge 47: Scarrbancke 47: Stoneheap 47: Well Croft 47
Holme: Acre 18, 20, 25, 37, 80: Acre Inge 18, 20, 25, 37, 80: Great/Little Adamley 18, 20, 25, 37: Adamley Inge 18, 20, 25, 37: Ashdole 113: Banckwood 3: Barneside Lane Inge 44, 55, 57, 59, 67, 69: Broomefield 114: Coat 18, 20, 25, 80: Crimble 3: Croft under the House 18, 20, 25, 29, 33, 36, 37, 80: Crookelands 114: Deinroyds 70: Over/Nether Ebsonroyds 18, 20, 25: Ebsonroyd Inge 18, 20, 25, 34, 37: Farrfield 70: Greenhillbanck 157: Hanroyde 70: Heward carr 70: Hey 70: Hirst 3:

Kemphouse 70: Kilne coft 115: Lathcroft 3: Long 3: Mooreyngs 70: Moorelands 114: Netherbothoms 114: Over/Nether Newlands 18, 20, 25, 37, 80: Newlands Inge 25: Nookes 18, 20, 25, 37, 80: Overbinfield 5, 28: Paddocke 113: Parke 18, 20, 25, 37, 80: Ryebanck 18, 20, 25, 37: Ryefield 114: Scotroyd Leys 18, 20, 25, 37, 80: Springewod 3: Stubbinge 18, 20, 25, 37: Thompson 2: Well Inge 18, 20, 25, 37, 80: Whitley 18, 20, 25, 34, 37, 80

Horbury: Crosse 45: Stanner/Stony wells 81: Wees Pitt 4

Lightcliffe: Quarlers 21

Northowram: Anthonywell 9: Bancks 53: Overbancks 137: Nether Charwell 137, 138: Coalpitt 52: Hawroydes 137, 138: Longinge 137: Mainroyde 9: Little Ryeding 137, 138

Ossett: Adcuckroyd 4: Broadroyds 46: Burdleys 15, 57: Farr Arrundell Field 80: Haggsclose 46: Over/Netherhaygate 46: Upper/Netherhealds 31: Hill 31: Honnleys 46: Hoylehead 80: Upper/Nether inge 31: Kirkestye 47: Kittroyde 31: Longlands 46: Gt/Neare/Far Maplewell 41: Far Maplewell Inge 41: Mooreroyd 73: les Pildarse 4: Wheat 31

Rastrick: Gt/Little Inge 148: Salmon Crofte 10: Gt/Middle/Lowermost Inge 62: Inge Tongue 62

Sandal: Armitt Crofts 26: Faugh 25: Carson Inge 11: Roundynge 11: Syke Inge 9, 13, 17, 19, 23: Kilnehill 31

Scammonden: New, Overbrinke, Little Stubbinge, Stubbing inge 96

Shelley: Littleinge, Windmilhill 117

Southowram: Lawhillcloses 50

Sowerby: Bank 136: Littlebanck 34: Banck above House 34: Bents 62: Bent Inge 34: Cattayles 44, 54, 56, 59, 67, 69: Coytefield 62: Croft within which the house stands 62: Crosselands 95: Delfe Field 95: Faugh 44, 54, 56, 59, 62, 67, 69: Furrfield 62: Goofe 95: Halfeacre 14: Horsehey 61, 67: Littlehey 44, 54, 56, 59, 67, 69: Upper/Nether Roughhey 62: le Holme 136: Ingam Holme 95: Inge 136: Great/Little Inge 44, 54, 56, 59, 62, 67, 69: Lower Inge 95: Kilneinge/Lanerhill 136: Field on Laith 44, 54, 56, 59, 67, 69: Lathfield 62, 95: Two Parks 62: Rishey 25: Swift 61, 66

Stanley: Brigg, 41: Bullacre 41: Cowpasture 41: Dewceroyds 30, 31: Edd Croft 41: Fallsyke 45, 56: Grith Fields 41: Harry Carr 41: Horse 41: Laith Croft 23: Moldroyd 41: Penny yards 41: Threenooked 30, 31: Woodside 30*

Stansfield: Leys 91, 103

Thong: Padock 172

Thornes: Crosse 71: Long 78

Wakefield: Little Fallyng 5: Hodgson 5
Wooldale: Banck 158: Bentonyhill 157: Browe 158: Bryanroyd 158: Croft 158: Croft by house 157: Flat 158: Greenshillfield 158: Netherhilltopp 44, 54, 56, 59, 60, 67, 69: Inge 158: Longynge/Weetynge 157: Sow 168: Wardcroft 157: Wellynge 157
Coal viii, 19, 52, 138, 143, 160*
Common pasture 4, 61, 66, 67, 95, 136
Commons: (Austonley) 170, (Cartworth) 169, (Cumberworth) 162, 163, (Emley) 120, 163, (Flockton) 120, 164, (Fulstone) 166, (Hepworth) 125, 171, (Holme) 166, (Kirkburton) 161, (Longfield) 145, (Normanton) 128, 133, (Outwood) 127, (Rastrick) 107, (Scholes) 167, (Shepley) 162, (Thong) 172, (Wooldale) 168
Continuity of persons on court panels ix-xiii
Copyhold rents 7-8, 21, 56, 58, 64, 65
Cowpasture 45, 68, 71
Crofts: (Parrocke) 47, (Suncrofte) 1, (Tailer) 84, 89, (Walker) 68
Customary dues for use of common 120 (Flockton), 133 (Normanton)

Days' work 61, 67, 70, 108, 116
Digging on common 83, 127, 130, 131: on roads 83, 87: for clay 131
Ditch repairs 83, 86, 88, 106, 108, 147, 150
Dog-worrying 168, 170, 171, 172
Dower 73-4
Draw well 159

Eggs 140
Enclosure 9, 12, 45
Encroachment on common 73-4 (Austonley, 127 (Outwood)
Enquiry into transfer of copyhold 80-1
Exchange of land 78-9

Failure to claim copyhold land 22, 24, 60, 64
Failure to repair 154
False weights 83, 86, 127, 131
Fencing 83, 87, 88, 91, 106, 107, 108, 109, 118, 119, 120, 125, 128, 132, 133, 149, 163*, 164*, 167, 171
Fictitious lease 11, 12, 13*, 18*, 19-21, 23, 29, 32-3, 44*, 48, 54, 75, 77-8
Fields: (Alverthorpe) Cliffe 8, 13, 17, 18: Humble Jumble 8, 12, 13, 14, 16, 18, 22, 23, (Crigglestone) 127, 130, (Earlsheaton) Arundell 9, 80,

(Hepworth) Berristall/West 70, 125, (Horbury) 45, 68: Le Milnefield: 4, (Hoyle) 96, (Ossett) 4, 41, 46-7, 57: Two Farther/Two Nearer Hartley 79: Quarrell 73, (Stanley) 41, 60, (Thornes) 35, 39, 42, (Wooldale) 158
Fines on officers for negligence 21, 37, 58, 128
Furnace-house 44, 55
Forestalling 140

Gate-hanging viii, 73, 120, 128, 132, 151, 165
Governors of Free Grammar School, Wakefield 3
Guardianship 11

Hedges 56, 65
House parts 44, 55, 73, 94, 114

Indentures 9, 25, 60, 61, 66, 75, 96, 137
Inmate 107

Jointure 37, 162

Kiln at Halifax 142: at Stansfield 145
King's highway 101, 102*, 143, 145-6

Lanes 4, 40, 56: (Barms Hill) 152, (Barraclough) 50, (Bradley) 151, (Brighouse) 150, (Harwoodfield) 87, (Hopper) 153, (Jack Bridge) 102, (Lydgate) 155, (March) 162, (Newbrigg) 153, (Pule) 152, (Quarmby) 109, (Salter) 154, (Stocke) 99, (Thornhill) 155, (Tuall) 99, (Woodhouse) 30
Lease 68, 79, 80, 113, 158*
Leave to inherit 10*, 14, 22, 29, 30, 34, 60, 67-8, 96, 157
Leaving customary ways 87, 103-4, 111, 116-7, 119, 121-2, 125, 152-3, 154, 156, 160, 163*, 164-5, 167-71

Meadows in Holme: Broad Lane Close, Greatbothome, Knacker 3, Whamynge 115
Milk 138
Mills 95, 117: (Boy) 6, 27, 68, (Flockton) 120, (Hinchliffe) 124, 170, (Mixenden) 143: fulling mill at Warley 68
Moors: (Dirtcar) 40, (Emley) 164, (Thornes) 71, (Westgate) 19, 75

Occupations:
attorney 138: barber 15: blacksmith 40, 94*: book-binder 136: cardboard-maker 19, 40: card-maker 4: chapman 137: clerk 2, 14, 15, 22, 47, 48, 63, 71, 73, 96*: clothier 15, 19, 37, 40, 45, 68, 76, 137, 138*, 148: cloth-worker 4, 5, 42, 60: cordwainer 41, 47, 49, 57: fell-monger 40, 77: flax-dresser 16, 22, 26: grocer 34*: pewterer 4: rope-maker 29: roper 73: salter 2: shoemaker 30: stapler 46: tailor 31: tanner 8, 12, 23, 31, 137: wheelwright 10: whitesmith 35, 38
Offer for vacant land 23*, 36, 48, 69*

Packway viii, 154-5
Pasturing on private land 125
Path repairs 99, 108, 124, 147, 149, 150, 152, 153-4
Peat digging 138-9
Pinder: Crigglestone 127, 130: Dewsbury 54: Horbury 129: Ossett 85: Rastrick 149: Sandal 58
Pinfold: Stanley 130
Poor of Wakefield x, 5
Presentments at the Court Baron 7-8, 12, 14, 17, 21, 24, 27-9, 37, 43, 56, 58, 64-5, 74, 82

Remainders 2, 11, 41-2, 49
Repairs 68, 158: to roads viii

Sale 9, 34, 68, 78, 93
Scabbed horses 131, 133
Seizure of land 58-9
Settlement of land 114, 115, 136, 138
Shotts: Horbury: les Holmes 4, Littsbanck 45, Longsouthfield 68
Ossett: Cherrytree 4, 46, Haggsbutts 46, Hanging butts 46, Kirkstye 47, Oldfield 46, Ryecroft 4, Sowdell 46, Storgate 46, Wheatley 46
Smithy 94, 95, 137
Spinster 2, 4, 25*, 30, 40, 71, 79, 136, 148
Stiles xiv, 84, 89, 120, 149, 150, 152
Street repairs 83, 86, 97-9, 101, 135, 140-2
Surety 15

Transfer of land disallowed as wife not examined by steward xi, 33
Tree lopping 122
Trust ix, 50-3, 57, 63, 71-2, 138

Undermining of wall 78, 82

Voidance of reversion 10, 15, 26, 31, 32, 34-5, 37, 40, 41, 47, 63, 73, 76, 81, 114, 159
Waif 91, 103
Waste land: Alverthorpe: 16, 38, 45, 48: Ossett: 41: Sandal: 40: Sowerby: 61: Soyland: 14: Thornes: 60
Water in its ancient course 140, 141, 150, 152, 162, 168
Water on the highway 84, 89, 125, 150
Watercourse 61, 66
Wayleave xiii, 44, 45, 52, 55, 56, 57, 69, 95, 96, 138-9
Widow 2, 8, 10, 14, 19, 23, 26, 31, 32, 35*, 36, 37, 39, 42, 45, 47, 49, 50, 52, 56, 60, 65, 68, 71, 73*, 138, 153*, 163
Wills viii-ix, 35-6, 48*, 49-53, 63, 71-2, 76